The Edge

Walking the Ulster Way
with my Angels and Demons

Dermot Breen

Published in 2017 by Shanway Press,
15 Crumlin Road, Belfast BT14 6AA

Cover design: David-Lee Badger
Cover photo: Johnny Baird

ISBN: 978-1-910044-14-8

Dedicated to Jacqui,
my beautiful wife,
soul-mate and angel.

Contents

Foreword

"I would walk even further than Harold Fry
if I thought it could save you".

These were the heartfelt and desperate words I had written for my wife, Jacqui, on her final Christmas on this Earth. Jacqui was dying from ovarian cancer and we both knew that she only had weeks left to live. Her life was going to end. My life was going to be shattered. Both of these facts were now inevitable. When I first penned those words to Jacqui, they were conceived out of a great sense of love and a terrible feeling of impending loss. I knew that there was no way on this Earth to save Jacqui. However, I could never have anticipated the incredible journey that single sentence would take me on, or the significant role that the resulting pilgrimage would play in helping to save me from despair. Literally, a walk to the edge and back!

For those of you who don't know, Harold Fry is a fictional character from Rachel Joyce's wonderful novel T*he Unlikely Pilgrimage of Harold Fry.* It was this book that provided the inspiration for my very own pilgrimage. Of course, I never in a million years ever expected that I would undertake a pilgrimage. The very word "pilgrimage" conjured up in my mind thoughts of religion, spirituality, shrines, searching, beliefs, faith, temples, and devotees – words that had all become fairly alien to a lapsed Catholic such as myself. But life, unfortunately, doesn't always go to plan and it doesn't always take you neatly in the direction of your own, or others, expectations. Sometimes fate or destiny, call it what you will, rudely intervenes and your whole life is suddenly upended to such an extent that you no longer know which way is up or down, never mind in which direction you should now be going.

For me and Jacqui, fate very rudely intervened in our perfect lives on the night of Thursday 23 January 2014. We were both lying in bed reading at the time, when Jacqui suddenly turned to me quite alarmed and said that she felt a large lump in her abdomen. She took my hand and, with some trepidation, I let her place it on her stomach. There was no mistaking it. It literally felt as if a large hard-boiled egg had been implanted into Jacqui's abdomen. It was a hell of a shock for us both and first thing the next morning Jacqui made an appointment to see her doctor and was subsequently seen that afternoon. We were at first somewhat reassured when the doctor's initial examination indicated that it may have been a simple temporary blockage in the bowel and we were even more reassured when the lump gradually disappeared over the next couple of days. However, the doctor had wisely referred Jacqui for further tests and unfortunately that initial reassurance quickly dissipated when we were informed in March that she had ovarian cancer and, in the words of one consultant, the type she had "was a very tricky one to treat".

One year later, on Sunday 18 January 2015, my best friend, soul mate and wife, was taken from me by the ovarian cancer that had been diagnosed only ten months earlier. The sense of profound loss was, and still is, heart-breaking. Thankfully I had lots of friends and family to help me through, including my son, Matt, and daughter, Hannah, who were obviously grieving also and trying to adjust to life without their wonderful and much loved mother. Initially there were lots of practical things that needed to be attended to and that kept me occupied and even distracted to some extent. A death to be registered, a funeral to be arranged, ashes to be collected, scatterings and committal of the ashes to be undertaken, bank accounts to be closed, employer to be notified, phone companies to be contacted, the list was seemingly endless – the bureaucracy of death. I still remember the surreal feeling and the sense of disbelief I experienced when I was referred to as a 'widower' for the very first time in my life. But that was now what I had become. After years of casually ticking the 'married' box on forms, I now had to pause and move the pen or curser to the 'widower' box and reluctantly acknowledge my new status. A new status that, unlike my former standing, had been thrust upon me without me having any choice or say in the matter.

After dealing with all the red tape, I had an overwhelming urge to do something more positive to celebrate Jacqui's life. Jacqui had very bravely written her own reminiscences to be read out at her funeral service and I had promised her that I would get them printed up "afterwards" to give to close friends and family. This promise developed into a commitment to produce a personal memoir celebrating Jacqui's life and this project became my obsession for the next few months. I completed the memoir around Easter time and I distributed it around friends and family to raise funds for cancer research. I returned to work after this and tried unsuccessfully to settle back into the old routine. It clearly wasn't enough. I felt very strongly that I needed to do more to ensure that Jacqui's life was remembered and honoured in some special way. I also wanted to raise more funds for cancer research, which both

Jacqui and I had believed was the only way that cancer was ever going to be defeated. All sorts of madcap ideas entered my head, such as surfing all the known surf spots around the coast of Ireland or cycling the Camino de Santiago in Northern Spain. Both had their attractions, but I realised that any venture involving surfing might be seen as me just enjoying my normal pastime, while a trip to northern Spain might be regarded by some as a nice little holiday in the sun. Anyway, this needed to be a more local venture. I wasn't yet ready to be away from home for a prolonged period of time and, besides, I had a job to hold on to. My venture would have to be fairly local and would have to be capable of being fitted in and around my working life. I also felt that it would have to be a real challenge. That's when the idea of my pilgrimage started to take shape.

Jacqui and I had loved the book *The Unlikely Pilgrimage of Harold Fry*. We had both read it a couple of years before – well before Jacqui had ever been diagnosed with cancer. In the book, the main character, Harold Fry, sets off unexpectedly one morning to walk a distance of 627 miles to visit an old work colleague who is terminally ill with cancer. It might sound like a depressing read, but it is ultimately a very uplifting story. On what was to be her last Christmas, in December 2014, I gave Jacqui a copy of the book's sequel, *The Love Song of Queenie Hennessy*. She started to read it, but she set it aside after the first 25 pages or so. It turned out to be the most inappropriate choice of present in the history of mankind, as the story was largely set in a hospice. I felt awful, but thankfully she didn't mind too much and made light of my blunder. What she loved though were the words that I had written inside the cover of the book, "I would walk even further than Harold Fry if I thought it could save you". Jacqui knew that I was never a great walker. Our walks together, while always enjoyable, were often much shorter than she would have liked as I generally ran out of steam much sooner than she did. So she really appreciated the sentiment behind the words I had written. Recalling this, with the inevitable tears in my eyes, I thought that perhaps I could honour Jacqui's memory and also help save others by walking even further than the fictional Harold Fry. When I began looking at possible walking routes in Northern Ireland, I couldn't quite believe it when I discovered that the complete Ulster Way route is 625 miles long, just two miles short of Harold's walk! The decision was made for me in an instant. Like most people from these parts, I had certainly heard of the Ulster Way and had even spotted the occasional Ulster Way sign while driving around the countryside, but beyond that I knew very little. Thankfully there is an excellent website at www.walkni.com/ulsterway, which is maintained by Outdoor Recreation Northern Ireland and it told me practically everything I needed to know about the route.

The challenge I set for myself was to walk the entire Ulster Way over the summer months of 2015 in memory of Jacqui and to raise money for cancer research. But I would start and finish at Greenisland Primary School, where Jacqui had taught for 25 years. This would add on a few extra miles to my journey to ensure that I exceeded the distance walked by Harold Fry. It turns out that 625 miles equates to 1,000 kilometres, so my challenge also became known as "1000K4J", shorthand for 1,000 Kilometres for Jacqui.

Because of my work commitments, I completed the various legs of my walk mainly over weekends, although I also took some leave from work, particularly towards the final stages. I started my walk on 12 June 2015 and finished it on   September 2, 2015. What follows is an account of my experiences preparing for and undertaking my pilgrimage, intermingled with some associated material that I hope the reader will find interesting. I had discovered that attempting to capture my thoughts and feeling on paper had been helpful, even therapeutic, and although I had never before seriously considered poetry as a medium for expressing myself, it seemed to lend itself very well to my state of mind at the time. I was quietly encouraged in my endeavours by my sister-in-law, Christine, who is a much better poet than I could ever hope to be and for a long time she was the only person I shared my efforts with. Maybe that's the way it should have remained, but my circumstances over the last year have given me a certain "devil may care" attitude and so I have decided to include the odd verse in this book. Dubious literary ability aside, they do at least offer a fairly honest and contemporaneous insight into my emotional state in the aftermath of Jacqui's death.

My objective was, and still is, to raise as much money as possible to support the fight against the awful disease that is cancer. The latest statistics indicate that one in two people will develop cancer at some point in their lives. All author profits raised through the sale of this book will be donated to Cancer Research UK (CRUK).

Dermot Breen
March 2016

The End

Sunday 18 January

On the day before Jacqui died, I had no idea we were so close to the end. I had been receiving a lot of texts and messages from friends and family enquiring after Jacqui. Everyone was obviously very concerned that Jacqui had gone into a hospice only a few days earlier, but at one point I remember apologising to Jacqui, as I seemed to be spending so much time on my mobile replying to people, rather than devoting my full attention to her. Being Jacqui, she was of course very understanding. But she then suggested that I should declare the next day a phone free day and that I should send out a general text to everyone to let them all know. I thought this was a great idea and promptly did as Jacqui had suggested. That evening Jacqui was feeling quite relaxed and insisted that I return home to get a good night's sleep. I did as she asked and have regretted it ever since. I had no idea then what the following day had in store and I don't know if Jacqui had either; on reflection she may have had, and her suggestion for a text free day may have been some sort of a sign or premonition, but I honestly cannot be certain. We both knew that her time was short, but I for one, certainly didn't realise just how short.

Early the following morning, I received a call from the hospice at Whiteabbey to say that Jacqui had an unsettled night and that a familiar face might help her relax. The nurse was quite calm and didn't suggest anything other than that it would be a good idea to come out as soon as I could. There was no trace of urgency or panic in her voice, but I suspect that this was her way of ensuring that I didn't panic and made it out to the hospice safely. I couldn't understand this sudden change from the night before, when Jacqui had seemed so relaxed. But I got my daughter, Hannah, up and we both got ready as quickly as we could and headed out to the hospice. While I have to admit to being quite anxious on the drive out, I really wasn't expecting things to be so serious or imminent. But the full realisation of what was happening suddenly became clear when we arrived in the hospice ward. This was it. The time we had been dreading. I contacted my son Matt, who was in Portrush, and thankfully a good friend drove him the 55 miles to the hospice. We all sat with Jacqui and chatted - about what, I really can't remember - but over the next hour it was clear that she was getting steadily weaker. Jacqui indicated that she didn't want Matt and Hannah to stay. She was being a protective mother right up to the end and wanted to spare them the final moments. Jacqui, Matt and Hannah all said their goodbyes to each other, with hugs and tears. It was truly heartbreaking to see. The tears I experienced then are only matched by the tears rolling down my cheeks as I write this now. Matt and Hannah left the ward and then it was just me and Jacqui.

I felt totally helpless as Jacqui slowly slipped away from me. All the while trying to be strong for her, to comfort her, to allow her to pass away peacefully, telling her that she didn't need to worry, it was alright for her to go; while at the same time my whole being was silently screaming out to her not to leave me. We kissed and I hugged her very gently and held her hand as I watched the light fade from her eyes. This wonderful woman who I had spent the last 35 years with, loving, living, sleeping, eating, sharing, walking, travelling, parenting, crying, laughing, was suddenly very still; her breathing seemingly paused. I waited and waited for Jacqui to take her next breath. But it never came; and the seconds kept ticking by. And that was it. The love of my life had taken her last breath. She was at peace. I was at sea.

The Sea

You gently slip the mooring rope as I look on disbelieving
Reluctantly letting go when you know you have no choice
Cast adrift, the distance between us gradually widens
Salt water between us offers no resistance to the parting
There is no line on the jetty or grappling hook to reach
The craft has no oars and knows only one direction of trave.
I can still see your eyes open wide but do they still see me
I bow my head and silently give you permission to leave
When I look up a mist has formed and my vision is blurred
The gentle swell, the rhythmic ebb and flow, has suddenly ceased
I call to you but there is no response
Who is adrift, me or you

I am quickly surrounded by family, your loved ones and mine
They keep me back from the edge, from the dark water below
I want to fall, want the current to take hold and drag me to you
But warm bodies hold me firm and prevent me from slipping
Night falls and they drift away with words, prayers, kindness
But I must remain and watch out for you on your lonely journey
A private room at last, courtesy of the angels here on earth
Window open to keep you cool, something you've been longing for
A silent vigil, a night of strange calm and peace, no more hurt
And as morning breaks, a blackbird sings, news I can't retain
I speak to you but there is no response
Who is alone, me or you

Your body has returned in a basket woven with grass from the deep
You are so cold to touch and your secret smile has disappeared
People come and go, some want to see you and to say farewell
Others simply want to be near and remember who you were
One last journey to plan now and so grateful we spoke before
Wear something bright you said and let it be a celebration
Three dark suits with three red scarfs followed you all the way
Hundreds were there to see you go but I never felt more alone
Your woven carriage quietly dropped from view as your song soared
Your image still there on display to hide the fact that you were gone
I cry openly but there is no response
Who is falling, me or you

I am home now with only memories and dust for company
Your treasures fill the house but only make it feel more empty
So many to tell, your existence on earth slowly being erased
Papers filed, forms completed, accounts closed, will activated
Our time together was so perfect before darkness invaded our lives
Then ten months of hope, followed by two months of hell
You were so brave and selfless, an inspiration right to the end
Heartbroken to be torn away but accepting of the way things were
I am comforted that you have no more drugs, needles, discomfort to face
But I wake each morning to no one beside me and my pain starts again
I weep for you but there is no response
Who is at peace, me or you

I return to the sea to escape the earth and these earthly feelings
Thankful for the water to wash away both my tears and worries
The waves demand attention and allow some temporary escape
At times I'm overwhelmed by both surf and bitter-sweet emotions
After, I return to the shore, cold as death but still stubbornly alive
Back to the land, but knowing you won't be there to welcome me
A band of gold lost from a finger made thin by worry and cold
Salt water rubbed into my wounds, loss made more emphatic
I will come back to these sands to walk with you one last time
When I am ready to mix dust with grains in this, our special place
I cry when alone, so no one hears
Who is lost, me or you

Escaping

Wednesday 13 May
My initial experience of long distance walking was also nearly my last.

It had now been almost four months since Jacqui had been taken from me. I had endeavoured to keep myself as busy as possible during that time. I found that the more I kept myself occupied during the day, and the more exhausted I was going to bed at night, the better. It allowed me less time to dwell on the pain and heartache that was constantly bubbling just below the surface. Of course this only had a limited effect and all too frequently, and in spite of my futile efforts to control it, feelings of devastation and hopelessness would break over me and I would be nearly drowned under a wave of despair that would be so powerful that it would leave me physically weak and emotionally drained. These metaphors may appear over dramatic, but I can find no better words to describe the suddenness and power with which such emotions could overwhelm me. Being a keen surfer, I know all too well the feeling of being "wiped out" by a huge wave. During those seconds, which often feel more like minutes, when you are at the complete mercy of the ocean, you feel like little more than a rag-doll in a washing machine. You are hit suddenly by the breaking wave, forced mercilessly underwater by the sheer power and weight of the water and held in its grasp and twisted and turned and disorientated until its energy eventually weakens and you are finally released from its grip. Only then can you make your way to the surface and gasp desperately for a much needed lungful of air. Being "wiped out" by a wave of grief felt very similar to me; only instead of the weight of water causing the havoc it was the weight of emotions – and it lasted much longer. And in the surf of course, when I felt that I had been battered enough by the ocean, I could simply paddle for shore and escape the waves. The waves of grief could not be escaped so easily. However, I did find that keeping occupied did help. I had certainly been busy since Jacqui's death. There had been so much to sort out and organise regarding Jacqui's affairs and I had then immersed myself in producing her personal memoirs for family members and close friends. But those tasks were now all complete and, although I was now back at work, I knew that I needed something more in my life to keep me focused and give me a sense of purpose.

The previous evening, the idea for my Ulster Way walk had been beginning to take shape and it was buzzing incessantly around inside my head. I was feeling particularly restless and I just knew that I had to escape the house, escape work, escape everything for a bit. I checked the forecast for the following day and saw that it was to be a good one and so, on the spur of the moment, I decided that I was going to walk from Belfast to Lisburn to test myself. The Lagan Towpath between Belfast and Lisburn is actually a part of the Ulster Way route so it seemed an appropriate training ground. I sent my boss a text apologising for the short notice but asking if I could take the following day off on leave. He quickly replied to say that wouldn't be a problem. I didn't say why I wanted the day off. I imagine that if I had, he might have questioned my sanity and declined my request in the interests of my own wellbeing!

Before turning in for the night, I made my rudimentary preparations. I printed the relevant maps and route directions from the Ulster Way website, packed my iPod, some snack bars and a flask of water into a small backpack, and set out the boots and clothes I was going to wear. The boots I chose to wear were a leather pair that I had worn quite often for short walks and I had always found them very comfortable. Matched with a pair of thick socks bought from a well-known high-street department store, I believed that these would serve me well. This was my first big mistake!

Anyway, with my gear all ready for a quick getaway in the morning, I headed off to bed and set my alarm for seven. Of course, as it turned out, the alarm wasn't needed as my anticipation levels were so high. I wasn't sleeping particularly well anyway due to the fact that the bed seemed very cold and empty without Jacqui. I rose before the alarm went off and after getting dressed and having a quick breakfast, I grabbed my backpack and headed out the front door. Now my "plan" up to this point had been to drive down to Stranmillis and join the towpath there. However, again on the spur of the moment, I decided to leave the car and walk from the house to Stranmillis. After all, this day was all about walking and testing myself and it would only add about three miles onto the ten miles of the Towpath. This was my second big mistake!

So, I set off on foot, as nature intended. I felt quite superior as I marched along the pavement, smugly watching the daily commute slowly crawling towards Belfast City Centre in the usual variety of vehicles. It was certainly a liberating feeling to be free of the car and on foot at this early hour and escaping the mass morning migration to work. However, although I was enjoying physical freedom that morning, my mind was still wrapped up in the constricting chains of grief. I would have very gladly swapped my illusion of freedom with any one of the drivers or passengers passing me by if it meant that my life could be returned to normal and I could have Jacqui back by my side. Such thoughts occurred to me frequently and although I realised that they were totally futile, they were impossible to avoid. Denial and reality were constantly at battle in my head. However, I knew deep down that what had been normal for so many years was now lost forever and that somewhere along the way, no matter how much my heart railed against it, I would have to adjust to a "new" normal without my love. So I marched on resolutely and, just over an hour later, I arrived at the Stranmillis end of the Lagan Towpath and left the traffic far behind as I joined the path that would hug the banks of the river Lagan for the next ten miles to Lisburn. It was turning out to be a lovely day and I had my iPod for company and it felt good to be off the city streets and starting this beautiful and tranquil stretch of the walk.

Grey squirrels, noisy ducks, quiet moorhens, graceful swans, stone bridges, the lock-keepers cottage, tumbling weirs, cellophane covered fields, blue skies, green banks, tall trees, a long-legged heron, slow moving water, grand buildings past and present – all these things and more provided a feast for the eyes as I travelled the length of the towpath. Four hours later and I was in the city of Lisburn. I had managed it. Legs, feet, everything felt good and I was feeling quite pleased with myself. It was around lunchtime and I thought I had earned a proper sit-down lunch, so I headed into the city centre and found a pleasant little café run by a friendly Polish couple and treated myself to the all-day breakfast. As I finished my cup of tea and rested my legs, I considered my next move. I could check the bus times and get a bus back into Belfast or I could phone for a taxi and be dropped back to my front door. But it was a beautiful day and it was still only around 2pm. I felt that my legs still had a good few miles left in them yet and so I decided to walk back to Belfast again. This was my third and biggest mistake of the day!

Looking back on it now, as I have done so many times since, this decision was the absolute height of madness. I really should have been satisfied with what I had already achieved in walking all the way from my home in Belfast to Lisburn. It was my first long distance walk ever and I should have let it be at that – after all, 13 miles wasn't a bad effort for starters. However, I was gripped by some kind of obsessive compulsion to push myself to the limit, regardless of the consequences. I believe that the trauma of my recent bereavement had lowered my defences and I obviously wasn't thinking straight. Either that or I was simply bonkers; and I'm not entirely ruling that possibility out.

Anyway, I made my way back to Union Bridge in Lisburn and joined the Towpath once again to start the downstream journey back to Belfast. After about five miles, the soles of my feet were starting to burn and my boots seemed to be pressing down on the tops of both of my big toes. It was uncomfortable at this stage, but not painful, and so I kept going. However, after another couple of miles things had become progressively more uncomfortable, now verging on painful, and I now realised that completing the walk back to Belfast was going to be a much bigger challenge than I had expected. I was too scared to take off my boots and socks at this stage to inspect my feet, for fear that I might not have been able to get them on again! So I marched, or rather hobbled, onwards.

There were a number of points along the Towpath where it passed over or under a public road and where I could have quite simply abandoned my walk and phoned for a taxi to come and collect me. But call it madness, stupidity, resolve, or determination. Call it what you will, but I simply kept on going. I myself favour calling it sheer bloody stubbornness! I had decided I was going to walk back to Belfast and nothing was going to stop me – no matter what damage I did to my feet in the process. By the time I reached Stranmillis again, my feet were in pretty bad shape. The confident and striding gait with which I had set off earlier in the day, had now been replaced by a rather hesitant and pathetic shuffling movement. Yet again I could have summoned a taxi to pick me up at this point, but yet again I pushed on stubbornly. At least my subconscious managed to find a nanoparticle of sense at this stage and, rather than attempting to walk the remaining three miles home, I opted to walk the shorter distance of one mile over to the Ormeau Road to get a bus. I think that somehow a taxi ride home would have equalled defeat in my muddled mind, while using the bus was a more acceptable and honourable way to complete the journey. What an absolute idiot!

When I reached the Ormeau Road, I looked down it in the direction of the city centre and spotted a bus coming. It was too far away to see the number or destination displayed on its front, but there was a good chance it would be the 7A that would drop me close to home. I gritted my teeth and quickened my step, ignoring the pain in my legs and feet, and made for the closest bus stop, determined to reach it before the bus did. And I made it just in time too – but only to find out that it was the wrong bloody bus after all.

I patiently took a seat in the bus shelter and tried to hold back the maelstrom of emotions that hit me like a wave at this point. What the hell was I doing? Why was I so stubborn and stupid? What good was this doing me anyway? It was never going to bring Jacqui back! How was I ever going to be able to walk the entire Ulster Way after this disaster of a day? Did I really want to go home? Was all this walking just an excuse to avoid going home? Where was home now anyway? Without Jacqui, the house where I lived no longer really felt like home. More than anything at that moment, all I really wanted to do, with all my body and soul, was to fall into Jacqui's arms and give her the biggest hug ever and tell her how much I missed her. It wasn't the first time and it certainly wouldn't be the last. I felt the wave starting to break over me and, although I did my best to hold my emotions in check, the tears simply would not be stopped. Sitting there, with my head in my hands and sobbing uncontrollably, I was glad that there was no one else waiting at the bus stop at the time, but I'm sure that I must have received some strange looks from anyone passing by.

About twenty minutes later the 7A bus finally appeared and I struggled, both physically and mentally, back onto my feet and climbed on-board. Twenty-five minutes later I arrived back at the house, eleven hours after setting out that morning. And on this occasion it did feel like home because my daughter, Hannah, was there to welcome me and she prepared me a lovely evening meal, while I had the hottest bath that my feet and legs could endure. The next few days were pure agony. My introduction to blisters was as immediate as it was painful and the ache in the muscles of my legs was so intense that the only way I could walk down a flight of stairs for the next few days, was to proceed backwards while clinging onto the handrail for support. I recovered from the worst of both of these conditions after three to four days. However, it was literally months before the nails on both of my big toes returned to their normal colour. I had dipped my toes in the pilgrimage pool and they had come out black! But I wasn't going to let that, or anything else, put me off. Despite my initial experiences, I felt compelled to undertake my pilgrimage round the

Ulster Way. I really needed this challenge to keep me going, needed the focus and purpose it presented to keep my head above water. Without it, I feared that I would simply give up on life.

The Right Stuff

I felt that my initial attempt at preparing myself for my pilgrimage was an unmitigated disaster. I had made some pretty fundamental errors – I think that's the kindest thing that could be said about my early approach. But as is often the case in life, the trick is to learn from your mistakes. So I used the next four weeks to put things right.

The first thing I had to do was to invest in some proper gear, starting with the boots and working up from there. In this regard, I found the staff in the local Cotswold Outdoor store in Belfast very helpful and knowledgeable. A few hours there, talking to experienced people and trying on various items, was time very well spent. I made a few visits to this store, doing my usual online research in between, and ended up with a good pair of lightweight and waterproof walking boots, two pairs of good quality hiking socks, two pairs of liner socks, trousers with detachable legs for the warmer weather, water resistant trousers for the wet weather, waterproof leggings for the even wetter weather, walking poles, a compass and a number of re-sealable waterproof bags. My top half was already well covered as I already had ample T-shirts, fleeces and waterproof jackets, although I did purchase a lightweight waterproof cape, which proved to be invaluable on more than one occasion. I also already had a small, lightweight backpack with well-padded shoulder straps and Hannah had bought me a two litre water bladder, or hydration pack to give it its technical name. I was reluctant to use it at first, but once tried I became a bladder convert, as it was so much easier to drink from the tube rather than having to struggle to get a water bottle out every time I wanted a sip. Another essential item added to my backpack was a pack of Compeed plasters to help cushion any further inevitable blisters. One other thing that I bought, in a moment of uncharacteristic optimism, was a hat to protect me from the sun – this, unfortunately, turned out to be by far the least used item I had purchased. The sales assistant was positively beaming when I headed towards the check-out till with my pile of intended purchases and her beam then transferred to my face when she informed me that I was entitled to 15% discount as I was walking for a recognised charity.

Right, now that I had the proper gear, it was time to do some proper training. And that didn't mean trying to complete the whole walk in one go again. No, a much more measured approach was now called for. It was time to build things up gradually. I had decided that I would start my pilgrimage on Friday 12 June 2015, which meant that I had about three weeks to get up to speed, as it were. In the evenings after work, I went out for short walks of two or three miles when I could and then at the weekends I would try to fit in one or two longer walks of around eight to ten miles. I would like to say at this point that I was incredibly disciplined and took my training seriously, but, to be honest, I can't. As it turned out, this wasn't a great problem – in fact I was later to find out that you can sometimes do too much training! A lot of my spare time was actually taken up with pouring over the maps and the descriptions of the routes and working out the logistics for the walk. When was I going to walk? How was I going to get to the start points each day? How far was I going to walk each day? What was I going to do when I reached my destination at the end of each leg? As I moved further away from Belfast and my home, where was I going to stay overnight? What was the back-up plan if something unexpected happened? All these details and more had to be thought through and worked out. If my physical preparation was a bit casual, this certainly couldn't be said of my logistical planning and preparation – years of working on countless operating and corporate plans for a public sector body certainly stood me in good stead here.

Looking back on it, the value of all this planning and preparation in helping me through my grief was perhaps more significant than I realised at the time. It forced me to focus on the challenge I had set for myself and provided me with a real purpose in my life at a time when I often felt that my life no longer had any reason or value. It distracted me from dwelling on the enormity of my loss and motivated me to get up in the morning and to keep going during the day. Often I would plot and plan late into the night – not going to bed until very late so that I could hopefully fall quickly into the exhausted, deep sleep I craved.

However, having said that, Jacqui had been such a huge part of my life and losing her had left such an enormous void that no amount of work was going to totally insulate me from the sheer devastation and bleakness I constantly sensed, lying just below the surface. All too often my emotions would rip through the paper thin walls I had built around myself and feelings of utter loneliness and hopelessness would at once overwhelm and totally consume me. Sometimes it felt as if I was swimming in an endless open ocean, no shore in sight, caught in an unending and powerful rip current, just trying desperately to keep my head above the water. And then, every so often, the huge, looming, dark shadow, lying in wait under the surface, would grab at my feet and suddenly and violently pull me under the water where I would struggle hopelessly until I was released. Only then could I once again make it back to the surface to catch my breath and continue with my unending swim – until the next inevitable attack. And swimming in open water is a very good analogy, because where I had once felt that I had solid ground beneath my feet, I now felt that nothing was stable – everything around me had shifted and was continuing to move – there was nothing firm and stable to hold onto – I had to keep moving forward in order to avoid drowning in despair. But without a doubt, having my challenge to focus on, and to plan for, did help me immensely.

Before I set off on my pilgrimage, I had a full walking schedule pretty much planned out on paper. I knew on which days I was going to walk, the start and finishing points for each of those days, and roughly how long it would take me to walk each day. For the early part of the walk, I also had arrangements in place to ensure I could get to the start points at an agreed time as well as arrangements in place for pick-up at the finish points. I also had arrangements in place to stay overnight away from home when required. In relation to transport, and more particularly in relation to accommodation, I only firmed up on plans for about a fortnight ahead as there was always the potential for my planned schedule to slip due to very bad weather or injury. As it turned out, this was a sensible approach to take. I would come to learn that a pilgrim needs to be able to cope with the unexpected and be prepared to be flexible. I was very heartened by the support I received from family and friends when it came to asking for lifts and a place to bed down for the night. As time went on, and word spread about my walk, I often didn't even have to ask for help, as people were coming forward and volunteering.

My walk was of course to be undertaken in memory of Jacqui. It was so important to me that Jacqui, and the special relationship we had together, should not be forgotten. But my walk was also to help raise funds for cancer research. So I also had to think seriously about publicising the fact that I was undertaking the walk for charity. After all, I could walk the Ulster Way and make it to the end and not raise a single penny if no one knew about it. I therefore set up a Just Giving page to allow donations to be made online and also created a Facebook page to help promote my challenge and raise funds. In all honesty, I don't believe that I could have raised anywhere near the sum I did without the use of social media. Social media certainly has its downsides, but it can also be, as it proved to be in my case, an incredibly useful tool to engage with many people I would never otherwise have reached. As well as writing a blog of my journey, I wanted to capture as many of the scenes as possible along the route so that these could also be shared on social media. So one of the most important items I decided to take with me on my pilgrimage was my trusted camera. It was a Canon SX700, which took excellent pictures and, even though it packed an impressive 30X optical zoom, was compact enough to carry in my pocket. My pictures also acted as a great aide memoir to myself as I tried to recall each day's journey in order to compose my blogs. Facebook became the primary communication platform for my walk, now well and truly branded "1000K4J", and it was incredible to watch the levels of engagement grow as the walk progressed and my updates were posted. Although it is no substitute for real human, face to face contact, there is little doubt that the messages of support that I received via Facebook really touched me and helped keep my spirits up during my pilgrimage.

However, before I fully appreciated the power of social media, I also resorted to a more traditional form of communication and decided to get a few hundred leaflets printed. These proved to be very useful in the early days as I dropped them at cafés and public buildings along the route and even took to handing them out to individuals I met along some of the busier stretches. Some of the messages posted along with donations left on my Just Giving page proved that it was certainly very worthwhile having the leaflets printed. Examples of the comments from total strangers included:

Hi Dermot, You gave us your last flyer on Sunday on the coastal path at Helen's Bay. I wish you well on your walk for this worthy cause. Regards Bill

Dermot, Helena and I were dashing to church on Sunday, so we couldn't stop (!). We read Dermot's Story and it really got our attention. Sorry for your loss. Charlie & Helena

'Dermot's Story' certainly did not pull any punches – it set out what had happened to Jacqui and how the idea for my pilgrimage had come about after I had told Jacqui that "I would walk even further than Harold Fry if I thought it could save you". I had decided early on in the process of formulating my challenge that I was going to be as honest as I could in telling people why I was undertaking my 1000K4J walk. So I just told my story as it was and used this as the foundation for the leaflet, my Just Giving page and for Facebook. It was a story that seemed to resonate with many people and I make no apologies for being so open and for baring my soul in public. I suppose in a way I wanted the reader to feel my pain; to fully understand that someone very special had been taken away from me by this vicious and cruel disease called cancer. I knew that I was not the first to be left wounded by the death of a loved one. Not the first to have lost a life partner at too young an age. And my family was not the first family to be treated so cruelly by cancer. Goodness knows there were many others who have suffered similar or worse. But ultimately, I wanted my story to touch peoples' hearts to such an extent that they would pause for a moment in their busy lives and make a donation. It certainly seemed to have that effect. One final thing I did to help publicise my walk was to get a couple of white T-shirts with "1000K4J IN AID OF CANCER RESEARCH" printed in large black lettering on the front. I now had the means to advertise my walk wherever I went.

So my preparations were now as complete as they were ever going to be. The right stuff had been bought, some (perhaps not enough?) training had been undertaken, maps and directions were printed, my walking schedule had been drawn up, immediate transport and accommodation plans had been put in place, and the publicity machine had been started. Friday 12 June was upon me before I knew it. To say I was apprehensive would be a bit of an understatement. I had by this stage cranked up the expectations and I had now well and truly committed myself to my 1000K4J pilgrimage. To back out now would be unthinkable. In all honesty, the thought of backing out at this stage never crossed my mind. I did still harbour some doubts as to my ability to be able to complete what would be, for me anyway (and probably for most people), a huge walk. I couldn't easily forget my disastrous introduction to long distance walking – a mere glimpse of my blackened toes was a sufficient reminder should it ever slip my mind.

However, I was determined to do this for Jacqui and for Cancer Research UK. All that remained for me to do now was to start walking.

The happy Breen family. Hannah, Jacqui, me and Matt on Christmas Day, 2013

I look at this photograph now and see the four of us standing together smiling on Christmas morning in 2013, blissfully unaware of what the following months would bring. It's the last photograph of all of us together before cancer entered and devastated our lives, ripping our happy family apart. Jacqui loved her family and she loved Christmas and her smile here clearly reflects this. It's how I always try to remember her in order to keep later, more tortured images at bay. I often look at this photograph and my eyes inevitably drift to the clock on the wall behind us as I over and over again wish for the impossible – to turn back time. To go back to a time BC, Before Cancer, and put my arms around her once again. But then the partially open door comes into focus and I think of how you can never really contain things forever. Time does move on and loved ones do leave. It obviously wouldn't have made any difference, but I still wish I had noticed the door and kicked it shut before this photo was taken.

Getting ready to set off from 'Jacqui's playground', with the staff of Greenisland Primary School

Looking across the River Lagan and the city of Belfast, with its hills in the background

A Single Step

The day to start my walk had finally arrived. Just what had I committed myself to? One thousand kilometres, or six hundred and twenty five miles, suddenly seemed like a huge challenge for a novice walker such as myself. Not for the first time, I quietly asked myself if I was indeed wise in the head. No backing out now though, even if I wanted to. So many people were already aware of my challenge that I simply couldn't let them down before even starting. And of course this walk was dedicated to Jacqui and that, more than anything, would see me through.

My pilgrimage was to begin with a 14 mile stretch from Greenisland Primary School to Belfast. Greenisland Primary School is actually located a few miles off the Ulster Way route itself, but it seemed like a very appropriate place to begin given that Jacqui had taught there for 25 years! In addition to this, the school had opened a new outdoor play area earlier in the year and dedicated it to Jacqui and erected a special plaque in her memory. My children, Matt and Hannah, and one of Jacqui's sisters, Christine, and I had been very honoured to be invited down to perform the opening ceremony in March. Following the opening, Christine had also presented the "Jacqui Breen Memorial Cup for hard work and enthusiasm in Primary 1" to its two inaugural winners. It was a very proud day for us and the memory of it reinforced even more in my mind the appropriateness of my chosen starting point. I could imagine Jacqui's amusement at such a fuss being made over her, as she had always been a very modest person, but I know that deep down she would have been delighted to have been honoured in such a very special way.

Thankfully, the Principal of Greenisland Primary School, had very kindly agreed to my starting the walk from Jacqui's playground, but had wisely suggested leaving it until the end of the school day. This meant starting a bit later than I would have liked, but I didn't mind at all under the circumstances. In fact, it also worked in my favour as it meant that I now only had to take a half day's leave from work rather than a whole day – I was going to need to ration my leave for use later in the walk. Nikki, a good friend and work colleague, had kindly agreed to drop me out to the school. When we I arrived that afternoon, I was delighted to see that so many of the school staff had resisted the temptation to dash off home for the weekend as soon as the school bell had rung, so they could bid me bon voyage from Jacqui's playground.

We all gathered in the play area for photographs and I recalled the Chinese proverb (metricated for my purposes) "A journey of a thousand kilometres begins with a single step". I placed my hand on Jacqui's plaque and vowed to return to it at the end of my walk - if I made it! I felt a heady cocktail of emotions at this point. In one sense I was pleased to be finally getting my long planned pilgrimage underway and delighted with the grand send off I was receiving. But this pleasure was inevitably undermined by the deep and dark seam of sadness that now ran through my being. I truly wished that I never had to embark on this journey at all. It was only because Jacqui was no longer here, a fact brought into stark relief by the plaque I was now touching, that this journey had ever had to be conceived in the first place.

I wished with all my heart that this was just another perfectly normal Friday afternoon and that Jacqui was still here at school, sharing jokes and laughter with her colleagues as they finished up for the day and made ready to head home for the weekend. I wished that I was still at work also, experiencing that usual Friday feeling and looking forward to getting home to Jacqui, to gather up our things before heading to our holiday home in Portrush for the weekend. In many ways, this was a pilgrimage that I now needed to do, but it wasn't one that I ever wished to do. I put my brave face on and gently removed my hand from Jacqui's plaque. And then I took that first single step and just kept going towards the school gates with a full entourage in tow.

Part of me still believes that they really wanted to make sure that I was truly serious about doing the walk and that I wasn't just going to take a lift back into Belfast with Nikki as soon as I left the school grounds. In fact, three of the staff, Mandy, Jayne and Dorothy, followed me along the upper road for a couple of miles before they were finally convinced that I was really going to continue without the need for a constant escort! I am jesting of course. In all honesty, the school provided me with a brilliant send off and it was great to have the company of some of Jacqui's colleagues at the very start of my pilgrimage. We walked together along the very busy B90 until the sidewalk came to an end and then, in the interests of road safety, I said farewell to my escorts and continued solo along the roadside, stepping up onto the grass verge frequently to avoid the heavy traffic.

Thankfully, it was only about another half a mile along the B90 before I joined the Ulster Way route proper and was able to escape off the busy road. Entry was via a rather inauspicious gap in some palisade fencing along the roadside, as it picked up the National Cycle Network Route through the Three Mile Water Park in Newtownabbey. I was now taking my very first steps on the actual Ulster Way route and, although accessed through a rather unpromising "gap in the fence", it still felt like a significant moment as I left the normal highway to join the 1,000 kilometre long circuit that would literally and metaphorically give my life direction for the next two and a half months. It was truly remarkable just how quickly the constant noise of the traffic I had endured along the B90 faded into the distance as I moved into the trees and bushes of the park. It was a pleasure to be welcomed into this refuge of nature and tranquility, which very quickly gave the impression of being very far removed from the hustle and bustle of urban life.

A sign close to the entrance of the park informed me that the Three Mile Water flows into Belfast Lough and that the river and the surrounding woodland provides an important habitat for a wide range of species, including bats, butterflies, otters, foxes and owls, as well as both sea trout and brown trout. However, I'm afraid that the only examples of wildlife that I spotted, as I meandered through the park, were some very energetic dogs and some very plump woodpigeons. Nevertheless, it provided a much more pleasant journey than the B90 could ever have offered.

I continued on through the park until I reached the Shore Road and then followed the Lough Shore Path into Belfast. Although I had driven along the Shore Road between Belfast and Newtownabbey many times, I had never been on the Lough Shore Path and it was quite a pleasant revelation. I enjoyed the walk along the North shore of the Belfast Lough and I stopped off at the oasis that is Hazelbank Park along the way for a snack and a short rest. On leaving Hazelbank Park, the path ran right alongside the M5 and then M2 Motorways for a few miles, but the journey wasn't as unpleasant as you might expect. On my left were the extensive mudflats of the North Foreshore, a Special Protection Area due to its abundance of bugs and birds, and to my right I enjoyed views of Belfast Castle and the Belfast Hills, including Cave

Hill and McArt's Fort, commonly known as Napoleon's Nose on account of its profile from a distance.

At the Fortwilliam Roundabout on the outskirts of Belfast, the path swung away from the motorway and led me along Duncrue Road and through an industrial landscape of warehouses and factories – this was definitely not the most scenic of routes. However, I soon reached the city centre area and there were a few more interesting things to see, including the Flying Angel sculpture at the Mission to Seafarers and the now abandoned St Joseph's Church, both of which stood rather incongruously among the new brick apartment blocks on Princes Dock Street. As the route skirted along the North bank of the River Lagan, I passed the Clarendon dry docks and newly restored pump-house, the Dividers sculpture, the Big Fish printed ceramic mosaic sculpture, the Lagan Weir, the Thanksgiving Statue/Beacon of Hope, known locally as "Nuala with the Hula", and the Belfast Waterfront concert hall. Instead of finishing at Belfast Central Station as originally planned, I pushed on for the extra mile or so to the Ormeau Bridge with its "ghost" bicycle mounted on the railings as a warning to cyclists of an earlier accident at this spot. The extra mile made it easier to get a bus home from this point, but, more importantly I thought, this was a mile that I wouldn't have to walk tomorrow.

It had been a lovely warm and dry afternoon and evening and the going had been fairly easy. I had managed to cover the distance in about five hours, which I was happy with. That was the first day complete and 14 miles covered. That only left another 610 miles or so to go – just to temper my enthusiasm! However, even though I still had a huge distance to cover on my pilgrimage, I was certainly pleased that I had at last made a start and that I had completed the first day successfully. It had been an emotional start, setting off as I had from Jacqui's school, but although I had walked away from her plaque that afternoon, I had still felt her presence with me every step of the way as I walked from Greenisland to Belfast. After having my tea and writing my first travel blog and posting it on Facebook, it was time to head to bed and rest the feet and legs in preparation for tomorrow's walk which would take me from Lisburn, along the dreaded Lagan Towpath again, to the Ormeau Bridge and beyond.

The Towpath

Saturday 13 June – Lisburn to Belfast

Although I had already walked from Belfast to Lisburn and back during my ill-fated training day in May, I had decided to travel the Lagan Towpath section once again as part of my 'official' walk – hopefully with less damage to my big toes on this occasion! The Lagan Towpath is described as an "arm" of the Ulster Way as it is not part of the main circular route that forms the majority of the Way. Instead it branches away from the main route in a linear style. This is one of three linear routes or "arms" of the Ulster Way; the Newry Canal and the stretch from Magilligan to Binevenagh being the other two. I decided to start this section of the Ulster Way in Lisburn and then walk into Belfast. Like the main "circular" route, it really makes little difference which direction you go in. After all, it is still the same distance whether you travel from A to B or from B to A.

So on Saturday morning, I drove myself to Lisburn and left my car in a small car park close to the Civic Centre. It was a gorgeous day as I set off walking from Union Bridge and followed the Lagan Tow Path all the way back into Belfast. Just downstream from the Civic Centre, I had a very clear sighting of a Kingfisher flying across to the opposite bank of the River Lagan. It was the first time I had ever seen one in real life and it brightened up my day right away. Even though I had my camera in hand when I saw it, it was gone in a flash and there was no way I was going to get a photo. This incident was all the more special due to the fact that one of Hannah's very special memories of her mum is when they had been out for a walk together on the Lagan Towpath near Belfast the previous year and had spotted a Kingfisher - a first for both of them. Jacqui had been so excited by the sighting at the time that the memory had remained very vivid in Hannah's mind. Jacqui was usually a very calm and placid person but her occasional sudden and unexpected outbursts of excitement were legendary and quite endearing – well most of the time anyway!

When Hannah was only about eight years old, we stayed with Jacqui's sister, Heather, and her husband, Terry, in London for a few days. While in the kitchen one day preparing lunch, Jacqui had been talking to Hannah about the famous TV chef, Jamie Oliver. It so happened that Jamie Oliver appeared on

TV later on that afternoon while Jacqui and I were watching. Hannah was in another room at the time and so Jacqui called to her to come and see. Now, when I say called, what I really mean is that Jacqui leapt up excitedly from the sofa and shouted "Hannah, Hannah, come quick. It's Jamie Oliver!!" You would have thought from Jacqui's excitement that Jamie Oliver had just arrived into the house in person. Unfortunately, Hannah was sucking on a boiled sweet at the time and in reacting to Jacqui's excitement she swallowed the sweet and it lodged in her oesophagus. All hell then broke loose and I had to quickly apply the "Heimlich manoeuver" to Hannah to dislodge the sweet! It was scary at the time, but became a source of humour over the years and any time Jacqui subsequently got over excited we just said she was having a "Jamie Oliver moment".

As well as the Kingfisher, there were a few other nice surprises along the Lagan Towpath. Janet, a very thoughtful work colleague, had put up a "Good Luck" sign along the path just before the Tullynacross Road crossing point. It was a wonderful gesture that really helped buoy me along. And then I met Jonny, another colleague from work, who had cycled all the way over from Whiteabbey. It was great to see him. Later, I was listening to a local DJ called Sonya Mac on my phone's radio as I was walking along and she was calling out "Woo Hoo's" for listeners that were doing something strange or unusual. So I sent a few texts to Hannah, who was at home, and a few minutes later my story was on the radio and I was getting a big "Woo Hoo" from Sonya!! She is a great supporter of Cancer Research UK herself and I was very grateful for the mention on the local radio station. I instantly nominated Hannah as my official Press Officer!

I stopped at the Lock Keepers Inn at lunchtime, luckily getting in just before the crowds arrived. As it was such a lovely warm and sunny day, I had my lunch sitting at one of the tables outside. Here I recalled the poem I had written back in February. It was shortly after I had gone out for a run along the Lagan Towpath for the first time after Jacqui had died.

Running on empty

I went for a run
Along the river path
Where horses once towed
Where we used to walk

Couples holding hands
Happy and carefree
Sunday strolls together
Life as it should be

The Lock-keepers Inn
Seats out in the sun
Crowded with people
A perfect location

Everyone looks fine
But God only knows
What grief in their past
Or grief yet to come

There on a bridge
In yellow and black
A stark warning sign
Danger Deep Water

Swirling waters below
Beckon me forward
Thoughts of reunion
You push me back

I turn to head home
On my solitary path
The river beside me
Setting the pace

Glad of the low sun
A reason for shades
To cover my eyes
To hide my tears

Memories surround me
I cannot escape
A life once so full
Now running on empty

Before leaving the Lock Keepers Inn and setting off again, I handed out a few of my 1000K4J leaflets to people sitting outside. Did I want their support and donations or did I crave their pity and understanding? I'm not sure – probably a mixture of both. In any case, I certainly wanted them to know what I was doing and why I was doing it. I know it's illogical, but I felt that people should somehow automatically know that I had lost the love of my life and that I was grieving inside, even if there were no visible signs of grief on the outside. It just didn't seem fair that the rest of the world could simply continue on doing normal things when my world had been totally devastated. How could something that had such a dramatic impact on my life have absolutely no impact on people sitting at the tables around me, only feet away? Of course, there is no reason why they should have known, just as I had no idea what was going on in their lives, good or bad. But it made me think about the Victorian tradition of wearing black for months or even years after bereavement. Perhaps it wasn't such a bad idea? It certainly told the outside world that all was not right in your world and perhaps even allowed the bereaved to benefit from the empathy of strangers, even if it was only a sympathetic look or nod of understanding. Anyway, my leaflet would have to suffice on this occasion.

As I was approaching the Stranmillis area, I contacted Hannah again and asked if she could drive to the Ormeau Bridge and pick me up in about half an hour's time. Now, how easy was that compared to my training day shenanigans? When I reached the bridge, I didn't have long to wait before Hannah and her boyfriend, Jonny, arrived to give me a lift from the Ormeau Bridge to Central Station. I had already walked that section yesterday, so I wasn't too keen on doing it again. At Central Station I carried out some minor repair work to my feet with the aid of a couple of Compeed plasters. Thankfully, there were no problems with the big toes this time, but a few small blisters had started to form. I then made my way past the Waterfront Hall, "Nuala with the Hula" once again, the Odyssey Arena (since renamed the SSE Arena), the SS Nomadic and around the superb, ship-themed design of the Titanic building, watching the bungee jumping taking place from a crane as I went. I then headed down past Belfast's iconic yellow Harland & Wolff cranes, Samson and Goliath, to the Dee Street bridge where I was picked up once again by Hannah and Jonny in the late afternoon sunshine. They then drove me back out to Lisburn to pick up my car and then we all headed home.

So that was my second day complete and another 14 miles under my boots. The weather had been fabulous all day. My legs and feet were tired but not so tired that I couldn't cut the grass in the back garden when I got back home. The chores still had to be done, and that also included my Facebook blog a bit later. The weather forecast for Sunday was also looking good and I was looking forward to it and the next leg of my walk that would take me from Dee Street in Belfast to the other side of Bangor in North Down.

Woods and Bays

Sunday 14 June – Belfast to Bangor

I woke early and, still half asleep, rolled over in bed to put my arm around Jacqui. Once again, I experienced the horrible sensation of emptiness spread through my entire body and mind as my arm failed to find the anticipated warmth of Jacqui's body, but instead landed upon a cold and empty space in the bed. It was becoming a familiar routine, but one that seemed to be beyond my ability to remember no matter how many times it was repeated. Sleep is supposed to allow the body and mind time out to restore and repair, but it could also play cruel tricks by allowing me to temporarily forget reality. Perhaps this was indeed part of the healing process? I don't know. But it seemed like every morning was a sort of "Groundhog Day", in which I repeatedly woke up time and again only to experience the realisation that Jacqui was no longer lying beside me, as she had done for practically every day for over 30 years. For just how long, I wondered, would I continue to reach out for something that was totally unreachable? After struggling once again with my inner demons that would have me lie in bed and close myself away from the rest of the world, I turned my mind to my challenge, my walk for Jacqui, something positive, something with purpose, a reason to get out of bed and face the world. It was never easy, but thankfully my desire to walk in memory of Jacqui's life was always stronger than the temptation to hide away and dwell on what was lost.

As predicted, it turned out to be a gorgeous day for the third day of my pilgrimage. Rich, one of my North Coast surfing buddies, picked me up from my home that morning in his cool red and black "surf-mobile" and transported me to the day's starting point at Dee Street in the Sydenham area of Belfast. My previous day's walk had finished by passing by some of Belfast's shipbuilding heritage at Harland & Wolff and today's walk started along-side some of its aeronautical heritage at Shorts Brothers.

The first couple of miles of the walk were along Airport Road, taking me past various industrial sites and a variety of oil, gas and petroleum storage facilities, so it wasn't the most scenic. But there were a couple of spots where nature stubbornly shone through, such as the poppies I spotted growing amongst the stones behind a wire fence along the roadside. More significantly, however, was the recently opened Window On Wildlife (WOW) nature reserve in the heart of Belfast harbour. Despite the urban surroundings, the shoreline is home to seals and many species of shore birds and wildflowers. Oystercatchers, cormorants, lapwings, redshank, eider duck and curlew are all common. However, these rare nature spots were very much diamonds in the rough along this mainly industrial landscape.

The scenery improved dramatically once I reached Holywood. Although pronounced the same as the American movie town of Hollywood, the Latin name for this town was originally Sanctus Boscus, meaning "Holy Wood". This was the name given to the woodlands surrounding a seventh century monastery that previously existed on the site of the present ruins of Holywood Priory. I was going to encounter many different types of woods and forests on my pilgrimage round the Ulster Way, some of them deemed holy, as was the case here in Holywood, but others reputed to be the home of fairies, witches and even devils! The rest of the entire route from Holywood on to Ballyholme was quite simply gorgeous, with the path hugging the coastline and revealing a new delight at almost every turn. When I caught the first glimpse of Helen's Bay in the glorious sunshine through the trees, as I rounded Grey Point, I could easily have mistaken it for somewhere in the Mediterranean.

Hannah and Jonny joined me at Crawfordburn Country Park and we had a bite of lunch here before the three of us set off together for the next six miles or so to Bangor. It was great to have their company. Crawfordburn Country Park is a beautiful area that boasts large areas of rich woodland and two beaches, the most famous of which is Helen's Bay. Helen's Bay and the nearby Helen's Tower are named after the mother of the first Marquis of Dufferin and Ava, who was famous as an arctic explorer in the 1800's. We passed two more small bays, the pretty Swineley Bay and Smelt Mill Bay, before we rounded Wilsons Point and turned into Bangor Bay to be confronted with an extremely busy Marina, which was basking in glorious sunshine.

We worked our way through the throngs of people enjoying a Sunday outing by the seaside and made our way along the seafront road and then around Lukes Point to Ballyholme Bay. As we rounded Lukes Point, it was with a sense of wonder that we noticed crossing jet streams in the blue sky above, almost as if someone had drawn a huge "X" in the air to mark the end point of our walk. Signs such as this one would become a regular occurrence on my pilgrimage and would grow in importance as I progressed round the Ulster Way. We reached our final destination for the day near the far end of Ballyholme Bay just after 4pm. From here, it was just a very brief stroll up one of the streets to meet up with Cyril and Judith, who provided us with plenty of refreshments while we rested in their back garden and soaked up the warmth of the sunshine, before making our way back to Belfast.

So that was the first weekend of my journey complete and I had already covered 43 miles. I began thinking, rather prematurely as it turned out, that this walking lark was straightforward enough, particularly now that I had prepared for it and invested in a few decent bits of kit. The past three days had been challenging at times but also enjoyable and rewarding. I certainly couldn't have hoped for better weather for the start of my venture and the support for my walk had been fantastic. I checked my Just Giving page and was delighted to find that, only one week after being launched, a staggering £1,500 had been raised. That was 30% of my £5,000 target already achieved.

However, the weekend had also been particularly poignant, as I had lost another very dear friend to the same cruel illness that had taken Jacqui in January. Rosaleen, who I had known for over ten years after she had come to work with me, had been a very good friend. Unfortunately, she had been diagnosed with ovarian cancer five years ago and had to retire from work as a result. We had become even closer in recent years, particularly after Jacqui's diagnosis, and she had been a great support and source of advice to both me and Jacqui. She had a great sense of humour and would never let things get her down for too long – she was very similar to Jacqui in many ways with regard to her spirit and determination. She had very bravely battled with cancer, and all the treatment that goes with it, for five years, but now her time had unfortunately finally run out. It was another heavy blow, but it just made me all the more determined to complete my 1,000 km walk and to continue raising funds for the vital work being undertaken by Cancer Research UK. I felt that Jacqui and Rosaleen would now both be with me all the way on my pilgrimage - my very own celestial cheerleaders! They would have just loved the idea of that.

Before the evening was out, I had to write my blog for the day and post it to Facebook along with the photos I had selected to illustrate my journey. Writing the blog was time consuming work but my small but growing band of Facebook followers seemed to be enjoying reading my updates and so I certainly felt it was worth doing. It also allowed me to keep a fairly contemporaneous account of my travels as I went. I just hoped that my followers could survive without any posts for a few days while I was back at work for the week ahead. However, it would give me ample time to get ready for next weekend's walk, that would take me down and across the Ards Peninsula, all the way from Bangor to Portaferry – or so I thought!

Weather Angels

Saturday 20 June – Bangor to Ballywalter

After a week at work, I was very keen to get back on my pilgrimage again. The plan for this weekend was to spend Saturday walking from Bangor to Ballyhalbert or Portavogie and then, on Sunday, all being well, I was going to get the running gear on and jog the rest of the way to Portaferry. Why jog on Sunday, you might very well ask? Well, Hannah had decided to enter a team of four for the Belfast Half Marathon in September to raise money for cancer research. Her boyfriend, Jonny, and Becky, a good friend of Hannah's since childhood, had already joined the team and she asked me if I wanted to join them also. The date was a few weeks after I planned to finish my walk and I did a bit of running anyway, so I readily agreed. I was quite proud that my daughter also wanted to do something for cancer research and I was only too happy to lend her my support. I had already started a bit of running training between my walking days and thought that I might even run a section or two of the Ulster Way instead of walking. But I was soon to find out that was most definitely a bad idea! I also thought that it would be good to leave my walking boots at home today and wear a lighter pair of trainer style shoes. The boots were great for rough ground, but they felt a bit cumbersome when walking on flat even surfaces, such as pavements and roads. This also turned out to be a very bad idea.

Anyway, after making another series of bad decisions, I drove from home to Portaferry on Saturday morning and met up with my friend John. I left my car there and John drove me through the dismal rain up and across the Ards Peninsula to Ballyholme, where I called in with Cyril and Judith again. The weather had improved at this point, although there was quite a bit of sea mist hanging in the air. John headed back home and I was chatting with Judith, when Cyril suddenly appeared in trainers, shorts and T-shirt. I hadn't been expecting him to join me, but was delighted to have the company and so we both headed off together down onto Ballyholme beach and turned east. We followed the coastal path round Ballymacormick Point for a couple of miles, crossing a secluded stretch of the walk owned by the National Trust, before coming to the very picturesque village of Groomsport. We then joined the busy A2 road towards Donaghadee.

We had another little excursion out along the coastline for about a mile or so at Orlock Point, following the nineteenth century Orlock Coach Road for a short section and passing under an archway, which had been hewn out of the rock by hand, before re-joining the A2 again. By this time the sun had burned through the mist and it was now an absolutely gorgeous day, with wall to wall blue skies. Cyril and I were met by my boss, Keith, who had walked about a mile out of his home town of Donaghadee to welcome us. He accompanied us into the town and led us to a lovely little coffee/gift shop, 'Home Sweet Home', run by his wife, Rhonda. There we were joined by Pip, another work colleague, and treated to a very welcome lunch courtesy of Keith and Rhonda. Refuelled, I once again set off with Keith keeping me company, while Cyril and Pip returned to Bangor.

Donaghadee was looking absolutely resplendent in the afternoon sunshine and I now began to think of my celestial cheerleaders, Jacqui and Rosaleen, as my own personal weather angels, who would do their best to watch over me and sweep the clouds and rain away whenever they could. I took lots of photos, particularly around the pretty harbour area where the stunning blue sky met a remarkably blue sea. We joined the A2 once again and headed further south along the east coast of the Ards Peninsula, with the Irish Sea on our left. We also enjoyed the super views of the Copeland Islands just off the coast as we went. There are three islands included in the Copeland Islands: Big Island, which is also known as Copeland Island; Lighthouse Island, which in fact no longer has a lighthouse; and Mew Island, which does have a lighthouse – it's all rather confusing and, some might say, very Irish. Apparently, the islands were used by smugglers who brought tobacco and spirits through the islands and into County Down, probably landing their goods at places like Orlock Point, up until the 20th century.

It was along this stretch of the A2 that Keith and I were also joined by Paul who had cycled over from Bangor to meet us. I was certainly enjoying lots of good company along this section of the Way. Keith had arranged for Violet, a reporter from a local paper, the Newtownards Chronicle, to meet us in Millisle and we stopped here for a while for me to give an interview, while sitting in the warm sunshine on a wooden picnic bench in a local park. I had also given a phone interview to the Larne Times the previous day. This was something I was quite happy to do. Any publicity was going to help raise awareness of the purpose behind my walk and therefore had the potential to draw in more funds for cancer research, which could only be a good thing. Keith had to leave at this point and he got a lift back to Donaghadee with Violet after the interview, while Paul opted to cycle alongside me for another few miles until the pavements ran out.

However, before leaving the picnic bench, I removed my shoes and socks to inspect my feet. Although I had been trying to ignore it up until this point, there was little doubt that my feet were beginning to suffer. My soles had been burning for the last couple of miles and it was now becoming clear to me that my choice of footwear for the day was turning out to be another costly mistake. Inspection of my feet confirmed what I suspected and I proceeded to apply the Compeed plasters where necessary to the blisters that had started to form. However, once my feet were patched up and re-shod, I hit the road again along with Paul, who had waited patiently on me completing my first-aid treatment. After a few miles, however, the pavement came to an abrupt end and Paul then had to say his farewells and head back to Bangor, while I walked on towards Ballywalter, hugging the verge and frequently having to step off the road to let the cars whizz past. I now understood why this section of the Ulster Way is described as a link section for which public transport is recommended. However, I made it safely to the village of Ballywalter, even though, in addition to the traffic, my feet and legs were now seriously conspiring against me. In addition to the tenderised feet, I had also now developed a pain along the shin of my right leg – something I had never experienced before.

As I was heading out the other side of the village of Ballywalter, towards my next milestone of Ballyhalbert, I felt a few sporadic, but heavy, drops of rain and decided to get the wet gear out of my rucksack; and not a moment too soon as it turned out. The heavens opened and there was an almighty downpour that lasted for about 15 minutes. My newly recruited weather angels had obviously knocked off early! I must have looked like a hobo with all my wet gear on, but it did its job very effectively. It was pretty miserable going though, as there were no footpaths once outside the village. The traffic was fairly fast moving and large puddles had rapidly developed along the roadside. I had to quickly become quite good at timing the passing of puddles so that it didn't coincide with the passing of a car. It quickly became obvious to me that many drivers weren't going to slow down in order to avoid drowning someone idiotic enough to be out walking in such weather! My feet were getting progressively more uncomfortable and now the pain in my right shin was getting quite worrying. I had hoped to walk at least as far as Ballyhalbert, which was only another three and a half miles away, but I now realised that it would be just too painful to carry on.

So I swallowed my pride and put an emergency call into Keith, who rescued me just about a mile south of Ballywalter and took me back to Donaghadee where he and his family, Rhonda and their two girls, welcomed me into their home for the night. They looked after me extremely well and treated me to a Chinese meal out in the town that evening. I tried my best to hide the fact that my feet and legs were in agony as I hobbled between house and car and restaurant. It was great to sit down at the table in the Chinese restaurant and take the weight off my damaged limbs. During the meal a good friend of Keith and Rhonda's came into the restaurant to pick up a takeaway meal and he came over to the table to chat briefly with us while he was waiting. Keith told him about my walk and before I knew it he was reaching into his wallet and handing me a donation. I was to experience many such spontaneous acts of kindness from people I had only just met as I walked the Ulster Way.

After returning to Keith and Rhonda's house, the girls headed off to bed and Keith, Rhonda and I relaxed with a few drinks before I turned in for the night to write my blog. Once again, I had taken lots of photographs along the way to give my Facebook followers a flavour of my travels. There was one I posted especially for Jennifer, a very brave friend, who was going through her own very personal battle with cancer and who had jokingly said that I needed to smile more in my photos. It had been a very tiring day, but also very enjoyable and it was great to see so many friends along the way. It was the longest day of walking so far and I have to say that I really felt it. My feet were badly blistered again and my right leg was quite sore along the shin. It was a slow and painful process manoeuvring around Keith's house and, despite my best efforts to try and disguise my mobility issues, I am quite sure they realised that I wasn't in the best condition for what I had planned for the following day. I would just have to wait and see how things were in the morning before deciding whether or not to set off for another days walking – I certainly didn't think that my planned jog to Portaferry was a realistic option any more. There was also another significant element that had to be factored into my plans for the following day. I needed to get to Omagh for my Dad's 91st Birthday and Father's Day celebrations.

Run Aground

Sunday 21 June

The following morning, I knew before even putting my feet to the floor that I wouldn't be walking anywhere today, never mind jogging. I had an uncomfortable night due to the pain in my feet and legs. When I did tentatively put my feet to the floor I realised that it was going to take at least a few days to recover from the damage I had inflicted upon myself. When I eventually stood up and tried to walk a bit, the discomfort in my feet and the sharp pain in my right shin told me that I might be looking at considerably longer than a few days to recover. What had I done? I felt both frustrated and foolish. This was a repeat of the stupidity I had demonstrated on my first ill-fated training hike from home to Lisburn and back. Would I never learn? I slumped back down onto the bed. Once again I had pushed my body too hard, too fast. I realised now just how foolish I had been to start running midweek in early preparation for the Belfast Half-Marathon in September. It had obviously put too much of a strain on my legs, particularly my right leg – I later had it confirmed that I was suffering from shin splints. And once again I had set out on a long walk wearing the wrong type of footwear! The shoes I had walked in the day before, had provided ample support, but I now realised that the soles were too thin to cushion my feet sufficiently from the hard pavements and roads and that the uppers were too closed in to allow my feet to breath properly, particularly during the hot weather of the previous day.

I clearly had no option but to eat humble pie and admit defeat. I had deluded myself into thinking that, after my meagre training efforts and my successful first three days of walking the previous weekend, I was now somehow suddenly a seasoned walker who was very much in complete control of his mission – that I was somehow now an unstoppable force. The reality was that after only four days walking and having only completed 59 miles, I had been brought to a grinding and embarrassing halt. I began to have serious doubts about my ability to complete the challenge I had set myself. Maybe I wasn't really cut out for long distance walking after all? Perhaps it was time to admit that to myself and to others and to abandon the walk all together? But, the doubts didn't last for long. No, I was determined to complete this walk come hell or high water; for Jacqui, for Cancer Research UK and for everyone who was supporting me.

I slowly and painfully made my way downstairs to inform Keith that I wouldn't be jogging or even walking today. He took one look at me and agreed that was probably a wise decision. He very kindly rustled me up a hearty breakfast, did a great job at keeping my spirits up, and then offered to drive me all the way down to Portaferry to be reunited with my car. At least my misfortune meant that I was now no longer under pressure to complete the next leg of the walk in sufficient time to allow me to get back home, get cleaned up and head to Omagh for my Dad's 91st! I now had ample time to do all I needed to do, albeit at a much slower pace with my tired and injured limbs, to arrive in Omagh in good time to raise a glass to my marvellous father. It's an ill wind that blows no good!

Thankfully, Hannah did the driving to Omagh and back, so I could relax and put my feet up, figuratively speaking. During the journey, I reflected on the fact that my father had been the same age as me (54) when he had lost his first wife, my mother, to cancer. My mum, Elizabeth, but known to everyone as Betty, had also been a primary school teacher, just as Jacqui had been. These coincidences seemed on one level to be just that; coincidences. But I have never really been able to shake of the thought that there was something deeper behind this strange case of history repeating itself. I certainly never truly appreciated the depth of the pain that my father went through when he lost my mother until I lost Jacqui and was forced to experience that same pain first hand. My sister-in-law, Christine, articulated these unusual circumstances beautifully in a very poignant poem, called "The boy", which she wrote shortly after Jacqui's funeral service. The boy in the poem is, of course, my son Matthew. I'm not sure how I would feel if he ever started dating a primary school teacher! I certainly hope he never ever has to experience the same pain felt by his father and his grandfather.

The boy

I see a man
Unashamedly weep
Like a boy
I see a boy
Hurting like a man
I see an old man
Who has suffered
The same hurt
As the man.
The man
Now suffering
As his father did.
The boy now hurting
Like his father did.
Three generations
United in grief.

Christine Mitchell

The following day I was back in Belfast and I visited Noel Rice, my local physiotherapist at the Belfast Physio and Sports Injuries Clinic, who had helped me out on previous occasions, mainly for back pain, which I have been prone to over the years. In my early thirties I had stooped down to pick up a paperback book from a low shelf at home and ended up reading it on the floor for the next couple of hours, while I waited for the GP to arrive to dose me with painkillers! Ever since that painful incident, I have had to be quite careful with my back. I have found that surfing, which I didn't take up until I was in my forties, helps maintain my back in very good condition – it's great for strengthening the core muscles, which is a great aid to combatting back pain. Anyway, I digress - back pain was not the issue on this occasion. Noel quickly confirmed what I had suspected all along, which was that I had a nasty case of shin splints in my right leg and that rest and ice were the only things that would help. A couple of weeks would probably do it. He also advised against any more running until I had completed my walk. He didn't actually call me stupid, but I thought I could read it in his face! Noel is a great guy though and he agreed to be my official 1000K4J physiotherapist for the duration of my walk, although I sincerely hoped not to have to call on him again anytime soon. He also wouldn't take any payment for seeing me and instead made a donation to my fund raising pot – as I said, he's a great guy.

The next couple of weeks were largely uneventful. I returned to work, taking the lift rather than the stairs whenever I could, and keeping an ice pack applied to my right shin four to five times a day. I also returned to the Cotswold store to invest in a good pair of walking shoes to use on the roads and pavements, as a suitable alternative to my boots for when I eventually got back onto the Ulster Way again. As expected, I wasn't fit enough to walk the next weekend, but I sincerely hoped that my legs and feet would be well enough improved to get back on the road the weekend after that, following a two week rest. I said that these couples of weeks were largely uneventful, but there was one remarkable thing that happened that still stands out clearly in my mind. On July 2nd, I received the following message from Rachel Joyce, the author of *The Unlikely Pilgrimage of Harold Fry*:

Dear Dermot,

I have heard about your walk and Jacqui too and I wanted to offer you all my support and encouragement. Harold Fry would be very proud of you. Maureen would suggest you don't wear yachting shoes. Let me know if you would like a signed copy or two and I will send them.

With best wishes, Rachel Joyce

PS Do remember to sit down once in a while.

I had absolutely no idea at the time how she had got to hear about my walk, but I later found out that a few of my friends had surreptitiously got in touch with her to let her know, which was a lovely thing to do. I was absolutely thrilled that she had got to hear about my endeavours and even more so that she had taken the time to send me a message of support. What's more, she also made a donation to my Just Giving page and then sent me a package of a number of signed copies of her books for me to raffle off to raise further funds for cancer research. She also included in the package a copy of "Harold Fry" especially for me, with a lovely personal message written inside the cover. If only Maureen's (Harold's wife) advice about unsuitable footwear had come a little earlier though. The shoes I had worn on my ill-fated walk from Bangor to Ballywalter were not quite as flimsy as yachting shoes, but they were certainly just as unsuitable. However, towards the end of the second week, my feet were well healed and I felt that my shin had sufficiently recovered to try again – gently though!

Of course, I had now missed three days that I had previously been scheduled to walk. However, rather than reschedule everything from this point on, I decided to simply continue with the walk as planned and postpone the sections I had missed for the time being, until I had an opportunity to go back and cover them. This would mean that the route wasn't going to be walked in a neat consecutive order. But surely as long as all the ground was eventually covered, it didn't really matter in what order I walked the sections –the same distance would be covered regardless. So, for now, I was content to skip the three sections concerned: Ballywalter to Portaferry; Strangford to Killough; and Killough to Newcastle. The approaching weekend would therefore see me jumping ahead to Newcastle to take on the formidable Mountains of Mourne. I was certainly eager to get started back on my 1000K4J pilgrimage again. I had missed walking with my weather angels!

I had also missed the focus and purpose that the walk had given me. There was inevitably more time for dark thoughts to get a hold and I found myself lying in bed very late on those mornings I didn't have to get up for work. The absence of my challenge, even on those few days, left me without direction again and made it easier for feelings of despair to settle in and for the dark demons to take over. Often I felt that there was little I could do other than to surrender to these feelings of hopelessness and despondency and simply allow it to run its course, however long that might take, be it minutes or hours. I would just let my mind and body be taken over by the waves of emotion and let myself be tumbled and beaten until the storms eased and I was once again able to lift my head. Although, it was probably necessary to go through these episodes as part of the overall healing process, it would also be good to get back out on the road again and once again have a real purpose to get up for.

Hitching

Saturday 4 July – Newcastle to Spelga Pass

The weekend came round soon enough and before I knew it I was driving towards the Mournes on a rather gloomy Saturday morning to meet up with Jim, my main guide for the day. Visibility was reasonable at first as I headed cross country via Ballynahinch and Castlewellan, but as I started driving up into the lower slopes of the Mournes I began to encounter some fairly thick fog. I had arranged to meet Jim at Ott Car Park, which was not far from Spelga Dam. However, this was not a part of the country that I was familiar with and the combination of the ever thickening fog and my dodgy map reading skills, left me running a bit late. Thankfully Jim had put on a bright fluorescent coat and had stood by the roadside to wave me down as I approached the designated car park. If it hadn't been for Jim's foresight, I might have missed the rendezvous point, so thick was the fog at that time of the morning.

After greeting each other and Jim batting away my apologies for being late, I transferred over to his car, leaving my car parked for the day at Ott Car Park. Jim then drove us both into Newcastle, picking up another friend, Audrey, at Trassey Car Park along the way. We parked in Newcastle town and the three of us made our way over to the Newcastle Centre, where Jim had arranged for me to meet a delegation of local councillors and members of the local Cancer Research UK (CRUK) Fundraising Committee. It was quite humbling to realise that these folk had all come into town that morning specially to welcome me to Newcastle and to wish me well on my walk round the Ulster Way. Mark McMahon, NI Senior Local Fundraising Manager for CRUK, had also arrived to show his support and he was going to walk with me for a few miles this morning also. A reporter and a photographer, both from the Mourne Observer, were also there and I was happy to spend a little time chatting with everyone and posing for a few photographs. Any opportunity to spread the word about my walk and possibly increase the funds raised for cancer research was to be warmly welcomed. After basking in the publicity for a bit, I reckoned it was high time to begin the days walk. So the four of us, Jim, Audrey, Mark and myself, all set off just after 10am, waving back to the townsfolk as we went. It stayed quite misty for the first hour or so, with the sun only making occasional and tantalisingly brief appearances. However, my weather angels soon got to work and the mist eventually burned off completely and started to reveal the Mournes in all their spectacular beauty.

Mark had his sights set on tackling Slieve Donard today. Slieve Donard is from the Irish Sliabh Dónairt, meaning "Donard's mountain" and is named after Saint Donard, who was said to have made the summit his hermitage many years ago. At 850 metres, it is the highest peak in Northern Ireland. Thankfully though, for my sake anyway given its height, Slieve Donard is not on the Ulster Way route and so we therefore soon parted company with Mark as he headed southwards towards Donard, while Jim, Audrey and I kept moving eastwards along the Ulster Way path as it wound its way through Tollymore Forest Park. Apparently, according to my Ulster Way directions, Oak wood from this very forest was widely used to fit out the interiors of the mighty White Star shipping liners, including the ill-fated Titanic, which was built in Belfast in 1911 and sank on its maiden voyage in 1912. I couldn't help thinking that perhaps balsa wood might have been a better choice! Another impressive mountain loomed to our left as we proceeded; this was Slieve Commedagh, the second highest summit in Northern Ireland at 767 metres and, thankfully, it also was not part of the Ulster Way route. So far, it seems that I was doing a pretty good job of avoiding the more challenging aspects of the Mournes, which suited me fine given that I had only just returned to walking after a fortnight of rehabilitation.

Both Jim and Audrey were experienced hill walkers and were quite familiar with the Mournes. Despite Jim's best efforts though, this was not a walk to be hurried! I stopped countless times for photographs and to simply take in the wonder of the views around us. Audrey too was happy to take things at a more gentle pace, given that she was in between treatments for cancer. I was so pleased that she was able to join us on the walk as far as Meelmore Lodge, where we stopped for a bite to eat. After lunch, Audrey headed back to her car nearby and Jim and I headed on for the last couple of hours together. Jim was an excellent guide and I will forever more think of him as Sherpa Jim. In the now glorious afternoon sunshine, we followed alongside a number of long stone walls as we went and we also spotted sections of the remarkable Mourne Wall running up and over the mountain peaks to our left. This 22-mile long wall was constructed between 1904 and 1922 by the Belfast Water Commissioners to enclose a 9,000 acre area, including the water catchment area for the Silent Valley Reservoir, which supplies Belfast with much of its water. The wall is, on average, about 1.5 metres high, built from natural granite stone using traditional dry stone walling techniques, passes over 15 mountains and took 18 years to complete. It was only mid-afternoon when Jim and I arrived back at Ott Car Park. As planned, Audrey had driven up to Ott to meet us and to take Jim back to his car in Newcastle. I thanked Jim and Audrey for their company and bade them both farewell as they headed off back to the town at the foot of the Mournes.

And that was meant to be it for the day. From here, I had originally planned to drive on to the Mourne Lodge a few miles away in Attical, where I had booked in for the night. However, the day was just too beautiful to head indoors so early. So instead I rested for a bit and then drove the couple of miles round to Spelga Pass and parked up in a little unofficial lay-by. I then did something that I hadn't done since I was a teenager – I tried to hitch a lift! I stood by the side of the road and put my thumb out. After about a dozen cars had passed with their drivers doing their best "I don't see you" looks, I was about to give up. But then a lovely lady and her young daughter pulled up in a people carrier. The lady driver put a window down and asked where I was going. After I told her, she said she could take me part of the way and to jump in. As I was climbing into the back seat behind her young daughter, she jokingly asked, "You're not a mad axe murderer are you?" Now I've no idea what she would have done if I had said "Yes", because I was already in the car by that stage. But I just laughed and explained that I was walking the Ulster Way for charity.

I was very grateful for this lift and the subsequent lift from a guy who had just completed a practice run for the upcoming Seven Peaks Challenge Race in August. Known as the Seven Sevens, this is a classic long race in the Mournes and gets its name from the fact that it takes in the seven highest peaks over 700 metres in the Mourne Mountain range. The 19-mile long route through this granite mountain range is certainly not for the faint hearted. He was a very fit looking guy though and I wished him all the best for the race as he dropped me back at Ott Car Park.

From this point, the Ulster Way directions offered me a choice of two routes. There was the more straightforward route along the road, essentially going back the way I had just been taken by my two hitch-hiker friendly drivers; or there was the official route across open mountainside. The directions pointed out that the mountain route is not way-marked and cautioned that you should only consider this option in clear weather and if you are an experienced mountain walker with good navigational skills. Well the weather could not have been better and how was I ever to become an experienced mountain walker with good navigational skills if I didn't give it a go. So throwing caution to the wind once again with my "devil may care" attitude, and casually forgetting the trouble that such an approach had brought me before, I set off to tackle the mountain route that would introduce me to Slievenamuck, Spaltha and Spelga Mountains. Now I'm not altogether sure that I did in fact encounter all three of these mountains, such was my inexperience and rusty navigational skills, but I somehow managed to make my way to Spelga Pass never-the-less. I suspect these mountains would have been a doddle for the Seven Peaks man, but, even though this section was only about two miles long, I found it the most challenging section yet. It was quite steep in places and the grass track was barely discernible for a lot of the way. However, it was also the most spectacular section yet. The views were just incredible and the photos I took could hardly do justice to the sheer grandeur of the landscape all around me.

The descent down into Spelga Pass, although providing great views over Spelga Reservoir and Spelga Dam, was a lot steeper than expected and I was really glad that I had invested in a pair of walking poles. They proved to be invaluable for negotiating the challenging terrain as well as helping to save the knees and shins. I had to work very hard to avoid "runaway train" syndrome – where it would become impossible to resist the downward momentum and I would be forced to run, hop, jump or do whatever just to stay on my feet as I careered down the slope. Thankfully, I eventually made it down safely, taking a slower and longer zigzag route whenever possible, and made it back to my car for about six-thirty; rather knackered but extremely satisfied. I then drove on to Attical, where the wonderful Mairead White welcomed me into the Mourne Lodge like an old friend and cooked me the most delicious meal I had had in a long while. The Mourne Lodge is a community based venture and an excellent place to stay if you are looking to "get away from it all". Mairead is one of life's saints and in 1999 she was awarded an MBE for her voluntary community work. She is a volunteer who runs the lodge almost single handedly and at the same time cares for her sister full time. As well as giving me a donation towards cancer research, she provided me with a voucher for a stay at the Lodge for two to help raise further funds. Her hospitality was such that it meant it was very late by the time I posted my blog for the day, but I didn't mind a bit. All in all it had been a very long but very rewarding day. It was great to be back on the road again and what a fantastic day and breathtaking route to return with.

Fog and Bog

Sunday 5 July – Spelga Pass to Rostrevor

The next morning, I was woken by the alarm on my mobile phone at 8am. I had enjoyed the best sleep I had had for some time while staying at the Mourne Lodge and I was very pleasantly surprised, on stepping out of bed, to find my right shin pretty pain free for the first time in two weeks. I had expected the opposite, maybe even deserved the opposite, after having pushed on for the extra couple of arduous miles the previous day from Ott Car Park to Spelga Pass. This was definitely a good sign!

During a superb breakfast cooked by the wonderful Mairead, I parted most of the other guests from some of their hard earned cash after Mairead insisted on telling everyone about my pilgrimage. Although extremely grateful for all the kindness being shown to me, I couldn't help thinking about how strange all this was. When Jacqui was alive and well, we had loved heading out on Sunday mornings for a leisurely breakfast in one of the many little cafes in Belfast or Portrush, depending on where we had been spending the weekend. This was usually followed by an equally leisurely stroll through Botanic Gardens, along the Lagan Towpath or across the beach to Whiterocks. Now, here I was spending this Sunday morning having breakfast in the company of strangers in a remote part of the Mournes and about to undertake the next stage of my walk, which was anything but a leisurely stroll. It was indeed a dramatic change in circumstances and how I wished I could turn back the clock, even for just one day, so I could once again hold Jacqui's hand and hear her voice. I missed her so much, but I did my best to chat with the other guests and to hide the pain that was forever present just below the surface.

After breakfast, I gathered up my belongings, said my farewells to Mairead and her sister, and drove back the few miles to Spelga Pass. Although my drive was through thick fog most of the way, thankfully Spelga Pass itself was clear of fog when I left the car at the same "lay-by" as the day before to pick up the trail again. Looking back up at the mountain route I had followed the previous day though, I could see that it would have been impossible to have attempted it this morning, as it was completely shrouded in low lying cloud. I was very glad that I had taken the opportunity to tackle it during the previous day's sunshine – the gamble had paid off on this occasion.

For the first couple of hours of today's walk, I really thought that my two weather angels had abandoned me, but it turned out that Jacqui and Rosaleen were just having a little Sunday morning lie in. The first part of the day was very tough going with the rain being quite persistent and the ground around Hen Mountain, and later between Pigeon Rock Mountain and Rocky Mountain, being very boggy in places. I was so glad to have my waterproof boots on and my walking poles to hand. Ironically, the driest part of the morning's walk was along a track called New Bog Road. I did another pretty good hobo impression for a while as I tramped through the wilderness with my big blue waterproof hooded cape tied tightly around my head and the body of it billowing around me. It brought to mind the big yellow cape that Jacqui used to sometimes wear in her student days. In fact, she was wearing it the very first time I met her and it certainly helped to get her noticed and provided a good talking point by way of introduction! I always referred to her as "Big Bird" when she wore it, as it reminded me of the tall yellow bird character from popular children's TV show, Sesame Street. But she wore it well and she certainly looked better in her big yellow cape than I did in my big blue one. At one point I stopped to clear up litter that someone had carelessly discarded in a shallow ditch by the side of my route. I just couldn't bring myself to walk by and leave it, despite the dreadful weather and the fact that I already had my own stuff to carry. Just how some people can discard litter in a beautiful place like the Mournes is really beyond me! I managed to gather up the litter and secure it to the end of one of my walking poles in the remnants of a black bin bag – my very own bindle to complete the hobo look.

While heading over the pass between Rocky Mountain and Tornamrock, my two weather angels finally woke from their heavenly slumbers and peered down to see how I was getting on back on Earth. They must have then immediately set to work sweeping the clouds aside because the sun broke through properly and I was even able to shed a few layers and pack away the wet gear for the remainder of the day. The section I had just walked was easily the toughest yet, due to the weather, the difficult terrain and the distances involved. However, setting that aside, three things in particular stood out for me that day. First was the realisation that the section had started with me crossing a footbridge over the start of the longest river in Ireland, the River Bann, at a point 80 miles from where it eventually enters the sea on the North Coast near Coleraine. Secondly, was my meeting with three lovely ponies. Initially we were separated by a deep ditch, thick undergrowth and a stone wall, but such was the desire for contact on all our parts, in this bleak and desolate mountain wilderness, that we all gradually worked our way round and through the various obstacles until we were able to greet each other properly. I don't suppose they get to meet too many people in this remote and isolated corner of the world. I took a photo of my three "Spelga ponies" and this was to become one of my favourite images of my entire Ulster Way walk, and one that would later be reproduced in a lovely water colour painting for me by my good friend, Nikki. Thirdly, was my encounter with the ram equivalent of Billy Goat Gruff who appeared to be guarding a footbridge over the Rocky River. He reluctantly stood aside to let me cross, although I remained very wary of his formidable horns. As soon as I got over to the other side, he strode back onto the footbridge himself, as if to make it very clear that this bridge belonged to him. I was very happy to move on and leave him to guard the centre of his own little kingdom.

After a long trek over open hillside, during which a bank of thick fog rolled down off the hills towards me, it was with much relief that I finally made the descent to the track at the base of the valley on the other side of Rocky Mountain. This track then took me along the base of Altataggart Mountain and eventually into the dense pine trees of Rostrevor Forest. The name Altataggart translates from the Gaelic as "Hill of the Priest" and refers to the fact that this mountain was the site of clandestine religious worship during the period of penal law in the eighteenth century. The rest of the route to Kilbroney Car Park in Rostrevor was really a breeze by comparison to what had gone before. I still had about five miles to cover but it was mainly over well-defined tracks and good quality forest paths with only occasional steep parts. My intrepid guide from the day before, Sherpa Jim, walked out from Kilbroney Park to meet me a couple of miles out and I was very glad of his company for the final stretch. As we made our way along the path, there were occasional breaks in the trees to our right, which allowed good views over the Kilbroney River Valley and we were eventually able to see the town of Rostrevor in the distance and pick out Kilbroney Church on its northern edge. This church lies on the site of a former convent founded by St Bronach in the sixth century, and is the location of the legend of St Bronach's Bell.

The story tells of an invisible bell that rang in the churchyard during storms, continuing St Bronach's work of looking out for sailors in trouble. The apparently supernatural origin of the noise was explained in 1795 however, when an ancient oak tree blew down, revealing a ninth century church bell that had been hidden in its branches during the reformation.

We arrived at Jim's car in Kilbroney Car Park in the late afternoon to complete my walk for the day. I had no intention of doing any extra miles today and was very happy to be chauffeured back to my car at Spelga Pass by Jim. Not for the first time, I was surprised at how little time it takes to cover the same distance I had just walked by car – it is without a doubt much easier and quicker by car, but the opportunities to appreciate and enjoy the landscape do not even come close.

Later that evening, when back at home, I couldn't help reflecting on the similarities between my experiences walking in the mountains and my experiences in trying to deal with grief. I could be walking along in the sunshine when, with little warning, the mist might suddenly descend from the mountain and envelope me and I would suddenly feel disorientated and lost. Similarly, I could be trudging along in the rain with my head down when all of a sudden the clouds would clear, the sun would break through, and I would feel able to raise my head and smile again. Then I could be walking along quite normally on a firm pathway when unexpectedly I would enter boggy ground and be stopped in my tracks until I could somehow find the strength to plough on through it. I only hoped that in time, I would start to learn how to recognise the difficult areas ahead and learn how to negotiate my way around them if I could. And, most importantly, when I got tired and felt like giving up, there were always good friends who were prepared to walk by my side and lend me a helping hand. I was certainly blessed to have many such good friends.

Anyway, that was another weekend's walking successfully completed and another 26 miles added to the tally, bringing the total distance now walked to 85 miles. The following day was Monday and so the plan was to get back to work for the week, but with an eye being kept to any opportunity to catch up on the sections I had previously skipped due to injury.

Narrow Waters

Wednesday 8 July – Ballywalter to Portaferry

Well, as it turned out I managed to squeeze in a little mid-week walk after all. With the weather forecast for Wednesday being fairly good, I decided to take a day's leave from work and catch up on one of the sections I had skipped previously due to the shin splints in my right leg, which had now improved greatly. That morning I met my friend Ronan in Portaferry and he drove me to the very spot about a mile south of Ballywalter, where Keith had rescued me from a couple of weekends before. Ronan had hoped to walk with me for a bit on this stretch a few weeks ago, but that had to be abandoned due to my injuries at the time and, unfortunately for him, he was working today. So I gave a quick wave to Ronan, who then set off for work, and I then pulled on my fluorescent jacket and set off along the A2, hugging the right hand verge of the road as I went.

Nearly all of the route today was along roads, some with quite fast moving traffic, and I had to remain alert at all times and be ready to step up onto the grass verge (where one existed) to wait for oncoming traffic to pass. Once again, I could understand why this section is described on the Ulster Way website as a link section, which it doesn't encourage you to walk, but instead suggests that you take public transport - it certainly would have been quicker, but I suspected that my Facebook followers probably would have got bored pretty quickly of looking at selfies of me sitting on a bus! And I would also have missed out on my encounters with many of my four legged friends along the Ulster Way, including the many lovely, friendly ponies and donkeys I met on this section, which would have been a great shame.

After passing through the sleepy village of Ballyhalbert, another couple miles brought me to the slightly busier fishing village of Portavogie, which is from the Irish Port a' Bhogaigh, meaning "harbour of the bog". It was very nice to get off the road and down onto the beaches either side of Portavogie for a while to enjoy the wide open stretches of sand and admire the colourful beach-huts that looked out over the sea. I stopped at a monument to fishermen lost at sea near the harbour which was rather poignant. There were twenty-seven names inscribed on it, including three Young's, four Donnan's and six Adair's! In common with most fishing towns and villages, Portavogie has had its share of tragedy. From Portavogie, it was about another three and a half miles to the village of Cloughey, where I was met by friends Ruth and Noel, who had brought me a delicious picnic lunch.

We enjoyed this at a picnic table in the park above Cloughey Bay and opposite Kirkistown Castle Golf Course. Although it was a bit windy, it was lovely and sunny and the food and hot drinks were greatly appreciated. After lunch, I bade farewell to Ruth and Noel, and also to the Irish Sea, as I started to head westwards across the Ards Peninsula towards Strangford Lough. After about five miles of walking along fairly narrow rural roads, and passing the picturesque Lough Cowey (when is a lake not a lake, but a lough?), I finally reached the shores of Strangford Lough and enjoyed the views across the water to the Mourne Mountains in the distance. it was strange to think that just a few days ago I was walking over those same mountains that now just appeared as pale blue bumps on the horizon. They looked very small, but having watched Father Ted numerous times, I knew that they were in fact just far away!

I followed the narrow road along the shoreline of Strangford Lough, heading south for the next two and a half miles towards Portaferry. Strangford Lough is the largest inlet in the British Isles and is linked to the Irish Sea by a long narrow channel or strait called The Narrows. The channel is only 0.8 km wide and, as a result, has some of the fastest tidal currents in the world at up to 8 knots. In 2007, this tidal energy was harnessed by the world's first commercial marine tidal power station. However, with such strong tidal flows, sailing into and out of Strangford Lough is not for the fainthearted and is best attempted at the turn of the tide, when the movement of water has slowed sufficiently.

As I approached Portaferry, I watched the ferry make its familiar crossing to the other side of the lough. Portaferry is a small town situated on the southern end of the Ards Peninsula, close to the Narrows. The town is well known for its passenger and car ferry service, which operates daily at 30-minute intervals between the villages of Portaferry and Strangford. A ferry has plied the Narrows from at least 1180 making it the oldest continuous ferry service in the world. Portaferry was also once renowned for its very popular aquarium, Exploris, but unfortunately this had closed due to financial difficulties prior to my visit.

I arrived back at my car, which was parked in the village square, just before the rain started to come on. My weather angels had been looking out for me yet again! So that was the Ards Peninsula sections now finally completed – it had only taken me three and a half weeks! And I now had a total of 98 miles under my feet. I still had to catch up on the two-day stretch from Strangford to Newcastle which I had also skipped previously. But the coming weekend would see me back in Kilbroney Park to start tackling Rostrevor to Newry, and then the Ring of Gullion.

Guiding Light

Saturday 11 July – Rostrevor to Flagstaff

The first day of a three day hike around the Newry area started at Kilbroney Park, just outside Rostrevor. After parking my car in the outskirts of Newry on Saturday morning, my next door neighbour, Barbara, drove us both to Kilbroney Park. Here we were welcomed very warmly by three representatives from the Newry Cancer Research Fundraising Committee, Gervase, Paddy and Noreen, and a photographer, Liz, from the Newry Reporter. It was really great to meet these dedicated folk and to hear some of their stories. It just served to remind me that I was very much a novice at this fundraising venture and that there were many, many dedicated people right across the country who had been involved in the fight against cancer for a lot longer than I had. I would dearly loved to have spent more time with them all, but Barbara and I had a little walk to be getting on with. So I hurried things along, got the photographs taken and waved goodbye to them all as we set off out of the park and onto the main road to Newry, but not before pulling on the reflective vests that Gervase had brought along and insisted that we wear, even though we would be on good sidewalks all the way to Newry!

The walk alongside the main road was pretty enjoyable for the first few miles, with the wide, calm waters of Carlingford Lough and the deep green forested hills of Slieve Foye to our left. I hit a big milestone after just two miles when I estimated that I had completed the first 100 miles of my walk! Only another 530 miles or so to go! Over the next few miles, we passed the old outdoor swimming pool in Warrenpoint, which Barbara, who was originally from Newry, used to frequent in her childhood, and later an impressive sculpture of an Irish elk at a roundabout. I really thought that Barbara was going to climb up on to the elk at one point to get her photo taken, but she thankfully restrained herself to just posing beside it! The next features of interest were Narrow Water Tower and Narrow Water Castle. Narrow Water Castle is the private home of the Hall family who have lived there since 1670. Apparently, they originally lived in the Old Narrow Water Tower, on the water's edge, which was a fortification built to prevent river-borne attacks on Newry.

The rest of the road into Newry became a bit tedious, with little by way of features to distract from the monotonous trudge and the noisy traffic constantly rushing by on the dual carriageway alongside us. We had been hoping to cut away from the road at the start of Greenbank Industrial Estate about two miles out of Newry and pick up the path of the old Newry to Warrenpoint railway line, but try as we might, we could not locate the entrance indicated on the map. This was unfortunate, particularly for Barbara, as she had fond memories of her grandfather working on this stretch of railway. I was, however, reminded of a much darker memory associated with the line; that of the Armagh train disaster of 1889. Although the train involved in the disaster actually crashed outside Armagh, it had been on route to Warrenpoint for a Sunday school excursion on that fateful day on June 12, over 125 years ago. The train had to negotiate a steep incline as it was leaving Armagh, but the steam locomotive was unable to complete the climb and the train stalled. The train crew decided to divide the train and take forward the front portion, leaving the rear portion on the running line. The rear portion was unfortunately inadequately braked and ran back down the gradient, colliding with a following train. Eighty people were killed and 260 injured; about a third of them children. They had been heading for a day out by the sea, but I imagine many ended up screaming in horror instead. It was the worst rail disaster in the UK in the 19th century and remains Ireland's worst railway disaster ever.

Denied access to the old railway line path, we instead had to make do with the dubious delights of wandering through the Greenbank Industrial Estate itself. However, on the plus side we did stumble across the "Fun House", an indoor play area for young children. It also had a cafe and we both badly needed a sit down and a coffee – I remembered Rachel Joyce's advice at the end of her message earlier in the month, "Do remember to sit down once in a while". The noise coming from the various birthday parties did little to deter us from the pleasure of the soft settees and chance to rest our weary feet! The children were having a fantastic time running around and screaming with excitement. It was quite a contrast to my earlier visions of screaming children caught up in the railway disaster. I wisely decided not to take any photographs in the Fun House for fear of being branded a pervert by irate parents and being hauled out and thrown in the lough. This was a pity though, because I really would have enjoyed posting a picture of Barbara next to the ball pit with her shoes and socks off, massaging her feet while the kids ran past with the funniest looks on their faces.

After suitable rest and refreshments, I cracked the whip and we were off again and it wasn't long before we reached Newry proper, with the spire of Newry

Cathedral never far from view. Barbara told me an amusing story about how, as a child living in Newry, she and her friends used to dare each other to go up to the door or even step inside, fearful all the time of being struck down by lightning, being as they were "from the other side". I told Barbara about the time that I first told my father that I was dating Jacqui and that she was "from the other side". He initially wasn't too pleased and I remember him asking me how on earth I could ever have let such a thing happen! As it turned, my dad couldn't have been more charming and welcoming when he first met Jacqui. I still remember bringing Jacqui home to Omagh with me to meet my family for the very first time back in 1980. I had of course phoned ahead to say that we were coming – I wasn't going to just arrive unannounced with Jacqui for such a momentous occasion. I was still nervous though! My brief phone call hadn't really given me any clues as to how we were going to be received. However, Jacqui was her usual calm and composed self. She always took the view that if someone didn't like her, then that was their problem, not hers. Mind you, I never met anyone in all the 35 years that I knew Jacqui, who didn't warm to her right away on first meeting her. And so it was with my father.

It was a lovely warm summer's day when we arrived and, just as we came round the corner of the house and into the backyard, my dad appeared. He had just come up from the garden, where he spent a lot of his time and was a fabulous grower of a wide range of fruit, vegetables and flowers as a result. When he spotted us, a huge smile broke out on his face and he made a bee line for Jacqui and shook her hand warmly (we weren't the hugging type of family back then!) and told her how delightful it was to finally meet her! You could have knocked me down with a feather at that stage. They then started up a conversation about gardening, Jacqui admiring the lovely display of sweet-pea along the fence at the edge of the yard and my father immediately picking a few choice blooms for her. As introductions go, I don't think it could have been any better! My dad really loved Jacqui and thought the world of her. Her background or religion was never an issue for him again – I don't believe it ever truly was in the first place. Barbara and I then had a very interesting conversation about religion and politics and I think we probably put the world to rights; and all without the aid of alcohol too.

We didn't go into the centre of Newry, but instead the route took us over the canal and then on a long, slow and tiring climb up the old Dublin Road back

The sunny coast of North Down, looking towards Wilson's Point, en route to Bangor

A stunning blue sky meets a remarkably blue sea at Donaghadee Harbour

Blue sky in the Mournes, looking out over Spelga Reservoir

My lovely 'Spelga ponies', close to Spelga Pass in the Mournes

to where I had left my car. I had just reached it and was about to get in, when a white Toyota pulled up alongside with the window down and a man I didn't recognise at the wheel. I thought they were probably looking for directions but it turned out to be Camilla, a work colleague, with her husband and children. They had been on their way to Newcastle, when they had spotted me struggling up the road. It was really lovely to see them and so nice of them to stop and show their support.

The next bit was quite complicated so suffice to say that I moved my car to Flagstaff about three and a half miles further on and Barbara then left me back to the Dublin Road to walk the final stretch while she returned home to Belfast. Fortunately, despite a pretty awful weather forecast for the day, the only significant rain we had seen was when we had been driving between places. It seemed like my weather angels were looking after me again.

The final stretch to Flagstaff, along the slopes of Fathom Mountain, was quite pleasant. Although the roads were very narrow for the most part, they were also quite quiet and I rarely had to step in to let traffic go past. In fact, it was quiet enough to allow me to relax and put the ear phones in and listen to some music, with my iPod on shuffle. However, there was one unpleasant incident as I was passing a rough lay-by where a couple of cars were parked with young lads inside them. The engine of one car was idling and as I came up behind it the driver revved the engine loudly and sent a cloud of exhaust fumes in my direction. It seemed such a purposeful action and as I walked past the driver's window I showed him a universally recognised sign of displeasure and walked on. The incident perhaps angered me more than it should have, but the more I thought of the lad watching me approach in his rear view mirror, waiting for his moment, the more I wanted to turn around and kick one of his headlights in with my waterproof boots. Did he not realise what I was doing? Did he not know what I had been through? Did he not appreciate the grief I was suffering? "Of course he doesn't" Jacqui whispered in my ear, "How could he, love? Just keep on walking my dear, he's just a young lad trying to look big to his friends". She didn't actually whisper in my ear, but I could hear her calming voice none the less. Jacqui was always very calm and understanding. I had witnessed this at first hand for over 35 years and I suppose her positive influence over me certainly wasn't going to disappear any time soon. So without so much as a glance back, I just walked on. But this minor incident had never-the-less clearly rattled me. A few minutes after this episode, and quite by chance, a song called "The Guide" by Borne, a little known Australian band, came on my iPod. As they sung "You are my angel. You are my guiding light", I smiled through my tears and kept on walking.

About an hour later, I reached the end point of my walk for the day at Flagstaff viewing point at just before seven. After taking some time to explore the viewpoint and enjoy the superb panoramic views of Newry, the Mournes and Carlingford Lough set out before me, I got into my car and drove back to the old Dublin Road yet again, this time to check into Lismore House B&B. Later, I enjoyed a lonely but very nice Italian meal in Newry city centre and then headed back to the B&B to write my blog and to try and get some rest before setting off again in the morning for Forkhill at the foot of Slieve Gullion. However, restful sleep eluded me this night!

Dear Jacqui,

Despite the B&B I'm staying in tonight being really comfortable, I just couldn't sleep. So I thought I would write you a letter instead to let you know what's been happening. It's been a while since I've do'd that - still have trouble deciding between done and did so I've used the my usual hybrid "do'd" which, as you know, I've used as a stand in over the years – I can hear you laughing now at my silliness and patiently correcting me once again! I guess I'll never learn. Remember when we first started seeing one and other all those years ago and we used to write to each other quite a lot during our spells apart – and even when we weren't – just because it was a romantic thing to do! It seems so quaint and of it's time now in this modern day world of mobiles and internet. Anyway, I'm starting to ramble – in more ways than one, but more about that later. I just thought it would be nice to write to you once again and I really hope you enjoy reading it.

Since you went away, Matt and Hannah and I have been trying our best to cope in our own ways. Matt has been trying to carve out a new life for himself in Berlin along with his best buddy Finn and, although he's had a few setbacks, things are generally going fairly well for him. Hannah has deferred her final year in psychology at Queen's for a year and taken up her part time and voluntary work again. Jonny and his family have been a great support to her. Matt and Hannah both miss you beyond words, as I do, but I am very proud of the way in which they are soldiering on and trying to be happy in their own ways, just as you told them to be before you left. I know you will be very proud of them and happy for them also.

For my part, I have decided to do this walk round the Ulster Way. I know, how ridiculous; me who previously could hardly walk the length of himself without complaining! Anyway, sure it's only 625 miles long. That's why I'm staying in this B&B in Newry at the minute. I've over 110 miles done so far and, despite some early setbacks with blisters and shin splints, I think I'm now getting into the swing of it and even starting to enjoy it. You will be pleased to know that I started off my walk from your wee school out in Greenisland.

The staff and pupils and parents from the school have been very supportive. In fact that's the main reason I wanted to write to you, to tell you how much love there is for you back here. I have been blown away by the messages I have received from friends, colleagues, parents and pupils, both past and present, and of course from both our family and wider family circles. There are just too many kind messages to forward on to you but I just want you to know that there has been a virtual tsunami of love and affection directed towards you - I know that your modesty would have made very light of such an outpouring of love, if you were still here to witness it, and I know that pride is frowned upon where you are now, but I can tell you that it has made me, Matt and Hannah extremely proud indeed.

Anyway, back to the walk. I know, you still can't believe it! But it's true, your beloved is slowly but surely making his was round Northern Ireland on foot. I'm doing this for three main reasons. Firstly, to give me some sense of purpose and to keep me sane, well as sane as I've ever been. If I didn't do something like this, I honestly feel that it would allow my grief from losing you to totally overwhelm me and drag me into a black hole from which I would never emerge. Tempting though this might be at times, to just to let go, I know that it is not what you would want me to do. Secondly, I'm doing it for you my love, every step I take is in your honour. 625 miles is actually 1000 kilometres, so I've given my walk the tag 1000K4J.

If you bump into Jesus, tell him the J stands for Jacqui, just in case he gets the wrong idea – he has plenty of people walking for him, but this one's strictly for you my dear. The third reason I'm doing this, and I know you will support me 100% here, is to raise money to support the work of Cancer Research UK in its fight against cancer. We both knew that there was nothing we or anyone else could do to keep you here, but we also agreed that it was so important for us to do whatever we could to help prevent others having to make the same dreadful journey.

Barbara and I stopped off yesterday in an indoor children's play area on the outskirts of Newry for a coffee (don't ask, it's a long story). Seeing all *those happy children at play and then having the dreadful thought of how many of them might be visited by the dark monster of cancer at some stage in their lives served to reinforce the importance of cancer research once again. A horrible thought I know, but with the latest statistics now showing that one in every two people will be touched by cancer during their lives, we can't bury our heads in the sand. So I know without question that you will totally forgive me for unashamedly using your name, photos and even personal stories to support our fundraising efforts.*

We have raised over £4,000 already in just over 4 weeks which is pretty incredible! The generosity of people never ceases to amaze me - some of whom never even knew of us before, but who were sufficiently touched by our story to dig deep into their pockets. Although you haven't been actively involved in the fundraising, I can assure you that the love and affection that many people still hold for you has been responsible for a good proportion of the money raised so far.

The support I have been getting from people during my walk has also been incredible. So many friends have already helped me with lifts to starting points and from finishing points, have walked with me for parts of the route, have put me up for the night and have provided sustenance, both nutritional and emotional. Not sure if you can get Facebook where you are (in many ways I sincerely hope not!) but if you can then you'll be able to see all the support I've had to date from your friends and mine. I have walked quite a few miles on my own also, but I have never really been truly alone as I have always felt your presence by my side.

I even sensed that you had whispered some words of wisdom in my ear yesterday on the way to Flagstaff. Oh, and by the way, thank you to you and Rosaleen for protecting me from the worst of the weather so far - I call you my weather angels! I was so sorry Rosaleen had to leave also. Jim misses her terribly, as I miss you, but we also know you will be good company for one and other. The other angels are probably in stitches already and desperately trying to hold onto their halos!

Anyway, that's enough rambling for now as I have to get on with my rambling (what do you mean, my jokes haven't improved!). It's been light for quite a while now and I will have to get up soon and get ready for the next leg of my walk round the Ring of Gullion. I'll meet you on the path.

> *All my love for ever,*
> *Dermot*

Hound of Ravensdale

Sunday 12 July – Flagstaff to Forkhill

Although my room at Lismore House had been very comfortable, I hadn't slept very well as there had been too many thoughts going round in my head. I no longer had Jacqui by my side to talk to and confide in and that's why I had decided to write to her instead. I also, perhaps unwisely, posted my letter to Jacqui on Facebook. (although, how else was I meant to post it!). Once again, I was baring my soul in public, but if it helped bring in much needed funds for cancer research, then it was a step I was prepared to take. It had certainly helped me to put down my thoughts "on paper", but needless to say, it was a poor substitute for talking to her and I was still feeling rather low when I got up that morning. Ever since Jacqui had died, I felt like there was a huge part of me missing. Not a limb or something external. Not something visible or obvious by its very absence. No, something internal, something deep inside – part of my very being. Even the word "missing" doesn't fully describe the feeling. No, not just missing, but removed. Removed by the very cancer that had taken Jacqui. Forcibly removed; stolen; snatched; ripped out. Not surgically removed in a clinical fashion, leaving a nice clean wound that can quickly heal, but removed in a most brutal fashion. Hacked, gouged, twisted and scrapped with a blunt implement, leaving a torn, ragged and messy hole that continued to suppurate and cause pain. A hole that couldn't easily be filled and a wound that seemed resistant to treatment. Too ragged and raw at times to even be touched. But with the right care perhaps even the most difficult of wounds can be healed over time.

It is said that time is a great healer and I only hoped that time might heal this wound of mine. That the hole would somehow be filled with something; it would never replace what had been removed, but it might at least lessen the terrible feeling of emptiness. That the wound would become less inflamed and eventually heal over to form a scar that I would be content to hide away from the rest of the world. I genuinely felt that the support and love that had come my way since setting off on my pilgrimage, from friends and strangers alike, did have the power to heal. It was undoubtedly another reason, in addition to Jacqui's memory and fundraising for cancer research, that my walk was so important to me and why I was determined to complete what I had set out to do.

Once I had gathered myself sufficiently, I headed downstairs to be provided with a hearty breakfast cooked by my host, Michael. He was very friendly and quite chatty and although he never knew it, he helped to lift me out of the dark place of despair I was in danger of sliding into. I had told him about my charity walk when I had booked my room weeks before and he had already reduced the price of the room for me, but before I left, he also give me a cash donation. Yet another example of the support and love that came my way!

After breakfast, I gathered up my gear and then drove to Forkhill where I met Ian, who had come down from his home in Banbridge. I switched to his car and he then left me to the point where I had finished the previous day, at Flagstaff Viewing Point. After checking out the superb views himself, Ian headed back home while I set off on foot again.

I have to say that what lay before me was probably the toughest days walking experienced yet, and I had already had a few tough ones. There must be a section on the Ulster Way, which I had maybe yet to find, that is the hardest of all and if you were to start there all the subsequent sections would appear easier? I wasn't sure if I had found it yet, but today's walk was certainly going to be a strong contender. Anyway, this section started off gently enough along the road from Flagstaff and I was rewarded early on with an opportunity to visit Clontygora Court Tomb, a Neolithic tomb which dates back to around 3500BC, and which was only about 50 metres off my route. Still in place were the massive boulders that once formed the entrance to a more extensive structure that was used by an early farming community for collective burial. It was a very peaceful little spot on a warm sunny Sunday morning and I spent a little time there with my thoughts on how each of us only exist on this Earth but for a brief moment in time. This, I suppose, meant that I had rather better get going again!

The gentle start to my walk didn't last long and was soon followed by a number of long uphill climbs that seemed to go on forever, as I gradually made my way up the slopes of Black Mountain, the second highest peak of the Ring of Gullion. I also missed a turn off on Black Mountain, partly due to an unclear route marking on the map and some rather ambiguous wording on the route directions. But if I was to be entirely honest, it was probably more to do with my own lack of attention, due to a distracted and troubled mind. Anyway, it probably only added about another half a mile onto my journey. I took another wrong turning on the way down through the forest also, but this one was fairly quickly corrected. I really needed to pay closer attention to the details on the maps. The descent down through Ravensdale Forest, some of it alongside a small river in a deep ravine, was very pleasant, but it was still good to reach the bottom at Marble Bridge Car Park for a bite of lunch. I had already read through the directions for the rest of the day's journey and had assumed that the toughest bit was now complete. How wrong I was! There were two relatively short sections ahead of me that only took a line each to describe in the three pages of the directions for today's walk, but they turned out to be much more significant on the ground!

Over my lunch of energy bars and fruit, I decided to study the map a little more closely, as I had said I must. It was then that I realised that the route I had followed, which was marked in red on the map, in fact created the outline of a dog or wolf - I christened this the "Hound of Ravensdale". I also strongly suspected from the map that I had actually crossed over the border into the Republic of Ireland coming through Ravensdale, a suspicion that was soon confirmed when a green post van, as opposed to a red Northern one, passed me on the road. I reflected on the fact that a number of years ago, before "peace broke out" in the North, it probably would not have been quite so easy to cross over the border in these parts unnoticed. The going was pretty easy from Marble Bridge for the next number of miles. Just south of Jonesborough the route passed a mountain saddle known as Moyry Pass, or the 'Gap of the North'. This was once a major thoroughfare between the provinces of Ulster and Leinster. The pass was guarded by Moyry Castle, which was built in 1601, and I made a short detour from the route to visit the remaining ruins. There was an information sign at the site that referred to the Fianna, who were warriors in Irish and Scottish mythology, and I was intrigued to read that "In the days of the Fianna legends, the men of Ulster sallied forth through this valley to harry the tribes of Leinster" – it sounded like a medieval version of *When Harry Met Sally*.

Also on the sign was a copy of an unfinished map of the Moyry Pass made by a Norfolk born cartographer, Richard Bartlett, in 1602-03. The information beside the map recorded that, shortly after drawing the map, "when he (Bartlett) came into Tyrconnell the inhabitants took off his head because they would not have their country discovered." I was fairly sure that Tyrconnell referred to what is now County Donegal in the northwest of Ireland, which was far enough away to reassure me that I shouldn't have anything to worry about from the locals here in County Armagh.

After this brief history lesson courtesy of Moyry Castle, I then proceeded towards Slievenabolea, with the more imposing Slieve Gullion dominating the landscape as I went. A steady climb by road took me up over the shoulder of Slievenabolea, which derives its name from the Irish Sliabh na Bolacht, meaning "mountain of the cattle". Eventually, after doubling back a couple of times and scratching my head even more times, I found the style described in the directions that would lead me to a path through an unnamed forest. Unfortunately, whole swaths of the forest had been bulldozed since the map had been drawn – either that, or another cartographer had lost his head before his map was finished! Anyway, much of what I saw before me now was like the aftermath of a nuclear explosion, with remnants of trees scattered like match-wood. I skirted along the edge of the trees that were still standing and when I came to a wall, I reckoned it was safe enough to follow its line into the forest, without risking not being able to find my way back if I needed to.

The forest had quite a creepy atmosphere due to the nature of the light coming through the forest canopy and the very deep blanket of pale moss that covered the floor of the forest. The directions described the forest as having a primeval feel to it – I would agree, but spooky also. I wouldn't have been entirely surprised to have seen my Hound of Ravensdale bounding through the trees towards me, with its eyes burning bright and teeth bared. Emerging out of the trees, I came to another style and at this point the directions simply said "negotiate a corridor of gorse, then descend along the forest boundary." Sounds easy enough, but what ensued was anything but easy! The corridor of gorse was extremely overgrown, as was the pathway down along the forest boundary. A machete would have been a very useful addition to my backpack. It was extremely hard going and at one point I was unexpectedly attacked and had the flesh of my leg torn savagely by the claws of the Hound of Ravensdale! Well, I actually had my leg quite badly scratched by some nasty brambles, but it was still somewhat unexpected and painful. The pathway down was simply too overgrown to negotiate at all and so I climbed out over some barbed wire fencing and made my way down over some very rough ground littered with felled tree trunks. It was quite dangerous and I had certainly never dreamed that I would be faced with such challenging terrain when I set off round the Ring of Gullion. I made a mental note to let Outdoor

Recreation Northern Ireland, the custodians of the Ulster Way, know of the difficulties I had encountered on this section.

I was exhausted but very relieved to get down safely to the grassy track below and then back onto the paved roads for a few miles. However, before reaching my finishing point at Forkhill, I came across another heavily overgrown pathway, which I eventually had to retreat from and find an alternative route through a field of horses. I arrived back at my car in Forkhill in the early evening, nearly eight hours after setting off from Flagstaff that morning. I rewarded myself with an unhealthy chicken burger and chips from the local takeaway and then drove to the Butterfly B&B near Jonesborough, where I had booked in for the night.

I enjoyed a very relaxing evening and night at the Butterfly, which is owned by a couple originally from Holland and run mainly by the lady of the house, Wilhelmina. I was the only guest staying and so I received Wilhelmina's undivided attention and was welcomed with freshly made coffee and chocolate cookies upon arrival. The very large bathroom had both a shower and a Jacuzzi-bath. After walking 16 miles plus on a very warm day, which do you think I opted for? No question about it, the bubbles won, feet down. Just perfect to relax and soothe those tired and scratched legs of mine.

Marching

Monday 13 July – Forkhill to Carnbane

The following morning Wilhelmina prepared me a breakfast fit for a king. Of course, I couldn't help being amused by the sheer coincidence that had brought me to a Dutch couple's house on the day that thousands of Orangemen across Northern Ireland were celebrating the victory of Dutch King William of Orange over King James II at the Battle of the Boyne in 1690. The Twelfth celebrations, as they were known, meant that it was a public holiday in Northern Ireland and so I had a day off work to continue with my walk. Of course, today was the thirteenth of July and the Twelfth celebrations are normally held on the twelfth of July each year. However, this year the twelfth of July fell on a Sunday, which was still considered by many to be a day of rest in Northern Ireland, and so on this occasion the Twelfth celebrations had been postponed until Monday the thirteenth. It was all very "Northern Irish".

After breakfast, I said farewell to Wilhelmina, threw my bags into my car and drove to Newry Train Station. Here I met up with Ian again, who had returned for a second morning to drive me to my starting point for the day, back in the village of Forkhill. It was a damp, grey morning and I initially had my coat on when I set off on my journey out of Forkhill towards Slieve Gullion. However, it was so warm that I soon abandoned the coat and just put up with the constant drizzle, which was quite refreshing in fact. It was clear from the outset that it was highly unlikely that I was going to be able to cross over the summit of Slieve Gullion today. The mountain had all but disappeared under the morning's low lying cloud. Although disappointed, it wasn't a problem as the summit path is actually an alternative route to the official route which takes you round the lower slopes of the mountain. But having seen Slieve Gullion from afar in all its splendour during the sunshine of the previous day, I had been quite keen to go over the top. My son Matthew had been on the summit during a school trip a few years prior to my walk and had said that the views were fantastic. Today, unfortunately, the summit and most of the mountain were nowhere to be seen and, even if reaching the top was possible, the views from there would have been non-existent. My directions indicated that on Slieve Gullion's summit plateau lies Calliagh Berra's Lough. The pool is named after a woman famed in local folklore for bewitching the giant Finn McCool, the same giant of the Giant's Causeway fame. She tricked him into diving into the lough, and when he surfaced his hair had turned completely white. Legend has it that the same fate will befall any person who swims in the waters today. I vowed to return another time to get the complete Slieve Gullion experience, although I was sure that I would be quite happy to resist any temptation to put the legend to the test. I imagined that the water in the elevated lough would be pretty chilly at any time of the year.

I wound my way round the rural roads towards where the map indicated the mountain should be and eventually came to the gateway at the boundary of Slieve Gullion Forest Park. I seemed to have found the mountain okay because the next couple of miles were definitely upwards. Thankfully the pathways on the route today were much better maintained than the day before. Visibility was quite poor as I skirted round what is known as the upper driveway on Slieve Gullion, although the eerie mist certainly added to the mystical atmosphere associated with the mountain. The route led me across the southern slopes of Slieve Gullion, before descending through the Giant's Lair Children's Story Trail and into the Courtyard Centre. The Trail was excellent with its different "giant" props, witches' lairs and fairy houses at every turn and, together with the Centre, I imagine would provide a great day out, particularly for families with young children. There were even a few families around at the time I was passing through, and in spite of the dismal weather they seemed to be having a great time.

I stopped in the Courtyard Centre for a break and had a lovely cup of coffee and the most delicious smoked salmon and cream cheese bagel ever! Being outdoors, walking in the fresh air, certainly works up an appetite and things definitely taste so much better when you feel that you've earned them! However, every time I sat down in a café or restaurant to eat, the fact that Jacqui could no longer be with me was once again brought into sharp focus. I would sit alone and watch other couples and families enjoying their day out and the feeling of loss would swell within me until I was in danger of losing control of my emotions. I had to fight back the tears on these occasions – sometimes I was successful and other times I was not. Because of this, I always tried to find a seat facing away from the other customers if I could manage it. It was also the reason that I preferred to carry my own supplies with me most of the time. But sometimes the lure of a dry place to shelter, and the chance of something hot to eat, was too much to resist. After finishing my bagel, I left a few of my 1000K4J leaflets in the café and set off again.

I followed a series of country lanes for about three miles, passing Killevy Old Church on the way, until I reached the entrance to Camlough Forest. The route then zigzagged up around and through the forest for about a mile, bringing me close to the top of Camlough Mountain. I believe the mountain takes its name from the nearby Camlough lake, which in turn takes its name from the Irish Camloch, meaning "crooked lake". It was certainly hard going on the way up and the feelings that I had been trying to suppress since stopping for lunch in the Courtyard finally broke through. Suddenly, now that I was alone, I fell to my knees and wept freely. It was hard and painful and it took me several minutes to regain control. When I had recovered sufficiently, I slowly pulled myself back up onto my feet. As I rose, so did my weather angels and the skies suddenly started to clear for the first time that day. It was hard not to think that Jacqui and Rosaleen were trying to encourage me and it certainly helped. I gathered myself and headed on up Camlough. From this elevated position and with visibility improved, I was now able to enjoy decent views of the ring dyke that makes up the Ring of Gullion. This ring dyke was formed 60 million years ago by a massive volcanic explosion that obliterated the central volcano, but left a circle of hills, including Flagstaff, radiating around the main crater.

The last three miles or so of the walk were largely downhill as I descended towards the impressively tall stone arches of the Craigmore viaduct, which I first spotted away in the distance from the northern slopes of Camlough Mountain. Also from these northern slopes I could hear, for the first time today, the distant but unmistakable sound of Lambeg Drums, the traditional rousing backbeat to every Twelfth celebration, rising up from the valley below. On reaching Bessbrook, I passed though the extensive parkland and woodland of Derrymore House, which is owned by the National Trust. The Trust describes the house as a "late 18th-century thatched house in gentrified vernacular style" and it certainly makes for a striking property, with its bright yellow exterior and unique thatching, reputedly using water reeds specifically from the River Shannon.

From the beautiful grounds of Derrymore House, I emerged onto the roadways again and made my way to Millvale Road in order to pick up a cycleway that would lead under the viaduct. However, at a crossroads close to the entrance to the cycleway it was clear that an Orange parade would soon be passing, given the number of bystanders, parade marshals and policemen gathered in

The view out over Carlingford Lough from Flagstaff

St John's Point lighthouse with its distinctive wasp colours

The approach to Newcastle with the Mournes looking foreboding in the background

The beautifully serene Lough Corry

the vicinity. So I delayed my onward journey for about 15 minutes to enjoy that part of our collective cultural heritage, that has unfortunately caused so much division and has led to highly charged stand-offs and controversial re-routings. When the parade arrived, I even walked alongside one of the Armagh lodges for about 50 yards; before voluntarily rerouting myself down the cycleway when I reached its entrance. Jacqui would have been proud of me! As I proceeded along the path, I thought to myself, not for the first time, that we all really need to be much more tolerant of our respective cultures in this small corner of the world.

I soon passed under the arches of the very impressive Craigmore Viaduct. It was completed in 1852 to allow trains on the Dublin-Belfast line to span the Camlough River valley. It is around 400m long and boasts 18 separate arches, the tallest of which is 38m high, making this the highest viaduct in Ireland. I walked on and eventually made my way back to Newry Train Station to return to my car at 5.30pm. It had been another long day's walk, but it had certainly been a lot less physically challenging than the previous day. On the drive back to Belfast and looking forward to some much needed tea, I found my traditional route home along the Hillhall Road blocked by another Orange Lodge heading back from Lisburn. I'm sorry to have to admit that my tolerance was then somewhat tested, as I had to wait half an hour before I could continue with my journey home!

The following day was another holiday and a day off work, but I had decided to use it as a day to rest. Then it was back to work for a day on Wednesday and I planned to take a day's leave on Thursday to walk from Newry to Portadown along the Newry Canal Way.

Route Canal

Thursday 16 July – Carnbane to Portadown

I left home and my lonely bed in Belfast and drove to Portadown to meet Ian in the Meadows Lane car park early on Thursday morning. Ian was becoming a regular helper, this being his third day of involvement and I was very grateful to him for all his assistance. Ian drove me back down to Newry again and dropped me off at the days starting point on the edge of the Carnbane Industrial Estate.

I then set off for the long walk along the towpath running alongside the old Newry Canal. It was a beautiful morning, but I had been watching the forecast very closely and it seemed pretty certain that rain was going to come in from the south around lunchtime. I was hoping my weather angels could hold it back until today's walk was finished!

The Newry Canal was built in the mid eighteenth century to link coalfields in Tyrone, via Lough Neagh and the River Bann, to the Irish Sea at Carlingford Lough near Newry. The canal closed way back in 1936, but in more recent years the towpath had become part of a long distance footpath and also part of the National Cycle Network. Some restoration had taken place, and the canal had become a haven for wildlife, with some parts of it also used for coarse fishing. The walk along the pathway was pretty pleasant for the most part and passed through some lovely rolling countryside.

After around seven miles, I passed through the village of Poyntzpass and three miles further on brought me to the pretty little village of Scarva, where I had arranged to meet up with my daughter, Hannah, her boyfriend, Jonny, and his dad, David. They hadn't arrived yet, so I took the opportunity to rest on a street bench and enjoy the lovely blooms that bedecked the village and that had obviously helped Scarva on its way to the finals of the 2015 Britain in Bloom competition, a fact that was proudly declared on signs around the village. Scarva is famous as the location of the "Sham Fight" Pageant on the thirteenth of July every year. The Pageant attracts thousands of members of the Royal Black Preceptory, a group related to the Orange Order, who come to march and stage a symbolic (sham) re-enactment of the 1690 Battle of the Boyne. I had missed this year's event by just a few days, although I'm quite sure that there was no surprise in the outcome of the battle yet again!

Twenty minutes later, my co-walkers for the rest of the day's journey arrived and we enjoyed a very welcome lunch, courtesy of David, outside the Scarva Visitors Centre. Lunch out wasn't so problematic when I had the company of friends and family. There was a little rain at this point but thankfully we were sheltered by a large awning overhead. I just hoped that this wasn't the start of the heavy rain that had been forecast.

After lunch, however, the rain had stopped and all four of us set off along the towpath towards Portadown, which was about seven and a half miles away. The weather stayed very pleasant, but there was nothing particularly remarkable to see along the route, unless you count the local "Buckfast connoisseurs" we encountered, enjoying a bottle or two of the popular beverage on our approach to Portadown. Never-the-less, we all enjoyed the walk and sharing in each other's company as we went. David has quite a demanding job and I think he really appreciated having the opportunity to slow things down for a bit and get back in touch with nature once again - he still couldn't quite help checking his Blackberry every so often though! It also looked like one of my friends had been on the towpath before us, as a number of laminated copies of my 1000K4J flyer had been erected along the route. It was thoughtful actions such as this that gave me a real lift on my walk and I was very grateful to the kind person responsible, who I later found out to be Lorraine, a colleague from work.

About three hours after leaving Scarva, we reached the finishing point for the day in Portadown, just under the bridge at the town's Main Street. There were a few drops of rain starting to fall at this point, so we hurried back to where my car was parked a few hundred yards away and managed to climb in just before the rain became really heavy. Yet again my weather angels had watched over me and had held the rain back just as I had hoped! From here, we drove back to Scarva for David to pick up his car and then we all returned to Belfast.

On checking my JustGiving page when I got back home, I could scarcely believe that, only five weeks after setting off from Greenisland Primary School at the start of my pilgrimage, my initial target figure had been exceeded and over £5,000 had already been raised for Cancer Research UK. I was simply blown away by the generosity and support for 1000K4J and for Jacqui. I used Facebook to thank everyone who had contributed so far and at the same time challenged everyone to keep the momentum going by increasing my fundraising target to £10,000. I wanted my campaign to be shared as widely as possible. I had seen many examples of absolute trivia going viral on social media. This was so much more important. While my campaign never went viral, I'm happy to say that people did indeed rise to the challenge and I was truly humbled by the level of support given.

I now had a day back at work before embarking on the next two-day leg at the weekend, which would take me westwards from Scarva, through Armagh City and on to Aughnacloy village in County Tyrone – a distance of just around 38 miles, or so I thought!

Cathedral City

Saturday 18 July – Scarva to Killylea

The last few nights had been spent at home in my own bed. Each morning I once again reached out for the unreachable, waking to the realisation that Jacqui was not in bed beside me as I had momentarily thought. I wondered for how much longer my mind would play this cruel trick on me. I went to sleep each night mourning the fact that Jacqui was gone and by the time the following morning came round I had forgotten! How was this possible? How could such a momentous thing slip my mind, even for a split second? I wondered when my brain would stop being caught off guard by sleep and cease being fooled into forgetting something that filled nearly every waking minute of my day. However, although it did indeed seem cruel, in some perverse way I also hoped that it would never stop. Because if it did stop, perhaps it would mean that I was beginning to fully accept my "new normal" and that I was maybe ready to move on and leave Jacqui behind. That just seemed totally unthinkable to me.

Thankfully, I was up very early on Saturday morning to drive to Loughgall, where I met my assistant for the weekend, Deirdre. After parking up at her house and meeting her husband Gareth and their children, Deirdre drove me to the day's starting point just about a mile north of Scarva, back on the Newry Canal Towpath. It was a beautiful morning as I passed under a nearby railway bridge and headed along rural roads away from the canal and towards Tandragee. As well as being the home of Tayto crisps and Tandragee Castle, the village is also the home of the Tandragee 100, a motorcycle road racing event held each year on the local country roads, usually in the first weekend in May. I was amused to learn that the name Tandragee comes from the Irish, Tóin re Gaoith, meaning "backside to the wind". I very much doubt that it's naming had anything to do with the road race, given the centuries separating the events, but it nevertheless seemed to be entirely appropriate.

About a mile on the other side of Tandragee, the route took me away from the main Markethill Road and through Clare Glen. It was a very tranquil walk through this glen and, as I followed the river flowing there, I was entranced for a while by a little dipper waiting patiently on a rock for something tasty to swim into view.

Emerging from the glen, I once again joined the rural roads that gradually wound through rolling countryside for about the next nine miles – getting lost for a time but helped back on track by a friendly local, whose house I called at to ask for directions. However, it was shortly after leaving the Clare Glen that the rain came on, varying from light drizzle to moderately heavy at times. Well before reaching Armagh, I came to the conclusion that my weather angels must have had decided to take the day off! They were quite entitled to – it was six months to the day since Jacqui had been taken from her loved ones here on earth. I often wondered if that was how it was – us missing our loved ones who had passed away and them missing their loved ones who they had left behind. It was a depressing notion to think that the pain of separation might be felt on both sides of the veil that separates the living from the dead. Even worse than that thought though, was the notion that those who passed through that veil, including my Jacqui, felt and thought absolutely nothing at all, because "the other side" was just pure nothingness! We all hope and pray for a hereafter to some extent or other, but just as there are no guarantees in life, there are no guarantees in death either. Jacqui absolutely loved an old character, Mickey McGuigan, who featured in a BBC NI documentary "True North – Miraculous Tales" that aired a few years back. Mickey was an elderly County Armagh farmer turned writer and he had been documenting stories of miracles he'd encountered along the border.

At one point in the programme, reflecting on the hereafter, Mickey said, in his very distinctive rural accent: *"There's a lot of things that people can believe in. Just believe in what you think is right. Well lots of people believes that there's a heaven and hell and other people's says, there's neither. But, there's no one knows, till the last day. And then what can you do? If you meet someone at the golden gates and they tell you you'll have to go down below, you wouldn't like that. And then if you were asked to go up above, it'd be great. But if you meet nothing, there's no harm done. You'd go neither place."*

I believe that the simplicity of Mickey's words belied a great wisdom. People may have their strong beliefs, but no-one can know with absolute certainty what awaits us after death. I certainly can't, much as I might want to believe, or hope, that there is something beyond death and that someday I will be reunited with Jacqui. The weather certainly matched my mood as I trudged on, mechanically putting one foot in front of the other. I fought hard to shake off the gloomy mood and was helped a little by remembering to smile occasionally, just as my friend Jennifer had asked me to.

I eventually reached the city of Armagh, the ecclesiastical capital of Ireland, at around 4pm. Armagh is famous for its two cathedrals, both called St Patrick's. Saint Patrick's Church of Ireland Cathedral stands on the hill from which the city of Armagh derives its name Ard Macha, "the hill of Macha", who was a legendary pre-Christian tribal princess. Less than half a mile away, on the adjoining hill, is the grand French Gothic twin-spired St Patrick's Roman Catholic Cathedral.

After surviving the challenges of the Mourne Mountains and the Ring of Gullion, not to mention Clare Glen caravan Park, I very nearly incurred serious injury in this seemingly innocuous urban environment, when I stopped to take a photo of Armagh Gaol. The gaol is located at one end of the city's famous Mall, which is the extensive tree-lined promenade in the centre of the city, once used for horse-racing in the eighteenth century but now used for sports such as cricket, football and rugby. The gaol itself dates back to the 1780's, but closed its doors as a working prison in 1986 and has been ear-marked for a hotel development for some years now. Anyway, I stepped off the street and onto the surface of the Mall pathway to try and get a better shot of the gaol, but before I knew it, my feet suddenly left me and I was on the ground. Because I had my camera in my hand, my efforts went into protecting it rather than my backside. I scrambled to my feet again and thankfully suffered no serious injury, other than to my pride, as a small party of Asian tourists looked on with obvious concern. I gave them an embarrassed smile, brushed myself off and continued on gingerly around the Mall, nursing a pair of tenderised buttocks as I went! It seems that the normally excellent grip provided by the soles of my boots were no match for the resin type surface of the Mall.

After that I felt like a bit of a rest and something to eat, even though it meant sitting on the aforementioned tenderised buttocks. I stopped off at a café in the main shopping area for a coffee and a filled bagel. This city of two cathedrals had been my intended finishing point for the day, but I felt refreshed after my short break and I decided to push on for another couple of hours. Winding through the city streets, full of character and charm, and passing by both cathedrals on the way, I then headed out of the city to pick up the Navan Fort Road. As the name suggests, this road took me past the Navan Fort itself, which I had never visited before. No time like the present. It was only a relatively short detour from the road to climb to the top of the fort to enjoy the fine, albeit rather damp, views of the surrounding countryside. Navan Fort is one of Ireland's most famous and important archaeological sites. It was one of the great royal sites of pre-Christian Gaelic Ireland and the capital of the Ulaid, a people and dynastic group of early Ireland who gave their name to the province of Ulster. The fort consists of a large circular enclosure, marked by a bank and ditch, with a circular mound and the remains of a ring barrow (or burial mound) in the middle. The site is believed to have had a pagan ceremonial purpose and severed heads of the Ulaid's enemies were also said to be kept here. They seem to have been rather fond of separating folk from their heads in Ireland in days gone by!

Another couple of miles and early evening brought me into the little village of Killylea. I had only just arrived when Deirdre, who I had contacted earlier, drove into the village to pick me up and take me back to her home near Loughgall, where I was going to spend the night with her family. I was provided with my own en-suite room and Deirdre cooked me a lovely chicken curry and then served me up some delicious dessert followed by coffee. She even treated me to a few glasses of wine. It was a great place to stay! Tomorrow, it's onward to Aughnacloy, the "field of the stone", and perhaps beyond!

Wrong Turn

Sunday 19 July – Killylea to Altadaven Wood

I enjoyed a very restful night at Deirdre and Gareth's home in the supremely peaceful countryside outside Loughgall. One of their children had very kindly given up their bedroom for the night so that I would have somewhere comfortable to sleep – and very comfortable it was too. It was lovely to pull back the curtains first thing in the morning to be presented with an idyllic rural landscape stretching out before me for miles. At least that's how it appeared to this dyed in the wool "townie". I wondered how many local farmers looking out on the same scene would see only hedges to be cut, fields to be ploughed and cattle to be fed.

After breakfast, Deirdre drove me back into Armagh again, where we met Katie, a photographer from the Ulster Gazette. She took a couple of quick photos of me and Deirdre in the Mall and scribbled down a few notes. Thankfully there were no mishaps in the Mall this time – my backside was still a bit tender from the previous day's tumble! Then it was off in the car again to Killylea to begin my walk from yesterday's stopping point. It was a fine morning as I waved to Deirdre and turned to leave Killylea on foot. However, the rain soon started falling again. I imagined the rain as angels' tears, thinking again that even they must get sad at times to be parted from the ones they love.

The next hour made for rather gloomy progress as angels tears mixed with my own. I certainly don't relish these moments of despair, but in a peculiar way it is like a dark and heavy, but at the same time comfortingly familiar, cloak being placed over your shoulders. It reminds you that, although the physical connection may be broken, the spiritual connection remains and that the love that exists between two people doesn't simply disappear when one is taken from this world. However, after a few miles of this gloom, my weather angels decided enough was enough. Jacqui and Rosaleen were never ones to allow things to get them or others down for too long and they quickly sprang into action and swept the clouds away to allow the warm, bright sunshine to fill the landscape around me – it was beautiful and it really lifted my spirits.

However, I think the sun went to my head after a while. Somewhere between the villages of Tynan and Caledon, I took a wrong turn and veered quite a bit off the Ulster Way and ended up heading towards the village of Glaslough, across the border in the Republic of Ireland. By the time I had realised my mistake, I figured that it would be quicker to keep going on, and eventually link up with the route again in Caledon itself, rather than turning back. I had to flag down a couple of cars along the route to check directions. Both cars were driven by teenagers who looked much too young to be behind a wheel, but perhaps I'm just showing my age here. Although they were both able to give me accurate directions, neither seemed to have much concept of time or distance. Half a mile turned out to be closer to one and half miles and 20 minutes turned out to be closer to an hour!

Anyway, I finally reached Caledon village, after adding five miles and approximately an hour and a half onto my journey! At this point it was close to 2pm and I felt that I had earned a break and a sit down, as recommended by Rachel Joyce. I called into a little cafe along the main street and ordered a coffee and a scone. While waiting for it to be served, I got chatting to one of the locals at the table next to mine. He had perhaps 15 to 20 years on me and he had just finished his Sunday lunch. I didn't ask, but I somehow got the impression that this was a regular stop for him on a Sunday. He was curious to know how far I had walked and, without taking the time to explain my unintentionally extended route, I simply said that I had set off from Killylea that morning. He looked at me with a rather bemused expression, probably taking in how warm and flustered I looked, and ventured "but sure that's only three miles down the road". He was perfectly correct of course. I hurriedly explained to him that the Ulster Way unfortunately didn't follow the main roads and, when you also stupidly didn't follow the proper route, it added up to a lot more than three miles. *"Ye wanna get yersel wan a them jeepee things,"* he offered. I'm sure he meant GPS and he certainly had a point!

The onward journey to Aughnacloy was much more straight forward and uneventful and the weather and the countryside remained gorgeous. Aughnacloy is from the Irish Achadh na Cloiche, meaning "field of the stone", but the origin is unfortunately lost in the mists of time. Perhaps there is some Neolithic stone circle still waiting to be discovered? I arrived in the village a good hour or two later than expected. Never-the-less, given the good weather, I decided to stick to a plan I had discussed with Deirdre the night before and push on to complete the first seven mile section of the Sliabh Beagh Way. The complete Sliabh Beagh Way is a 40 mile long stretch passing over Sliabh Beagh Mountain. Although it is a two day walk, the first day is largely uphill and I reckoned that nipping seven miles off now wouldn't be a bad thing. So I headed off again out of Aughnacloy and wound my way around a mix of narrow country roads and forest tracks, weaving in and out across the border with the Republic of Ireland as I went.

It was a very pleasant walk and I hardly met a soul along the way. However, the peacefulness was very abruptly interrupted while walking though, what I imagine to be, the normally tranquil surroundings of Favour Royal Forest. In the year 2000, Favour Royal Forest was one of 16 sites chosen across Ireland to host new woodlands as part of the People's Millennium Forests scheme, which saw the planting of one native tree for every household in the country. However, I don't think the characters I encountered as I passed through the forest were too concerned about nature and conservation. I heard the roar of the engine before I saw anything and then suddenly there was an old red Renault Clio racing up the forest track towards me. It almost seemed like the driver, one of two lads in the car, accelerated as soon as he saw me and I quickly stepped off the track to let them fly past in a rush of wind, noise and dirt. As they passed, I noticed that the windscreen of the car had been entirely smashed out and also that there wasn't a number plate in sight – the engine sounded perfectly tuned though! A few minutes later I heard the car on its way back and this time I took shelter behind a tree as they flew back down the track.

Shortly after my encounter with the local speed demons, I emerged from the forest and joined the road again which, for the next couple of miles, gradually climbed up towards a small car park near St Patrick's Chair and Well in Altadaven Wood. Tradition relates that St Patrick said mass in the stone chair in Altadaven Wood, and blessed the nearby well. However, it's likely that the site's importance pre-dates St Patrick. The name Altadaven translates as "Glen of the Druid, or Devil" and archaeological evidence indicates that the chair was probably also used for pre-Christian rituals. I was late evening by the time I reached the car park and this was my final destination for today's walk. Having texted Deirdre about a mile back, I had only to wait another 15 minutes for her to arrive to pick me up. I should probably have used that time to make a quick visit to St Patrick's Chair and Well, but I was too knackered and maybe just a little wary of encountering more demons in the woods, whether speeding or not. So I just sat down on my back pack and waited on Deirdre to arrive and drive me back to Loughgall. After a farewell photo with her and Gareth, I set off in my own car back to Belfast for a meal, shower and bed. I slept well that night. After 28.5 miles in one day it was hardly surprising!

Castles and Towers

Tuesday 21 July – Strangford to Killough

After making a brief appearance back at work the day before, today it was back to South Down to start the first of two days tackling the Lecale section of the Ulster Way, which stretches from Strangford to Newcastle. I had of course skipped this two day hike a few weeks back due to my self-inflicted injuries. Lecale is from the Irish Leath Cathail, meaning "Cathal's territory", and gets its name from Cathal, a prince of Ulaid about 700AD.

I met Audrey, who had returned to support me once again, in the Quay Lane car park in Killough. Leaving my car there, Audrey then drove me to Strangford, where we met Marion and a number of other members from the local CRUK Committee at the Cuan Restaurant. Marion had arranged for a photographer from the Down Recorder to meet us, but unfortunately he was running late and it was another half hour before he appeared. After the photos were taken, the Cuan had laid on complementary coffee for us all, so we spent another 15 minutes chatting and drinking coffee before Audrey and I thought that it was high time we were moving. We said our thanks and goodbyes and headed out of the restaurant to begin the walk in earnest.

It was a lovely sunny morning and I was delighted that Audrey had decided to keep me company for the start of the walk. As it turned out, she accompanied me right around the headland to the north of the town, through dark and damp woodland tracks and over the rocky shoreline with views across to Castle Ward and Audley's Castle, which was used as Winterfell Castle in the very popular HBO series, Game of Thrones. When we reached the point where the main road branched off towards Glebe, Audrey and I gave each other a farewell hug and she then headed back in towards the town. I headed on along the Black Causeway Road, which ran inland for about two miles, before turning to meet the Shore Road at Kilclief Church and Castle. Kilclief Castle is really more properly described as a tower house and is one of many such buildings dotted along the shores of Strangford Lough, dating back to a period when Portaferry was a major port. Most were constructed during the fifteenth or sixteenth centuries, spurred on by King Henry VI's offer of £10 to anyone who would erect a tower to protect the coastline.

For the next three miles, I walked along the Shore Road with the ruffled waters of Strangford Lough to my left. When the tide is retreating here, 400,000 tonnes of tidal flow empties out of the narrow mouth of Strangford Lough. With such an immense volume of water on the move, it is little wonder that the Vikings named the inlet Strang Fjörthr, meaning "strong fiord". About a mile after passing Killard Nature Reserve, a popular spot for bird watchers, I reached the little village of Ballyhornan. I stopped here for a bite of lunch at a little picnic area looking out over to the nearby, uninhabited, Guns Island, while a couple of very hardy children played in the shallows of the lough below.

From this point, I left the tarmac and followed a fairly rough coastal path for the next two and a half miles or so. It was quite a rocky and jagged stretch of coastline and might have provided some superb views of the Mournes and the Isle of Man, both in the distance, if the weather hadn't been closing in. Along the way, I encountered a small herd of young bullocks that were grazing freely along the path near a small bay. They seemed very curious of my presence and some of them even started to make towards me. So, being a true townie, I decided to cut across the little beach below their grazing area, giving them as wide a berth as possible.

Before reluctantly moving inland again away from the coastal path, I passed another St Patrick's Well. Just how many wells did St Patrick have? I was at one near Aughnacloy on Sunday past and would encounter lots more on my travels. If bottled water had been invented in the fifth century, Patrick might have become a rich man and not bothered us all with religion. Imagine how differently our little country might have turned out then!

After about a mile of laneway and country roads, I joined the A2 and endured the traffic while hugging the verge for about half a mile until I arrived in the fishing village of Ardglass and thankfully meeting up with some sidewalk in the process. Ardglass contains more medieval tower-houses than any other town in Ireland, a total of four, reflecting its importance as Ulster's busiest port in the fifteenth century. The route then took me round by the harbour and the marina, past Jordan's Castle, one of the aforementioned medieval tower-houses, and then out the other side of the town on a quiet rural road heading westwards. However, it wasn't too long before I met up with the busy A2 once again as I approached Coney Island.

Apparently there are a number of islands of the same name in and around Ireland and even beyond. Coney is a medieval English word meaning rabbit – that's probably why there are so many of them; put two rabbit islands together and the next thing you know.....! Anyway, the Coney Island I was now passing was in County Down and is probably most famous for having a song penned about it by the Belfast singer and songwriter, Van Morrison. Is his song, Van waxes lyrical about travelling through the Lecale District, heading all the time ever closer to Coney Island. The song ends with the lines: *'And all the time going to Coney Island I'm thinking, Wouldn't it be great if it was like this all the time'*. Hmmm, I'm not so sure when you're doing it on foot along the dreaded A2.

Anyway, I soon passed by Coney Island and discovered that it's not actually an island at all, but a peninsula that is almost entirely, but not quite, surrounded by water. I stayed with the A2 for about another mile and a half, circling round Killough Bay, before entering the village of Killough itself in the early evening and making my way back to my car to finish walking for the day.

It had been a slightly less arduous day than Sunday's epic trek through the "field of the stone" and there had been much less chance of taking a wrong turn, with the sea almost constantly being over my left shoulder. And despite the frequent threat of rain, my weather angels had performed another excellent job of keeping the rain clouds well away from me throughout the day. My plan was to return to finish the Lecale section of the Ulster Way the following day, which would take me on to the popular seaside resort of Newcastle at the foot of the Mourne Mountains, or to quote from another famous song, by Percy French this time: *'Where the Mountains of Mourne sweep down to the sea.'*

The Bridge

Rocky, muddy, thorny, stingy, boggy, twisty, sweaty; and that was just the first couple of miles of today's walk! It was to be a difficult day after a difficult night.

I hadn't slept very well at all, which unfortunately was not an unusual occurrence. Most nights, my mind kept going round in infuriating endless circles and it seemed impossible to break free of the spinning and twisting emotions of anger, sadness and fear. Anger at how Jacqui's life had been cut so tragically short, sadness at the loss of Jacqui and the beautiful life we had together, and fear at what the future held for me now that Jacqui was gone. These feelings circled around each other and passed and wove over, under and through each other in a wild uncontrolled fashion that had me constantly twisting and turning in bed, unable to find rest or peace. It was like riding a mental version of a fairground Waltzer ride and despite my silent screams for it to stop, it just kept going, relentlessly swinging and swirling until I ended up dizzy and exhausted. Therefore, despite my lack of sleep, I was glad to get up early and drive to Newcastle for the next leg of my pilgrimage.

In Newcastle I met up once again with Sherpa Jim, who had returned to duty as my driver once again this morning. I left my car here and Jim drove me to Killough, kindly pointing out some of the turn offs for the walking route along the way. I bade farewell to Jim at Killough pier and set off to start my walk along the coastal path. Killough came to the fore in 2012, when a film shot in the area by Terry George, *The Shore*, won an Oscar for best live action short film. Some of the characters in the film were seen harvesting shellfish along the shore, so it was interesting to see oysters being collected and sorted by some of the locals as I walked along the path.

The coastal path gradually became a coastal track and then little more than a coastal impression in the grass, which became so indistinct at times that it was difficult to know the exact route to take! However, there was generally a way-marker or a yellow painted style in the distance to aim for and then it became a question of finding the path of least resistance in making my way towards it. The views around me were super and the weather was ideal for walking, but I found that the terrain was much tougher than I had expected and it made for quite slow progress as I headed towards the distinctive 'wasp' lighthouse at St John's Point. The lighthouse itself was about half a mile off route, but it seemed a pity to pass it by when I was so near. So I made the diversion to get an up-close look at the 40 metre high structure, with its black and yellow striped paint job. With the Mourne Mountains n the background, it made for a striking image.

I then made my way back and re-joined the official route, which took me up lanes and quiet country roads to once again join the dreaded A2. However, just before reaching the main road, I met a friendly local man out walking his two dogs and he advised getting down onto the beaches wherever possible to avoid the traffic. This seemed like a very good idea to me and so at the first opportunity, I cut down a lane, through some very quiet farm buildings and climbed over a gate to get onto Tyrella beach. Technically, this may have constituted trespassing, but I was prepared to take my chances. It was lovely to walk along the wide open sands of Tyrella and to watch a pony and trap being put through its paces in the silver shallows down by the shoreline.

Unfortunately, the very pleasant beach walk lasted for less than a mile and I then had to join the A2 again for about another mile before veering off down a quieter road towards the village of Ballykinler, which is bordered by an army camp to the west and south west. I could probably have navigated my way to Ballykinler blindfolded, given the constant sound of munitions being fired on the camps firing range just beyond the village. My directions told me that Ballykinler gets its name from the Irish Baile Coinnleora, meaning "townland of the candelabra" and I had visions of it being populated entirely by Liberace lookalikes. I was therefore slightly disappointed to find the inhabitants boringly normal – not a sequin or coiffed hairdo in sight. In fact, the name of the village derives from the fact that the lands of Ballykinler were granted by John de Courcy, around 1200, to Christchurch Cathedral in Dublin for the upkeep of a perpetual light (the "candelabra") before the crucifix there.

After having walked several miles towards the Mournes, and where the seaside town of Newcastle lay, it was a little disconcerting to start heading away from them as I left Ballykinler, leaving the sound of munitions behind. However, this was the only practical option. Tempting though it was to imagine taking a shortcut straight across the bay at low tide to Dundrum, a distance of only one and a half miles, the official route sensibly took me on a much longer route around the bay, a distance of four and a half miles. Jim had reminded me, on the way to Killough, that people had drowned while attempting to take a shortcut across the bay in the past! The bay can be almost completely empty of water at low tide, but can also fill up very quickly when the tide turns.

On the plus side, the longer route allowed me to enjoy a hidden gem of the Lecale Way. I left the tarmac behind quite close to the "apex" of the bay and joined the delightful Dundrum Coastal Path that followed the route of a disused railway line for almost two miles into Dundrum itself. This path provided a mix of leafy shelter from the sun interspersed with open views across the bay. At one point, I had a clear view of a heron wading deftly through the shallows in search of its next meal. Apparently, the heron instinctively adjusts the angle at which its heads strikes the water to compensate for the refraction of light at the water's surface, otherwise it would miss its target. Nature never fails to amaze me.

Barbara, my next door neighbour, had planned to meet me in Dundrum at around 1.30pm with a picnic lunch. However, it was now after 3pm and I was still half an hour away. So, after a few phone calls, we met near the start of the coastal path instead and I enjoyed a lovely basket of food and tea she had very kindly prepared – food tastes so much better when you have worked/walked for it and I certainly felt that I had earned it today – I think Barbara may also have got something to eat before I scoffed the most of it! Even a boiled egg, still in the shell, that had escaped the basket and rolled under the car seat was not allowed to get away.

After refuelling, it was back onto the beautiful coastal path again and Barbara walked with me along this stretch into Dundrum. We were both surprised and delighted to discover this very well-kept secret. The Dundrum Coastal Path follows the line of the old Belfast and County Down Railway, which once ran from Belfast to Newcastle, but closed in 1950 after operating for almost 100 years. It made up somewhat for missing out on our chance to walk the path of the old Newry to Warrenpoint railway line, when Barbara and I had walked from Rostrevor to Newry eleven days previously. As we reached the town, the rain started to come on and after a quick hug and goodbye, Barbara hurried back along the path to her car. She had hoped to walk further with me today but due to my very late arrival for lunch, she had no option but to cut her journey short. It was probably just as well, given the sudden change in the weather. As I struggled into my wet gear, the rain became quite heavy, which always made the struggle more urgent and inevitably, in my case anyway, much less efficient. A miserable trudge then ensued along the main road for a couple of hundred yards before veering off to the right and taking a street up to twelfth century Dundrum Castle, which overlooks the town and normally commands fine views south over Dundrum Bay and the Mournes. There were no views to be had today though, as the rain remained persistently heavy.

I left the castle and weaved my way down and round Dundrum town through public paths, laneways and streets and eventually joined a path that led me to Downshire Bridge. I had seen the three stone arches of this bridge on numerous occasions in the past when driving to or from Newcastle and had always wondered where it led to. Now I was finally going to find out. I just so wished that it was under different circumstances and that I wasn't doing it alone. In many ways I wished I never had a reason to cross that bridge, but cross it I must - I had to keep on pushing forward despite a niggling urge to give up sometimes. Miraculously, as I was crossing, the sun suddenly broke through the clouds and bathed the landscape before me in a beautifully soft and warm light! I don't really know what this meant, if indeed it meant anything at all. But I do know that I often found it impossible to look at such an occurrence and not see it as some kind of sign to cling on to and to draw some hope from.

When dealing with profound personal loss, it is perhaps too easy to read positive things into what are, in reality, everyday occurrences. However, if it helped me along, even in the slightest way, I was only too happy to go along with it and give into its comforting embrace. So, at that moment on Downshire Bridge when the sun "miraculously" appeared, it was, in my mind anyway, my weather angels lighting the way forward for me; beckoning me on across to the other side and giving me encouragement to keep going. I wondered if something similar occurs when you reach the end of the road that is your life and you are standing on that bridge between life and death. Do your loved ones that have gone before you light the way for you and beckon you across to the other side? I certainly hoped that was how it had been for Jacqui when her time had come back in January. I hoped that her parents were there to light the path for her and that they were there to welcome her home at the same time as I was reluctantly letting her go.

With the sun now out again, there were some lovely views back towards Dundrum, with the ruins of the medieval castle now visible on the hilltop overlooking the town. Once over the bridge, the track ran for about another mile before joining a long boardwalk that passed through the dunes of Murlough National Nature Reserve. The sand dune ecosystem of Murlough is 6,000 years old, and is regarded as the best and most extensive example of dune heath in Ireland, being designated as Ireland's first nature reserve in 1967. Before I reached the end of the boardwalk, the rain came on once again and unfortunately accompanied my emergence onto the beach, which had promised to suddenly reveal spectacular views of the Mourne Mountains. Nevertheless, with the dark skies forming, the Mournes provided a dramatic and brooding backdrop, reminiscent of Tolkien's Mordor, on my final approach to Newcastle across the sands and stones of the beach.

I think that this walk across the beach would have been quite nice if it had taken place in isolation. But, to be honest, after the distance I had already walked that day, this last stretch of almost two miles was closer to an endurance test! Thankfully the tide was out, which at least meant that I wasn't confined to the narrow strip of beach I might have been if I had been crossing at high tide. But the sand was very soft in places and, together with the large stones that skidded to the side as I stood on them, it meant that the ground was rarely firm beneath the feet. My already tired legs had to work extra hard to maintain my balance as I went. The challenge of walking this section made me think about the extra effort that I now needed to put into simply continuing with my life. Before Jacqui's illness and death, my life – our lives – had been like the boardwalk through the Murlough dunes. The path was clearly laid out and the surface was solid and secure. My life after Jacqui's death, was more akin to walking over this stretch of beach. The path wasn't clear at all and the surface was uneven and unstable. The things I had taken for granted in the past, the things that had provided stability and certainty in my life, had now shifted and no longer offered the security and sureness that they once had. The path that I had once thought my life was on, the path that I had once walked along so confidently with Jacqui by my side, was now an uncertain route that I had to negotiate alone. I longed for Jacqui's hand in mine as I continued my long, slow trudge over the stone strewn beach.

It once again started to brighten up as I got closer to Newcastle and a small section of rainbow even appeared over the Irish Sea to welcome me into the busy seaside town. Passing the Victorian facade of the well-known Slieve Donard Hotel, I left the beach by a set steps to join the wide pavement of the town's promenade and followed it until I crossed a white metal footbridge over the Shimna River. From here I made the short journey through the town and arrived back at my car, quite exhausted, but very pleased to have completed the Lecale Way and to have finally caught up with those sections I had previously had to skip. I was now fully back on schedule. I drove home, had some tea, started to write my blog, and crashed after the first couple of paragraphs.

The following day, I still couldn't understand why 16 miles, which was the distance indicated in the directions for Killough to Newcastle, had taken so long to complete and had seemed so difficult, even allowing for my lack of sleep the night before. So I went back to the maps and measured out the distance actually covered by the route. I discovered that the directions had underestimated the distance of the Lecale Way and that my 16 miles walk the previous day had in reality been 20.5 miles! I didn't feel quite so bad now, knowing that I had good reason to be more knackered than I had expected to be, as well as now having a good excuse for having been so late for Barbara's picnic lunch.

Bog Bouncing

Saturday 25 July – Altadaven Wood to Eshcleagh Lough

After a couple of days back at work, it was time to get back on the road again. The day started with a drive from Belfast to Lisnaskea in Co Fermanagh to meet up with my mate Brian. I left my car in one of the town's public car parks and Brian then drove me back to Altadaven Wood, where I had stopped five days before. Here we were met by a small welcoming party of members of the Ballygawley CRUK Fundraising Group – Iris, Roisin and Jean – who very kindly presented me with a generous cash donation. After taking a few photos, including some for the local press, Brian took his leave and I set off on the day's walk. I was joined by two of the Group for a short distance, before they had to return to Ballygawley. I was beginning to learn that the folk involved with CRUK are all very dedicated and supportive – all bound by a common bond, often born out of personal tragedy, but always distinguished by an unselfish desire to do something to make things better for others.

It was a very pleasant day as I headed on along a number of country roads that took me past Lough More and on a long steady uphill climb to the expanse of open, peat covered moor, that blankets most of the upper lands of Sliabh Beagh. There was a small picnic area at Braggan, at the highest point, and I stopped here to have a "Rachel break" and to take in the panoramic views across Counties Tyrone and Fermanagh in Northern Ireland and County Monaghan in the Republic. There were distant mountain ranges visible from this elevated position to both the North-West and the East, which may have been the Sperrins and the Mournes/Ring of Gullion respectively.

After my break, I followed a road, lane and then stone track for a few miles before leaving the surety of the hard surfaces to take on a less well defined route across the open moorland. On leaving the stone track, I immediately found myself walking over a short section of bare peat. This provided the most bizarre walking experience I have ever encountered. The turf was unbelievably springy and the sensation was akin to walking on the springs of an old fashioned type bed, for those old enough to remember. That the actual ground beneath my feet could be like that was quite amazing. You might feel that I am exaggerating here, but all I can say is that you should give it a go if you ever get a chance – add "bog bouncing" to your bucket list.

From here, unfortunately, the ground started to become a lot wetter and spongier, which together with the lack of a well-defined track, made the going rather slow and at times quite arduous. Thankfully, there were quite a number of way markers to indicate the general direction to head in most of the time, although some were difficult to spot from a distance. A small pair of binoculars might have been a useful addition to the kit bag. The most striking thing about this area was the feeling of sheer isolation and with its elevated position I really felt like I was at the top of the world – and the top of the world turned out to be composed of wet sponge!

I passed a couple of small loughs along the way before crossing over another section of moorland and then following the route around and through a series of forest tracks, which eventually brought me to a road at Muckle Rocks. Muckle is an Ulster Scots word for many or large, so I presume that the name means many rocks or large rocks. Nearby lies Shane Barnagh's Lough, which owes its name to a Co. Tyrone highwayman Shane Barnagh, also known as "Toothless Shane". Legend has it that he lived in the seventeenth century and assisted impoverished locals with his robberies, mainly from English gentry and soldiers. Because of this, Barnagh became a local hero in the style of Robin Hood who robbed from the rich and gave to the poor. One of his hideouts was apparently at the small rocky hillock near the lough, known as Shane Barnagh's Stables. Barnagh was eventually captured and executed by the English and his body was cast into the lough. Rumours persist of a horde of undiscovered treasure still buried near the lough.

However, I had no time to go chasing after rumours of treasure and, instead, it was back onto the blacktop for me. Along this road, I paused for a few minutes to look in at Mullaghfad Church, a remote, stone church with an external bell. This church dates from 1836, and must be one of the most isolated churches in Ireland. It has never had an electricity supply and just a handful of services are held there each year. There are a number of fine, ancient yew trees around the church, which apparently is not uncommon in old churchyards. There have been many theories as to why this is the case such as, they were regarded as sacred, as evergreens they were associated with immortality, they thrived on corpses, they ensured that animals didn't stray into the churchyards as they were poisonous, or they would protect churches from gale damage or even ward off evil spirits – take your pick!

Another mile beyond the church, I left the road to follow a series of tracks through Mullaghfad Forest. This brought me past Lough Cushy, Jenkin Lough and Lough Nadarra, before I emerged from the trees once again and joined the road at Eshywulligan. There were certainly some strange and wonderful place-names in this part of the world. Eshywulligan conjured up all sorts of thoughts of fairies or evil spirits in my head. I was therefore slightly disappointed to discover that it actually translates to reveal the rather more mundane and functional meaning of "O'Mulligan's low lying land". This was my first option as a stopping point for the day, but it was still early and the weather was fine. The forecast for the following day was petty terrible, so I decided to push on and complete another few miles while the going was good. This took me past Lough Nabull and up the steep hill of Carnmore, which plays a central role in Irish mythology. Legend has it, that when Noah took to sea in his ark, a second ship also set sail, containing Noah's son Bith, along with Queen Cesair and her fifty maids. The ship came to rest in Ireland and Sliabh Beagh is named in Bith's honour. His body is said to lie under Carnmore, which was once topped by a massive burial cairn. Carnmore, of course, simply means "Great Cairn".

Before reaching the top of Carnmore, I turned off onto a gravel track and followed it down to the shore of the beautifully serene Lough Corry. After taking a moment to enjoy the view and watch a fisherman, who seemed to be in his own personal nirvana, I headed on through Lisnaskea Forest, past Lough Eshcleagh and out onto a quiet rural road, where Brian magically appeared bang on time to transport me to his home at Killygorman.

Here I met Brian's wife, Florence, their three young children and Molly, their pet dog. After enjoying a much needed hot shower, I joined the family for a delicious meal. Their hospitality was just superb! After relaxing and chatting with Brian and Florence for a while, it was time to turn in and get some rest. All the rooms in the house were taken so Brian had fixed up the family caravan in the yard for me and it proved to be very comfortable indeed. Before lights out, I checked the weather forecast for Sunday. Unfortunately, it had not improved!

Misery

Sunday 26 July – Eshcleagh Lough to Lisnaskea

Well I expected Sunday to be a miserable day and I wasn't disappointed. Not even my trusted weather angels could hold back this particular front that had pushed in resolutely from the Atlantic overnight.

I woke very early to the sound of heavy raindrops falling on the roof of the caravan and was immediately transported back to my childhood days – an all too familiar sound from family caravan holidays in Bundoran back in the late 60's, early 70's. I lay there thinking about how simple and carefree life was back then, when I had no worries or responsibilities and death was unknown to me. But we all have to grow up and sooner or later death inevitably becomes part of life. Benjamin Franklin famously said that there were only two things certain in life – death and taxes. Neither are welcome and whilst one of them can be avoided to some extent, the other certainly cannot. Since those carefree childhood days, I had lost my mother, one of my brothers and now my wife. The rain drops drumming on the roof above me became the steady beat of a funeral march in my mind and I once again found myself sinking into a dark and bleak place. The tears came and my body was once again racked with grief as I stared into the abyss that was my seemingly hopeless future. I wished that I could quietly slip away from life and not have to think about what lay ahead. At times the thought of just opting out of living seemed so attractive. The appeal of returning to a state of innocence through lifelessness. Oh to just stay asleep and never wake up again. Why wake up to pain if you could stay asleep in blissful ignorance? But once again I reminded myself of why I was undertaking my pilgrimage and I fought against the desire to stay in bed and do nothing. Instead, I once again forced myself to get up and to face the day.

After getting dressed and composing myself, I joined Brian and Florence for a lovely continental style breakfast. Once again, the company of good friends really helped to lift me out of my dark mood and allowed me to face the day ahead with some optimism. Brian and I then left for Lisnaskea, where I dumped my overnight bag back in my car and we then headed back to the point where I had finished the previous day, close to Eshcleagh Lough. I was very glad that Brian, who knew the local area very well, was driving, as I certainly couldn't have found my way round the country roads quite so easily.

I waved farewell to Brian and then I set off in the persistent rain along the road towards Tully Forest. The road passed through the trees at the edge of the forest and I was looking for a way marker to indicate a right turn onto a forest track, which would take me into Tully Forest proper. I passed a couple of tracks off to the right but none of them were way marked. At the third such track I almost convinced myself that this was the turn I was looking for, but, search as I might, I could not see a way marker. After some deliberation in the pouring rain, I decided to stick to the road for another bit to see if I could find a way marked track further on.

However, after another ten minutes walking, no such track had appeared and so, in desperation, I called at a local house. An elderly gentleman opened his door to find a bedraggled hobo standing on his doorstep looking for help with directions. Thankfully he helped me get my bearings. I had suspected that I was on the road towards a place called Corraghy but he politely informed me: *"You're actually in Corraghy, son"*. In the shelter of his porch I was able to study the map a bit better and I could now see that the third turn off was indeed the one I should have taken. I thanked the gentleman for his help and headed back up the road, back the way I had come, reflecting on my good fortune that the message about elderly folk not opening their doors to strangers had apparently not yet reached Corraghy.

I arrived back at the turn-off again and discovered the way marker I had previously been looking for, hidden behind tall grass and weeds about 15 metres in from the junction. That was another mile clocked up unnecessarily, and in the pouring rain too! I felt like screaming. In fact I did scream. Not for the first time, I was reminded of the old acronym RTFM - Read The Fecking Manual – except in my case it was, Read The Fecking Map! I was now definitely going to invest in a decent mobile with GPS – that man at the café in Caledon had been perfectly right!

Anyway, I was now back on track once again and was able to trudge on through the forest and through the unrelenting rain, which was now accompanied by a chilly and blustery wind – some might say just another typical July day in Ireland! After about a mile and half, I emerged from the trees again and then followed a series of country lanes and roads for about four miles, making my way towards the small village of Donagh.

It was along one of these country roads, in the sheer misery of the pouring rain, that a car pulled up beside me and the lone woman driver offered me a lift – it appears that personal security is not a big thing in Co Fermanagh! She had obviously taken pity on me walking in such poor weather conditions. I asked her if she was sure that she didn't mind the inside of her car getting all wet and she replied that I needn't worry about that. I was suddenly exasperated with walking in this miserable weather and I just wanted to quit for the weekend and get back home. So, in a moment of weakness, and without really thinking too hard about what I was doing, I pulled off my cape and threw it and my backpack onto the back seat and quickly climbed into the passenger seat. The woman, who I reckon was in her early forties, introduced herself as Annie and asked where I was going. I told her my name and said that Lisnaskea would be great but anywhere in that general direction would be good. Annie said that I was in luck, as she was heading through Lisnaskea on her way to visit a relative in Florence Court. Annie seemed very friendly, someone who I would describe as homely, and we passed the next couple of miles easily, making small talk; me telling her about my walk and her appearing to be quite interested. However, I started to get a little uneasy as her questions became quite personal and, when her hand brushed against my leg for the second time as she shifted gear unnecessarily, I in turn shifted in my seat uneasily. I told her that I thought that the rain was easing a little and that perhaps I should get back to my walk after all. *"You can drop me anywhere along here, thank you,"* I added politely. Annie said that I was just being silly and that the rain was clearly on for the day. Her next words, however, really sent a shiver through my body. *"My own house is really quite close. I'll take you back there and you can get dried while I make you something nice to eat"*. Panicking, I quickly replied, *"Annie, I'm not hungry and I would really like you to pull over now, please"*. But she persisted, *"That's fine, we don't have to eat. We'll just get you nice and dry. We might have to get you out of those damp clothes"*. That did it. I was getting out of here at the next opportunity. Fortunately, she had to slow down on the approach to the next junction and, seizing my chance, I quickly opened the passenger door and jumped out, only just managing to stay on my feet. *"Mad cow"*, I shouted after her car as she raced away. Just as I realised that my cape and backpack were still on her back seat, the car skidded to a halt and I saw Annie get out, open the rear door, drag my gear out and dump it in the middle of the road. She then shouted back, *"You fecking men are all bastards"*, jumped back in the car and sped off once more.

At this point I snapped out of the fantasy I had wandered into. As it was, I have no idea what the lady driving the car was called because our conversation really went more like this: Her, *"That weather is awful. Would you like a lift somewhere?"* Me, *"Thanks for the offer, but I'm walking for charity and I'll just have to stick with it"*. Her, *"Ok then. Good luck"*. And off she went and I continued along the road and allowed my mind to wander as well as my feet. Now, for all I know, she might indeed have been some crazy woman out on the prowl looking for vulnerable men on the roadside to kidnap and take back to her lair to keep as her plaything! But I really don't think so. She seemed like a lovely woman, who was genuinely concerned as to my welfare on a really horrible day. And she didn't look anything like the Annie Wilkies character, played by Cathy Bates, in that movie based on the Stephen King book, "Misery". It's amazing how my mind could wander off into these realms of fantasy when tramping along the roads in the pouring rain for hours on end. Later in my pilgrimage, I was to experience fantasies much darker than this particular one, and rainfall was not always a prerequisite – as well as my angels, I also had my demons following me!

I arrived in Donagh (on foot!) at around lunchtime and was surprised to find that the rain had paused for a bit. This allowed me to have a quick 15 minute lunch break in a small picnic area, where I enjoyed the delicious sandwiches that Florence had prepared for me earlier. She had also packed me a large square of chocolate brownie which was just heavenly. I wished that I had more time to savour them, but before I had finished the rain started again and it was back on with the wet gear and back on the road. Donagh is from the Irish Domhnach, meaning "church", and, from the number of cars parked along the roads, it certainly seemed like the whole village and the surrounding district for miles around had turned out to attend the large Roman Catholic Church on the edge of the village. I was amused to note the usual sight of a handful of "moochers" hanging around outside the church smoking and chatting; never actually entering the church building but loitering close enough to the doors to hear the odd word drifting out so that they could, in their own minds at least, claim it as attendance and their Sunday mass duty fulfilled.

From Donagh, it was roughly another three and a half miles along country roads to reach Lisnaskea and back to where my car was parked. The directions talked of this stretch providing a "picturesque journey with occasional good views across the myriad islands of Lough Erne". I'm afraid to say that this was all lost to me with the landscape continually shrouded by a curtain of rain and my vision constantly blinkered by the hood of my jacket. However, I did have the pleasure of meeting a very friendly white horse along the way, which brought a little enjoyment to an otherwise miserable day. I finally reached my car in the early afternoon and, although it was quite early to finish walking for the day, it was with great relief that I was able to strip off the layers of wet gear and get into the shelter of the vehicle. Then, with de-misters set to full, and headlights and wipers on, I was off on the road back to Belfast.

It had been a difficult enough day, mainly due to the lousy weather conditions. I was certainly glad that I had walked a few miles extra the day before to shorten this day's journey – although adding the unnecessary extra mile back at Tully Forest didn't help. However, arriving back at home in Belfast, I once again reflected on the fact that no matter how difficult I found my long walks along the Ulster Way at times, in many ways the most difficult part was always that short walk I had to take from the car back into the house after having been away for a day or two. Stepping back into surroundings that were so familiar, but at the same time changed forever because of Jacqui's absence, was always difficult. The feelings of loss and abandonment rushed to meet me as I opened the front door once again. I always hoped that perhaps I had managed to lose those feelings out on the road somewhere; hoped that I had managed to leave them far behind as I marched on relentlessly through the rain. But my demons weren't so readily shook off; they were tenacious and resilient and always managed to cling onto me. So once again, I was "welcomed" home by loss and abandonment rather than by the person who I longed to be there to hug me as I came through the front door. Instead of laughs and smiles it was tears and despair. The one person who had made our house a home and who had made my life complete was simply no longer there. No longer there to ask how my day had been, to chat with as we prepared our tea together, to sit down beside and enjoy the evening meal with, to relax in front of the TV with, to later head to bed with, to snuggle up warm and safe and comfortable with, to wake up beside in the morning. Simple things. Taken for granted things. Lost forever things.

Your ways

Your face
Your smile
Your look
Your ways
I still see

Your voice
Your grace
Your laugh
Your warmth
I still miss

Your touch
Your kiss
Your embrace
Your love
I still want

Your body
Your mind
Your soul
Your spirit
I still sense

Your life
Your hopes
Your plans
Your dreams
I still hold

Halfway to Heaven

Saturday 1 August 2015 – Florencecourt to Belcoo:
This day should have been a day of celebration to mark mine and Jacqui's 28th wedding anniversary. Instead it was a physically tough and emotionally challenging day of walking alone in Jacqui's memory. The evil that is cancer had robbed us of our future together and it hurt to the very core of my being. Despite my heartbreak though, I knew that I had so much to be thankful for. The 35 years we had together, including the eight years we had been together before getting married, had been truly wonderful and we had been blessed with two lovely children, Matthew and Hannah. I can honestly say that I was a much better person for having known Jacqui. Over the years she managed to gradually dismantle many of my inbuilt prejudices and make me a much more tolerant and forgiving person - well, sometimes anyway! Jacqui had that effect on many people who had been fortunate enough to meet her during her lifetime.

After a week back at work, I had travelled back down to Brian and Florence's on the Friday night and, after being welcomed to join a little family celebration, I stayed overnight in their caravan once again. I had been keeping a very close eye on the weather forecast all during the week and everything was pointing to Saturday being the pick of the days, with heavy rain forecast for Sunday and Monday. So based on this information consistently being reported on TV, radio and online, I decided to switch my walking schedule for the weekend and walk from Florence Court to Belcoo via Cuilcagh Mountain on the dry Saturday and leave the road walking of Lisnaskea to Florence Court to the wet Sunday.

So, after breakfast on Saturday morning, I followed Brian's car in my own to Belcoo, parked up and got a lift back to the entrance gates to Florence Court with Brian. At this stage, the weather was lovely and I enjoyed the very peaceful walk up the long driveway towards the stately home and grounds, taking in the impressive views of Benaughlin Mountain in the distance as I went. The name of this mountain comes from the Irish Binn Eachlabhra, which translates to reveal the wonderfully evocative name of "peak of the speaking horse". Legend tells of a mythical white horse, the "Coppal Bawn", a powerful creature that came out of the mountain once a year on "Bilberry Sunday", the last Sunday of July, to speak oracles to people. Myth has it that a local twelfth century chieftain, Donn Bin Maguire, was tricked and abducted by the magic white stallion and afterwards he in turn lured and carried off many people to an underground lair, situated underneath Benaughlin Mountain. Apparently, mothers in this area used to warn their children not to stay out late, because "the white horse would come and take them away". It is also said that, up until recently, there had been a large white outline of a horse carved into the hillside, apparently visible from miles away. It was not a bit wonder, that my own mind had started to concoct bizarre fantasies as I travelled round this land that was steeped in folklore and legend.

When I eventually reached the end of the long driveway, I took the opportunity to drop off some of my leaflets in a recently opened new visitors centre. I then spent a bit of time in the grounds, alone with my thoughts. In September the year before, Jacqui and I had, what unfortunately turned out to be, our final holiday together. Jacqui was feeling great at the time and things were looking very positive as we enjoyed a few days break at the lovely Knockninny Guesthouse on the shores of Lough Erne, near Enniskillen. The weather had been fantastic and on one of our days we visited Florence Court House and spent a good part of the day wandering around the grounds, just relaxing and soaking up the sunshine and the tranquillity of the place. Now I sat for a few moments on the same garden bench close to the old sawmill that Jacqui and I had shared less than a year before, when we enjoyed the peace and quiet and spoke of our hopes for a future without cancer in our lives. At that time we had even booked a holiday to a beautiful little spot in Lanzarote for the following month, as Jacqui had been responding so well to her treatment. Unfortunately, circumstances changed for us quite dramatically within a matter of weeks and the planned holiday had to be cancelled just a few days before we were due to leave. On Monday 20 October 2014, the very day when Jacqui had been hoping to be relaxing on a sun lounger by the sea in Lanzarote, she was instead settling back into one of the reclining chairs in the Bridgewater Suite at the City Hospital in Belfast to begin a second round of chemotherapy treatment.

It still hurt so much that my best friend in life had been taken away from me far too early – before we ever had a chance to enjoy the freedom of retirement together and do all the things that we were so looking forward to doing in each other's company. Although we had travelled quite a bit during our years together, there was still so much we wanted to see and experience. Being free of many of the financial commitments, such as childcare and mortgages, and having an abundance of free time that retirement would bring, would have allowed us to travel so much more of the world together – as well as simply spending more time in each other's company in places closer to home, such as our beloved Portrush. This had now been denied to us by cancer. Future happy family occasions, such as weddings, births and christenings, had also been denied to Jacqui and would undoubtedly be bitter-sweet events for me as I would feel her absence more acutely at these times – all because of bloody cancer. People often advise the bereaved to not dwell on the loss, but to focus on the happy memories. Much easier said than done! For me at this stage, the pain due to things lost was certainly a much more powerful emotion than the pleasure from happy memories of the past. In fact, the happy memories only served to accentuate the loss. Although I never expected the pain of loss to disappear, I could only hope that, over time, the balance between pain and pleasure would shift so that at some stage the sweetness of the memories could be enjoyed without it being overwhelmed every time by the bitterness of loss. I wiped away the inevitable tears that these memories of dashed hopes brought to the surface and, remembering why I was here and what I had resolved to do, I forced myself off the garden bench and set off to conquer Cuilcagh Mountain.

After passing by the water powered sawmill and following a number of lanes and forest tracks, I came to a section of open farmland where I had to keep one wary eye on the cattle and the other on the increasingly rough and marshy ground. About an hour and a half after leaving Florence Court, I reached and traversed round the base of an impressive "mud-mound", known as Gortmaconnell Rock. I was tempted to scramble to the top of the rock, where a viewing platform promised panoramic views, but I thought, quite rightly as it turned out, that I had better conserve my energy for Cuilcagh.

I joined the Marlbank Loop Road for a mile or so before entering the long stony track at Legnabrocky ("badger's hollow") that led up through Cuilcagh Mountain Park. At this point, Cuilcagh Mountain still looked a very long way away. The name Cuilcagh comes from the Irish Cuilceach, which has been translated as "chalky". However, the mountain is mainly sandstone and shale, covered with bog and heather. It is possible that the name refers to the limestone rock on the lower northern flanks, where a number of streams disappear below ground at swallow holes that form part of the Marble Arch cave system, which I would encounter later.

As I started my approach to Cuilcagh, I noticed that the rain clouds were starting to gather ominously to the West. Roughly about a third of the way up, I came across a little orange roofed shelter and thinking little of it, other than that might be handy for somebody caught in a storm, I strode nonchalantly on by it. However, a few minutes later the rain clouds seemed to have accelerated towards me and it was as if my weather angels were saying, *"Look we've been holding this rain back long enough to let you reach the shelter, so for heaven's sake would you please just use it!"* So I turned and rushed back to the shelter and had only just got in and closed the door when the heaven's opened properly. It was certainly an opportune time for some lunch. I enjoyed my sandwiches and chocolate brownie, courtesy of Florence yet again – if not the best brownies in the world, then they were certainly the best in Fermanagh! There was a Perspex window in the door and I watched another poor walker struggling up the track in the pouring rain. I could do little, but wait until he arrived at the shelter and then at least open the door to let him in. He thanked me as he dived in, while at the same time cursing the weather forecast for getting it so badly wrong. His eyes were stinging from the sun cream, he had optimistically applied earlier, being washed into them by the rain. He had no sooner sat down, than the rain suddenly stopped and the sun came out again! He saw the funny side though and we exchanged a few pleasantries before I set off again leaving him to decide whether he would call it a day or not. I didn't see him again, so I have to assume that he decided he had enough and had headed back down to his car.

After climbing another tiring length of track, I eventually reached "the eighth wonder of the world" – the Cuilcagh Boardwalk. This is close to a mile of timber walkway and staircase that leads off the hard stone track and takes you over the extremely boggy ground of the lower slopes and then up the steep and equally boggy side of Cuilcagh all the way to the summit plateau. The boardwalk had only been completed quite recently and had been constructed to protect the rare blanket bog from erosion caused by walkers in this Special Area of Conservation. Now I know that having such a structure to walk on sounds easy, and I have no doubt that it is ten times easier than walking through the bog land itself, but let me assure you that it is still quite a challenge, especially after having walked about seven miles to get there. I certainly felt every one of the 450 steps that make up the incredible staircase – a stairway to heaven? The ascent certainly provided some fantastic views out over Fermanagh and Cavan and beyond. It also, unfortunately, provided good views of further rainclouds approaching.

Once on the plateau, it was then another half mile across very boggy and rocky ground to reach the triangulation pillar on top of the 665m high summit itself. The directions pointed promisingly to the prospect of magnificent 360° views on clear days over six counties (Tyrone, Donegal, Cavan, Leitrim, Sligo and Roscommon) in addition to Fermanagh of course. Unfortunately by the time I reached the pillar I had to make do with magnificent 180° views over only three or four, as the next storm front was advancing quickly and the other counties were hidden under dark cloud and heavy rain. The wind was also picking up rapidly ahead of the front and it was all I could do to take some photos and video footage without being blown off the top!

It was, however, also time for a little celebration as this was officially, by my calculations anyway, the half-way point of my walk round the Ulster Way. And, at 665 metres, it was also the highest point on the entire Ulster Way route. I couldn't think of many places more spectacular than the summit of Cuilcagh Mountain in County Fermanagh to mark this significant milestone on my pilgrimage. As I took in the fantastic semi-panoramic views from the summit, and remembered the wonderful person who had brought me here, the chorus of the famous Proclaimers song was resounding in my head:

But I would walk five hundred miles
And I would walk five hundred more
Just to be the man who walked a thousand miles
To fall down at your door

However, the weather conditions were worsening, so I cut short my celebrations and took shelter at the base of the pyramid of stones, on which the triangulation pillar is mounted, and waited for the worst of the storm to pass. After about 15 minutes, the wind had eased sufficiently to allow me to set off again, back across the plateau in the rain until I met the top of the staircase again. It was certainly a lot easier going down than it was coming up and I made my way fairly quickly back down the boardwalk and the stony track towards Legnabrocky again. On the way, I stopped for another "Rachel break" beside a little stone bridge over a small river flowing down the lower slopes of Cuilcagh. The weather had improved considerably by this stage and it was a very relaxing place to rest for 10 or 15 minutes and let the sun warm my face and the "water music" work its soothing magic.

A mile after exiting Cuilcagh Mountain Park, I arrived at the Marble Arch Caves Visitor Centre. I would have liked to have spent a bit more time in the Visitor Centre, but I needed to push on. So I quickly passed through the building and went out the rear exit to join the steps and pathway down to the famous limestone arch itself. Then it was on down through the beautifully tranquil Cladagh Glen along the banks of the Cladagh River for about the next half hour. After the hours of wilderness and being exposed to the challenges of the mountains, I loved the peacefulness and shelter provided by this beautiful river walk. The exit of the Glen brought me out onto the Florence Court to Blacklion road and, about a mile along this road, I was confronted with the broody, overhanging cliff, known as Hanging Rock. Thankfully, I had already had my picnic and didn't need to linger other than to take a few quick photographs. Another two miles of roadway brought me across the border briefly and into the village of Blacklion, before crossing the bridge into Belcoo and into "the North" once again. Here I collected my car again and headed back to Brian and Florence's for another superb meal, great company and a caravan for the night.

It had been a tough day. Physically challenging to be sure, due to the weather and the terrain, but also emotionally challenging. I know I hadn't made it particularly easy for myself. I had decided to walk on our 28th wedding anniversary, my very first without Jacqui. A date for celebration had now become one of commemoration. And in addition, there was also the inevitability that the location would bring memories of crushed hopes and dashed dreams rushing back to the surface. However, this day was always going to be difficult no matter where I spent it. I reckoned that I was much better to be out doing something positive and doing it in memory of the woman I loved, rather than languishing at home and feeling sorry for myself – even though the temptation to do just that was always present and had to be constantly fought against.

Blackbirds

Sunday 2 August – Lisnaskea to Florence Court
I had another very pleasant evening with Brian and Florence, when I met more of their extended family, had another super meal and discovered that, in addition to Florence being an excellent cook, Brian makes a very good Irish Coffee! After a good night's rest in the caravan, I was up early for breakfast and a drive back to Florence Court, with me following Brian's car in my own and trying desperately to keep up with him along the narrow country roads. I left my car in the grounds of Florence Court and got a lift back to a wet Lisnaskea with Brian to begin my walk.

It started off a damp enough day and, to begin with anyway, I certainly thought that I had probably made the right decision to tackle Cuilcagh the day before. I had even ditched the sun cream out of my rucksack thinking there was no way that I was going to need it on this wet Sunday. However, it later cleared up to be a beautiful day and any time I had a view of Cuilcagh Mountain, which was quite often, it was bathed in glorious sunshine! Having said that, it still turned out to be not too bad an idea to switch days, regardless of the weather. The route to Florence Court from Lisnaskea is entirely by road, some of which I imagine could be very busy on most days of the week – the directions even warned of extremely busy sections with many lorries passing due to heavy industry in the area. However, with it being a Sunday, the roads were quite quiet most of the time and I didn't have to step up on to the verges too often, which made for a more pleasant walking experience.

I encountered an extremely noisy donkey as I was leaving Lisnaskea that came charging down the field to meet me at the gate. I had honestly never heard the like of it before – at first I thought it was complaining and wishing to see me off, but it turned out to be really friendly and was perhaps just over excited to see a stranger passing by his field on a very quiet Sunday morning. I'm not so sure that any of the occupants of the nearby houses, perhaps hoping for a peaceful lie in, would have been just so excited to hear such a loud and prolonged braying, as opposed to praying, so early on a Sunday morning though!

About a mile from Lisnaskea, I came across the medieval ruins of Aghalurcher Church, which were both surrounded and invaded by quite a variety of trees and shrubs and gave the impression that nature was slowly and determinedly reclaiming its territory. People and buildings may come and go, but nature always wins out in the end. It is said that a church was originally founded here in the seventh century by St. Ronan. Aghalurcher comes from the Irish Achadh Urchair, meaning "the field of the cast or throw", taking its name from an old tradition of St Ronan's of throwing a stone to determine the site of his next church.

After negotiating a couple of narrow bridges over Lough Erne, at either end of Trasna Island, I came upon the village of Derrylin. The village appeared to be quite deserted when I arrived and it made for quite a surreal experience. As I approached, it was still quite a grey day and the ridge of Slieve Rushen Mountain looming above the village was lined with a multitude of windmills, like an army of fighting machines from War of the Worlds about to descend. As I had discovered with "Annie" near Donagh, your imagination can run away with you when you are out walking on your own for hours on end. But where were all the people? I came to a junction in the village and from there spotted a sign for the Blackbird Coffee Shop and I just couldn't pass that by - blackbirds had a very special significance for me. The male blackbird was always one of Jacqui's favourite birds – neat, sleek and completely black, except for its striking bright orange-yellow beak and eye-ring. They were frequent visitors to our back garden at home, particularly in the morning, and we often saw them and heard their lovely rich and warm song. The beautiful hymn "Morning Has Broken", which starts with the line "Morning has broken, like the first morning, Blackbird has spoken, like the first bird", was our choice of wedding hymn when Jacqui and I were married in 1987 and we chose the same hymn to be sung by the congregation at Jacqui's funeral service. On the first night after Jacqui died, I stayed by her side throughout the night in a private room at the hospice. As dawn broke the following morning, a bird started to sing its immediately recognisable song just outside our window. I pulled back the curtains slowly. The sky was just starting to brighten sufficiently for me to see and there, in a tree not ten metres away, was the unmistakable shape of a blackbird. Morning had broken and the blackbird had spoken. It was a small moment of joy amidst the terrible sadness of that time. Every time I see a blackbird now I immediately think of Jacqui and it was for this reason that I was drawn to this particular coffee shop in Derrylin.

The name Derrylin comes from the Irish Doire Loinn, meaning "oakgrove of the blackbirds" and I presume that this was why the Blackbird Coffee Shop was named as such. Florence had made me sandwiches again and I had it in mind to order a cup of coffee and ask if they wouldn't mind me having my own food on the premises, given the charitable nature of my walk. I therefore made my way over to the Blackbird, pleased to note the "Now Open" sign, and pulled open the door only to find the coffee shop completely empty of people – absent of any customers and staff alike. Where the heck was everyone? I called out – no response. I rang the bell on the counter – no response. I used the washroom at the back and then came into the shop again and called out – still no response. Very strange. There were still drinks in the cooler, cake and buns on the counter, and the coffee machine was on. The drawer of the till was lying open though and it was empty, as if the owner had gathered up all the cash and left in a hurry! Thoughts of the "fighting machines" on the hill crept back into my mind again. Anyway, I decided to have my lunch in the coffee shop regardless – I would just have to forego the coffee and instead sip on the orange juice I was carrying with me. I must have been there for close to half an hour and no-one appeared during all that time – no staff and no other customers.

The real reason for their absence had finally dawned on me while I was enjoying my solitary lunch. I left one of my leaflets on the counter before I left, with a note to say thank you for the use of the facilities. I then added a "PS" to say that I hoped that everyone had enjoyed watching the Fermanagh v Dublin football match! Practically every mile of the route so far from Lisnaskea to Derrylin had been festooned with flags in the Fermanagh team colours – they certainly take their football very seriously in this part of the world!

I made my way out of Derrylin, finally reassured to see one or two other humans as I went – they were obviously of the lesser spotted non-football fan species. I then started a long, slow climb up the road leading to Doon, getting closer and closer to the huge machines on the hill all the time. I have mixed feelings about these windfarms. They are certainly green in terms of using an inexhaustible and plentiful energy source, but they are not without environmental consequences in terms of noise and the obvious visual impact on the landscape. Whatever your opinion though on their merits or otherwise, there is no denying the grandeur of these mechanical marvels, especially when you get up as close to them as I did. I was completely mesmerised by the huge blades rotating on their massive stalks towering high above me. Very much man made though; no sign of any little green aliens from Mars!

It was a long walk up to Doon and a long walk "doon" again, skirting around Molly Mountain and many more windmills on the way. The road eventually brought me to the village of Kinawley, about seven miles from Derrylin, and from there it was another five and a half uneventful miles to my destination back at Florence Court, with the impressive "peak of the speaking horse", Benaughlin Mountain, once again ever present in the near distance. Just as I arrived back to my car the rain started to come on again, quite heavy this time – my trusted weather angels had been looking out for me once again.

From here, I made a quick call back to the Marble Arch Caves Visitor Centre to leave in some leaflets and then drove on to Belcoo, where I had booked in to stay overnight at the Customs House Inn. Here I met my sister, Teresa, and her husband, Brian, who had very kindly driven across from Dromore in County Tyrone to help me with my transport arrangements. We took both cars to Lough Navar Forest, where I left my car in preparation for my next day's walk, and got a lift back with them to Belcoo. We had a lovely meal together at the Customs House Inn and Teresa and Brian then headed back to Dromore, while I headed to my room and crashed. The following day was a Monday, but I had booked the coming week off from work and so I needed to be well rested for another day's walking ahead.

Sleeping Dogs

Monday 3 August – Belcoo to Lough Navar Forest

A good rest at the Customs House Inn followed by an Ulster fry in the morning set me up well for the day ahead. However, before leaving I had to thank the management and staff for their kindness and generosity. The manager, Clara, had already reduced the room rate for me and then the staff had a whip round and paid the remaining amount. So I had a £70 night at the Customs House Inn for free, which was fantastic. I have to say that, in my experience, the Fermanagh people are a very hospitable and generous bunch – when they're not busy watching the football that is!

It was a glorious morning as I set off up the main street in Belcoo. At the top of the street, I turned left onto the Garrison Road and after about a mile I came across yet another holy well named after St Patrick. This one was famous for healing properties, especially for blindness! I wondered if St Patrick had walked the Ulster Way – he seemed to have visited many of the same places I had! I had visions of St Patrick in his hiking boots and backpack, using his crozier as a walking pole and making his way round this heathen land from one refreshment stop to the next – the locals erecting "St Patrick's Well" signs as soon as he disappeared over the next hill or round the next bend.

From here I followed a long, slow climb up a country road, and I enjoyed some superb views of Lough Erne below as I went. I eventually reached Ballintempo Forest Park after about three miles. From here it was a matter of following a series of well-defined and way-marked forest tracks through Ballintempo, Big Dog, and Conagher forests in turn, with the altitude increasing gradually as I went. A sign along the route explained that Big Dog Forest takes its name from the larger of two small hills nearby, known as Big Dog and Little Dog. The names of these hills originate from Irish folklore, as they are said to be the giant, Finn McCool's, favourite Irish wolfhounds. Legend has it that they picked up the scent of a witch one day long ago and gave chase, but the witch used magic to escape and turned the dogs to stone. Now they lie forever side-by-side and form part of the landscape. Of course, the geologists tell a very different story. According to them, the hills are made up of harder, more resistant sandstone than the rock of the surrounding area and over the centuries the softer rock has been weathered away by wind, rain and ice, while the harder hills have remained standing proud. Certainly an altogether more plausible explanation, but somewhat lacking in drama and imagination – personally, I prefer the folklore.

Anyway, I decided to let sleeping dogs lie, and pressed on through the forests. There wasn't an awful lot to see along this stretch - one forest track looks very much like another and onward progress became a bit of a slog at times. I even began to hate the downhill sections more than the uphill sections. They just undid any height that I had already gained, and wasted any energy already expended, and inevitably meant more climbing ahead just to regain the height I had lost.

However, the drudgery was also sprinkled with some more pleasurable moments along the way. One such time was when I stopped alongside the small but beautiful Lough Formal in Ballintempo Forest for a bite of lunch. Here I sat on a wooden bench overlooking the lough and soaked up the gloriously warm sunshine. I really enjoyed the tranquillity of this place, but once again it was tempered with the fact that Jacqui was not by my side to share the moment. I had spent so many years seeing sights and experiencing new places in Jacqui's company, as opposed to in her memory.

Over the years, we had travelled extensively together to many places in Europe and North Africa, as well as places closer to home in the UK and Ireland. Practically everywhere I had seen over the last 35 years had been observed and appreciated through, not one pair of eyes, but two, and the experiences had been enriched as a result. Encountering these new places on my Ulster Way journey often felt like an incomplete experience to me without having Jacqui by my side to share them with. However, regardless of my inner turmoil, the beauty of Lough Formal on this gorgeous summer's day could neither be ignored nor denied. The surface of the lough was so still and an incredible shade of blue as the water reflected the beautifully clear blue sky above. I was also quite amazed at the thickness of the deep blanket of moss covering the forest floor just behind where I had been sitting. Here, I discovered a large, solitary red capped toadstool nestled under one of the pines. Looking deeper into the trees, it was easy to imagine it was still a home to witches and that dog walkers should perhaps still be wary of letting their dogs run loose in the vicinity!

On exiting Conagher Forest, some 18 miles after leaving Belcoo, I turned right along the Garrison to Derrygonelly Road and followed this for a couple of miles before reaching the car park at Lough Navar Forest, where my car was awaiting my return from the night before. However, I first made a very short detour across the road to visit Correll Glen, a designated nature reserve containing a delightful nature trail dominated by native woodland species such as Birch, Ash, Oak and Holly. I made my way carefully down into the ravine carved out by the fast flowing River Sillees and stood warily on the slippery rocks at the riverbank. I was transfixed for a time, mesmerised by the roaring river as it tumbled furiously down the Glen, its peaty water almost the colour of Guinness and the white turbulence, as it cascaded down over the rocks, only adding to the effect. There is a popular myth surrounding the River Sillees that St Faber, the patron saint of the Sacred Heart Church in Boho, had a pet deer that carried a number of sacred books that she had been entrusted with. One day, as she was travelling to Boho, the deer was harassed by some hunting hounds.

Whether these were the same hounds that had subsequently been transformed into Big Dog and Little Dog isn't known, but in order to escape, the deer jumped into the River Sillees and in the process ruined St Faber's books. The saint was appalled and so outraged that she placed a curse on the river to make it run backwards – quite unbecoming behaviour for a saint I thought. Previously, the Sillees ran from Boho towards the sea, but as the curse took effect, "the river writhed and recoiled" and now its route goes towards Upper Lough Erne rather than the sea. The second part of her curse was that the river would be bad for fishing and good for drowning. As I contemplated this, I could feel my inner demons beginning to stir and the dark waters starting to lure me closer. It was a few minutes before I came to my senses and the hypnotic spell the river had over me was broken. I cautiously retreated from the turbulent waters and made my way safely back, up and out of the Glen.

As I arrived back at my car, I was feeling more composed again. The weather was still quite nice and so I decided to drive round the Navar Forest loop and stop at the Magho Cliffs to take in the view. The cliffs were only about two and a half miles away and I had read about the wonderful views that could be had from the viewing point at the top of the cliffs. On a good day the view could stretch for miles, from over the islands in Lough Erne, to the Blue Stack Mountains of County Donegal and on a very clear day apparently you can see

Slieve League, the highest sea cliffs in Ireland, in southwest Donegal about 36 miles away. Unfortunately by the time I arrived, the weather had started to turn again, resulting in the views not being as spectacular as they might have been. I left hoping that when I visited the cliffs in two days time to begin my walk again, the weather might cooperate and the views might be more rewarding. I headed back to the Customs House Inn in Belcoo to pick up my overnight bag and then headed back to Belfast to enjoy a very welcome meal cooked by my daughter, Hannah. The next day was a much appreciated rest day and a time to recharge the batteries.

It was now over six months since Jacqui had been taken from me. In many ways it still just didn't feel real. In fact, it felt totally surreal most of the time. It was just so hard to comprehend that someone who had been so close to me for 35 years was no longer here. It was also very hard to accept the permanency of the situation; accept that Jacqui was never going to return. She wasn't away visiting friends or on a residential course somewhere, from which she would soon return home. She was gone – forever! Despite knowing this, I still half expected to see Jacqui when I woke up in the morning, when I came downstairs for breakfast, when I came back home from work or when I entered the bedroom at night. It was taking a long time for my brain to catch up with my eyes; for my mind to catch up with my sight. In some ways this could be viewed as the mind playing more cruel tricks, but on reflection, I believe that it may in fact be a defence or coping mechanism. There seems to be an inbuilt natural resistance to fully accepting that a loved one is gone in the early stages of bereavement – perhaps it's a way to allow for gradual adjustment to the full reality of the situation, rather than being hit with the full impact right away. Later on, I would come to see this process as being in some ways akin to descending a mountain and being able to slowly pick a safe route down the sloping face, as opposed to going over the edge of the cliff. You ultimately reach the bottom, the same ground level, but one journey is certainly slower and much less traumatic than the other. Whatever, coping mechanisms or inbuilt natural psychologies were at work, it was clear that Jacqui's presence was not going to leave me any time soon.

Forgetting

I reach over to place a hand on your shoulder
A simple movement repeated many times before
Seeking comfort there, finding disappointment
My hand sinks down to an empty pillow
I am still searching

Everything in the room is the same as before
Nothing disturbed, nothing missing, only you
I lie on the same side, an invisible barrier remains
I cannot intrude, your place still reserved
I am still waiting

Another meal alone at the table, TV for company
Same place mats, same cutlery, plates and glasses
Your chair still beside mine but a place set only for one
I reach across to place my hand in yours
I am still hoping

Picking apples from the tree we both planted years before
Bucket overflowing with fruit offering so much promise
Plump, juicy blackberries on brambles almost hidden
I turn proudly to show you the harvest
I am still forgetting

Dancing Fairies

Wednesday 5 August – Lough Navar Forest to Belleek
Wet wet wet, was the only way to describe today. I had left Lough Navar Forest two days before hoping that the weather might be better today so I could enjoy the potentially spectacular views from Magho Cliffs. I was to be sorely disappointed though. The weather was pleasant enough that morning when I arrived at the forest car park with my sister, Ann, but unfortunately it didn't hold. Ann had put me up the previous night in Omagh, served me a lovely breakfast and then driven me first to Belleek, to leave my overnight bag at the Fiddlestone Guesthouse, and then on to Lough Navar Forest. Ann walked a short distance with me along the main road into the forest and then turned back to head to her car and on to her work in Omagh.

A little drizzle of rain soon started to fall, gradually getting more persistent and, about two and a half miles later, I reached the viewing point at the Magho Cliffs to take in the panoramic views of low lying cloud! As with Slieve Gullion, I was just going to have to return at some other time to experience the promised views. I met another walker at the cliffs, and it was pretty obvious from his gear and demeanour, all alert and peacocky, that he was a much more seasoned walker than me. He had arrived at the top of the cliffs the hard way – by taking the path up from the bottom, a 215 metre climb. After agreeing that it was a miserable day, he pointed out that if you waited for the rain to stop before doing something in this country, you would never do anything at all. And then off he marched, utterly undeterred, while I paused to consider my next move. There was a gravel path along the top of the cliff and, looking at the map, I thought that it might be possible to follow this path and eventually join up with the official route after about two miles. The path ran fairly parallel to the official route and I thought it might be a more interesting journey than the forest road. However, I subsequently discovered that the nice gravel path ran out after about a quarter of a mile and transformed into a very boggy and not very well defined track. I tried it for about 20 metres, becoming less and less certain of its suitability as I went. I eventually did the sensible thing and turned back to the gravel path, and back to the "viewing" point, to join the official route once again. Perhaps, at 21 days into my pilgrimage, I was finally learning how to properly evaluate situations and make sensible decisions.

I followed the tarmac roads and then hard tracks around Lough Meenameen and then Lough Navar, with the rain getting heavier as I went. It was a case of keeping the wet gear on, putting the head down and trudging on, one foot in front of the other. I kept a lookout for any shelter along the way so I could stop and have some of the lunch that Ann had prepared for me, but it wasn't until I was close to the exit of the forest (some ten miles from the start) that I spotted my place of refuge. It was an alcove built into the perimeter wall of a rather grand looking private house on the edge of the forest. What the purpose of the alcove was, I have no idea, and it was barely adequate for sheltering, but it would have to do. Beggars can't be choosers and hobos can't be picky. I managed to have, even enjoy, my lunch in this rather bizarre location, looking out at the persistent rainfall and wondering what the occupants of the house would think if they knew that there was a hobo talking shelter under their wall. I always followed the principles of "Leave no trace" when out walking and so, in all likelihood, the occupants would never know that I had been there.

After lunch, I reluctantly left the shelter to step out into the rain again. From this point on it was sheer drudgery as I exited the forest park to follow the various roads for about 11 miles to Belleek. I couldn't even use my iPod to help relieve the tedium of the journey, as I needed to listen out for traffic approaching from behind. Once again, I had to carefully time my passing of large puddles as best I could to ensure that it didn't coincide with any passing traffic. Some drivers were very considerate and slowed down on approach, but others just didn't seem to give a damn that there was a pedestrian on the road, who really didn't care for a shower before getting back to his guesthouse!

I had never been out in such rain for such a prolonged period of time before. Nor can I ever remember my finger-tips going wrinkly before when out in the rain – even my wrinkles had wrinkles. I wondered if my weather angels had abandoned me for good! One thing that did manage to bring a wry smile to my face though, was the sight of hundreds of little fairies dancing on the road as I trudged along – that's what Jacqui always called the heavy raindrops as they fell into puddles and created little splashes that momentarily looked like little crystal figurines pirouetting. Even in the most miserable of situations there is often something of beauty and wonder to be found if you just allow yourself to see it. Despite the unrelenting rain, I took the dancing fairies as a sign of encouragement, smiled and pushed on.

However, by the time I reached Belleek, the rain had somehow managed to penetrate all my waterproof layers and I could feel my tee-shirt cold and wet against my skin. It had been without doubt, and dancing fairies aside, the most miserable day's walking so far. I was thoroughly soaked and thoroughly depressed by the time I reached my destination. Thankfully, a very warm welcome awaited me at the Fiddlestone Bar and Guesthouse. After having a hot shower and a change of clothes, I went downstairs to the bar, where Raymond the barman poured me a lovely pint of Smithwicks. A beer had rarely tasted so good! One of the local customers was very interested in my challenge and insisted on giving me a cash donation there and then. After this, I headed up the street for a very tasty chicken curry at the Forge Café – simple, but very welcome comfort food. I then returned to the Fiddlestone for another pint, which I sipped slowly as I attempted to catch up on my blogs, before turning in for the night.

Rivers and Loughs

Thursday 6 August – Belleek to Pettigoe

After a good night's rest at the Fiddlestone Bar and Guesthouse, both parts of which I made good use of, I enjoyed a full Irish Breakfast cooked by the owner, Cormac McCusker. I was the only one up for an early breakfast and so Cormac sat with me having a good old chat as I tucked into my protein packed fair, while he enjoyed a cup of coffee. I felt justified in having all these cooked breakfasts – I needed to keep my strength up after all.

Cormac told me that he had been out fishing on the River Erne, which flows through Belleek, from 5am that morning. There had been nothing biting, but he had still enjoyed the peace and tranquillity to be had sitting beside the river at that time of the morning. I asked him how the Fiddlestone Bar had got its name and he explained that it was from the Fiddle Stone at the nearby Castle Caldwell, which had been erected in memory of a local fiddler who drowned near there in 1770. A replica of the stone is mounted on a wall in the bar area. The carved inscription on the Fiddle Stone reads:

"To the memory of Denis M'Cabe, Fidler who fell out of the St Patrick Barge belonging to Sir James Caldwell Bart and Count of Milan, and was drowned off this Point Aug. 15, 1770 –

Beware ye Fidlers of ye Fidler's fate
Nor tempt ye deep lest you repent too late
You ever have been deemed to water foes
Then shun ye lake till it with whiskey flows
On firm Land only - Exercise your skill
There you may play and safely drink your fill."

This seemed a highly appropriate message to have hanging on the wall of a bar and I imagine that it must be one of the earliest versions of the "sensible drinking" message ever recorded!

Much as I would have loved to have whiled away the day with Cormac, I had a walk to be getting on with and he had other guests to prepare for, so I finished up my breakfast and headed to my room to collect my things. Cormac allowed me to leave my overnight bag to collect later and he had also very kindly prepared me a couple of sandwiches to take with me. There were always kind people looking out for me wherever I went. People like Cormac and others such as Mairead in the Mourne Lodge in Attical, Michael in Lismor House in Newry and Clara in the Customs House Inn in Belcoo, as well as my legion of drivers, fellow walkers and accommodation providers. And there would be many more to come. What forces were at work here? Was this just the natural goodness in people shining through or was there perhaps "someone up there" looking out for me? My logical brain favoured the former, but my vulnerable heart craved the latter.

I was to leave Belleek in much better weather than when I arrived. However, before leaving, I returned to the bridge to take a photo of the famous Belleek Pottery, which sits on the banks of the River Erne. It was certainly a better shot that the one I had snatched in the rain the previous day. The rivers surface was pretty calm and reflected the imposing nineteenth century facade of the pottery and the sky above beautifully. From here I then set off on a day's journey that would take me as far as Pettigoe. I headed out of Belleek along a small side road that followed the banks of the River Erne, which was occasionally visible through the trees, and then looped round the back of the town for two and a half miles before joining up with the main road to Pettigoe

.
The Ulster Way rarely takes the most direct route between towns and villages and this has its pros and its cons. On the plus side, it tends to keep you away, for the most part, from the busier main roads and allows you to enjoy much more of the tranquil countryside. On the downside, however, it certainly takes the long way round! For instance, the direct route from Belleek to Pettigoe along the main road is only 12.5 miles, but via the Ulster Way route it is 21 miles, which is quite a difference. But it's all academic really. If I didn't clock up the miles here, I would have had to do it somewhere else, and if you are going to do it you may as well do it in beautiful, quiet countryside. It can be quite relaxing and therapeutic.

Unless of course you happen to be a tourist out for an early morning walk, believing yourself to be the only one around, listening to your music through earphones, rolling the first cigarette of the day and lost in your own little world - when some pilgrim backpacker suddenly appears out of the blue from behind and nearly gives you a heart attack! At least that's the effect I seemed to have had on some poor elderly gentleman who was out for a gentle stroll through the countryside when I marched past him. I did cough and clear my throat as I approached him from behind in an attempt to alert him to my presence, but, I assume because of his music, he was totally oblivious until I was upon him. I don't think there was much tobacco left in the roll-up he was preparing, after he jumped and let out a yelp. Anyway I apologised for startling him and continued on, leaving him to try and recapture his lost peace and tranquility, and to begin his roll-up once again. I was sorry, but I'm afraid I couldn't help laughing to myself every time I thought about it – Jacqui would have been in stitches!

After rejoining the main road for about one and a half miles, I cut off to the left down a side road just at the end of Keenaghan Lough, noting the ruins of Keenaghan Abbey on the way. The name Keenaghan means "a mossy place" and the Abbey is said to be one of the oldest in Ireland, having been established about 880. The road took me around Lough Scolban, where I encountered a couple of very yappy little dogs that bounced up and down in turn behind their garden's low wall as I passed. Talking nicely to them only seemed to make them worse. I could still hear them going strong for about the next mile or so beyond their house. Oh, how I wished then that I knew the magic spell used by the witch on Finn McCool's wolfhounds in Big Dog Forest. Just think of how surprised and puzzled the dogs' owners would have been to have returned home only to find two wee dog shaped mounds in the middle of their front lawn!

After leaving the yapping sounds far behind and passing another number of loughs, I came to the picturesque Lough Vearty and stopped here to have my lunch in the lovely afternoon sunshine. There were lots of dragonflies flitting amongst the reeds near the shore here, but I found it impossible to get a decent photo of them as they darted about so fast. I sat on a large boulder in the glorious sunshine and enjoyed the lovely sandwiches prepared freshly by Cormac that morning, followed by some fruit and a little treat to finish off – I had become quite partial to the Raspberry Ruffle bars that Audrey had provided me with a good supply of. I set off again to almost immediately step across the border into County Donegal and to circle round the back of Rushen Hill, passing a few more loughs, including Breen Lough.

About seven miles from Lough Vearty, I rejoined the main road again for the final two mile stretch into the village of Pettigoe, a small picturesque village bisected by the Termon River, which forms part of the border between the Republic of Ireland and Northern Ireland. I walked through the village and picked up the road to Castlederg. I passed over the bridge at the River Termon, into "the North" again, and continued for about another half mile before being picked up as pre-arranged by my sister, Ann. She drove me back to Belleek so I could collect my overnight bag from the Fiddlestone and we then headed on to Omagh, where I would be based for the next few days. Needless to say, my sister looked after me extremely well.

Sanctuary

Friday 7 August – Pettigoe to Drumlegagh

After a night at my sister's home in Omagh, Ann drove me back to Pettigoe on the Friday morning and dropped me off at the pick-up point from the previous evening. It was a glorious day as I set off, heading away from Pettigoe towards Castlederg. This minor road I was on essentially followed close to the path taken by the Termon River for the next six miles and cut in and out of the border (often defined by the river itself) as it went.

I was acutely aware of the fact that, only four miles north of Pettigo, was Station Island, the location of the Lough Derg Pilgrimage, which is often referred to as St Patrick's Purgatory or simply Lough Derg. This small lake-island, renowned in Irish Christian tradition since the time of St. Patrick, has been receiving pilgrims continuously for well over 1000 years. The area around the lough was considered a place of protection for anyone in trouble and the monastery nearby offered hospitality to all. However, this particular pilgrim had his lunch safely stowed in his backpack and had no desire to trek the additional eight miles off route it would have taken to get to Lough Derg and back. So I kept right on the road I was going, following the banks of the Termon River. I believe that Termon is from the Irish An Tearmann, meaning "place of sanctuary", but I'm not certain if this has any connection with the protection reputedly afforded around Lough Derg in the past. Given their close proximity though, I wouldn't be surprised if this was indeed the case.

I had some very friendly encounters along this stretch of road. First there was a golden retriever that came bounding up from behind and then just lay down in front of me waiting to have its tummy rubbed. I happily obliged and after enjoying this for a few minutes, its tail sweeping a single angel wing in the dusty road, it simply got up and continued on its travels on up the road until it eventually disappeared around the next bend. Where it had come from or where it was going to I have no idea – perhaps it was seeking sanctuary. Then there was a very nice Southern couple that pulled up in their car as they were passing and offered me a lift. No wild imaginary stories from me this time though! After explaining that I was doing a walk to raise money for cancer research, the woman in the passenger seat reached into her handbag and handed me a few Euros. And lastly, there were some more lovely donkeys at the gate of a field, including a rather shy foal that would only briefly step out from behind its mother to have a quick look at me before retreating to its place of sanctuary once again.

I clearly couldn't get the idea of sanctuary out of my head. For the very first time it occurred to me that perhaps my own pilgrimage was partly a search for a place of sanctuary for myself. Since Jacqui's death I had felt like all the safe havens of the past, such as my home in Belfast, the holiday house in Portrush and even my place of work, had all changed significantly, or, to be more precise, my perception of them had changed significantly. They no longer provided me with the sense of security that they had in the past. I felt as though my anchor had slipped and that I was now adrift in a stormy sea with no safe port to head for. I longed to find somewhere where I could rest and feel safe and secure again. I wasn't sure how I was going to find it, or if indeed such a place even existed, but I felt that I was going to have to keep walking and keep searching until I eventually found my place of sanctuary - a place that could offer me some inner peace and renew my desire to live again. Perhaps, even as I thought this, part of me was beginning to realise that my place of sanctuary might not actually be a physical place, a destination on the map to be reached, but rather a state of mind, an acceptance of things as they are and not as I wished them to be. But for now, all I knew was that it was important to keep walking, to keep moving forward.

After following the river for about six miles, and shortly after passing Lough Cack, I crossed over the Termon River for the final time and headed south-east uphill, towards and then through part of Kesh Forest. After another couple of miles I came to Drumskinny Stone Circle and stopped for a short time to visit and take a photo or two. Drumskinny, from the Irish Droim Scine meaning "knife ridge", is a megalithic mini-complex, with a stone circle, a well-made kerbed cairn, and a stone row or "alignment", all neatly accommodated within a relatively small area. The stone circle is part of a complex of five in the immediate locality, dating back to around 2000 BC. The purpose of the circle, made up of 39 stones, is unknown but was probably linked to religion, astronomy or simply keeping track of the time.

From here, I followed the road around the wonderfully named Rotten Mountain. It was at this point that I began to realise that the funny place-name count was quite high on this section of the Ulster Way. I had already encountered Lough Cack, Drumskinny and Rotten Mountain. The map also showed a Lugmore, Near Scraghy, Doochrock and Fartagh nearby and I would soon be passing close to Bin Mountain. I have to be honest and say that I did a double take when I also spotted Cruntully and Balix Hill on the map!

After passing by Rotten Mountain, which was actually quite nice, I had to search for a bit to find a turn off into a lane to take me down to meet the main road to Castlederg. I found a laneway which seemed to be in the right location and heading in the right direction, but it passed through private farm property and was closed off with a locked gate, so I assumed that this couldn't be the correct turn-off. However, after checking further on up the road a bit, I concluded that there was no alternative route; none that would have avoided adding on a couple of extra miles anyway and I had already done enough of that. So I climbed over the gate and proceeded briskly down the lane to meet the main road and thankfully didn't encounter any angry landowners on the way. It was then another half mile walk before turning off into Lough Bradan Forest.

Lough Bradan Forest was two hours of tedium with endless stone grey roads through walls of green, with occasional glimpses of blue when I mustered the energy to lift my head sufficiently to look up at the sky. I'm sorry if this sounds like I was totally fed up at this point, but, to be honest, once you've seen one commercial fir forest, you certainly feel like you've seen them all. To add to the monotony, my iPod battery gave up about 20 minutes into the forest, denying me even of the distraction provided by my music. I was getting hungry, so I started to keep a look out for a place to stop and have lunch, promising myself that if I didn't find somewhere suitable within the next hour, I would just sit down wherever I happened to be at that point. With only five minutes of my self-imposed deadline to go, I finally found somewhere to sit just off the track, on a few logs in a forest clearing. Here I enjoyed the very tasty tuna sandwiches that Ann had kindly prepared for me that morning. The skies were a perfect blue above me at this stage and it was sunny and warm as I rested for a short time and remembered again the wise words of Rachel Joyce. I then set off through the tedious forest once more and eventually emerged out the other side, five miles from the entry point, to once again savour the freedom of the open landscape.

I continued on the hard stone roadway past Lough Lee and Lough Hill Wind

Farm and, after about half a mile, I left the roadway to take a trudge and squelch over the heather and bog of Bolaght Mountain. This was one of the rare occasions when I had to use my compass, although mainly just for reassurance. There wasn't even a semblance of a path here and the way-markers were sometimes quite hard to spot. I enjoyed the great views from the top of the mountain though and, making good use of my compass, I was able to pick out the Sperrins in the East, Cuilcagh to the South West and the Bluestacks and Donegal Highlands to the West and North. The distant but distinctive pyramid shape of Errigal was clearly visible in the northwest. I then made my way down over more bogland on the other side of Bolaght to eventually pick up what my directions referred to as an "old turbary track", which led down to a tarmac road about half a mile from the top. I must admit that I had never heard of such a thing as a turbary track before and I made a mental note to check it out once I got back to civilisation.

The narrow country roads then wound around the base of Bolaght for a couple of miles before descending further into the Fairy Water Valley to eventually join the main Drumquin to Castlederg road. Fortunately, I only had to follow this main road for about half a mile, as in this part of the world it seems that everyone, even women and old men, were "boy racers". However, I managed to make it unscathed to the next turn off towards Drumlegagh, where Ann, who I had contacted on my way down Bolaght Mountain, met me and drove me back to Omagh. Here, I called first on my 91 year old father and then my 94 year old Aunt Nelly before returning to Ann's for the night. When I asked my Dad if he had ever heard of a turbary track, he was able to tell me without hesitation that it was a deep-cut track through peat or turf, proving once again that you're never too old to learn from your parents.

Apart from the drudgery of hiking through Lough Bradan Forest, it had been a super day and I had been in a T-shirt and shorts for most of it. My weather angels had well and truly returned.

Family Matters

Saturday 8 August – Drumlegagh Rd to Gortin Rd

After breakfast at Ann's, my older brother Michael arrived up from Enniscrone to join me. Today, Michael and I were going to be walking in an area, which despite being on the doorstep of the home in which we grew up, neither of us had ever explored much on foot before. Michael drove us both out to the Drumlegagh Road, where he left his car outside a local house, after speaking with the owners, so that they didn't report an abandoned car with Southern plates to the police.

We set off together and headed up through the village of Drumlegagh itself and then turned right at the crossroads towards the southern reaches of the Baronscourt Estate. This has been the home of the Duke of Abercorn's family, the Hamilton's, since 1612. The Hamilton's house is a neo-classical mansion surrounded by ornate Italian-style gardens, and woodland. The 15,000 acre estate also features an 18 hole golf course and is home to a wild herd of Japanese Sika deer. It was a far cry from the bungalow in the estate in Omagh where Michael and I grew up, although I really can't complain as we had a very comfortable and happy childhood and never wanted for much. As we followed the road, we had a pretty clear view of our mid-point destination for the day, the rounded summit of Bessy Bell, a familiar sight from childhood days. We had a large window in the "west wing" of our bungalow in Omagh and, as a child, I had spent many hours gazing out over the Sperrins when the weather had been too poor to venture outside. Bessy Bell and a smaller hill nearby, called Mary Gray, were apparently named by Scottish immigrants who came to Ireland before making their onward passage to America. According to an old Scottish ballad, Bessy and Mary were the daughters of two Perthshire gentlemen, who in 1666 built a shelter to avoid catching a devastating plague. The girls were supplied with food by a young lad who was in love with both of them. Unfortunately he caught the plague and gave it to the girls, and all three of them fell ill and died. A very sad tale indeed. The original name for Bessy Bell was Sliabh Troim, which means "mountain of the elder tree", and which, it has to be said, is a lot less bleak.

After passing the lovely nineteenth century Baronscourt Church, with its striking lynchgate, we headed up through Upper Cloonty Wood, Manus Wood and Cashty Wood, climbing steadily as we went. As we made our way through Manus Wood, we came across a rather unique "garden bench". The bench was fixed half-way up a tree and, of course, my brother just had to get a photo of me perched on it. So I climbed up the steep vertical ladder and posed for a photo and at the same time enjoyed the superb views back across to Bolaght Mountain and the surrounding countryside that I had crossed the day before. Although we had a number of forest tracks to follow along this section of the route, they were certainly more varied and interesting than my previous day's expedition through Lough Bradan Forest, and having the company of my big brother along the way also helped considerably. After emerging from Cashty Wood, we joined a rough roadway and climbed steeply for about the next half hour, passing another wind farm on the way, until we reached the triangulation pillar on the summit of Bessy Bell, at a height of 420 metres. The last triangulation pillar I had encountered on my travels, at the summit of Cuilcagh, signalled a change in the weather and so it proved to be the case here also. The wind got up and the rain started to come in, and, although it wasn't particularly heavy, it was sufficient to cause us to pull on our wet gear. The summit of Bessy Bell is essentially open moorland and it provided little in the way of shelter, so even though it was around lunchtime, we decided to push on and descend through the pastures and farmland on the other side of the hill, to find a more sheltered spot before stopping to eat.

The going was a little boggy in places, but not too bad, and we made steady progress down through the fields, crossing a number of styles and passing under the turbines of Beltany Wind Farm along the way. We eventually joined a laneway that led us to a deserted farmhouse. We stopped here and sat outside the house on a stack of concrete coping stones to have our lunch, including the sandwiches that Ann had kindly prepared for us. Unfortunately the rain, which had eased off during our descent, soon started to get a bit heavier again and so our lunch was a little less leisurely than it might otherwise have been. After a brief chat with a friendly local farmer, who was heading up the lane on his quad bike, we got on the road again. It occurred to me, not for the first time, that so much of the Ulster Way depends on the good will of farmers like the one we had just met, who allow the public to freely tramp over their land. The next half hour saw us following a series of lanes and roadways until we arrived at a bridge over the River Strule, which brought back memories for both of us of teenage years canoeing down this river and under this very bridge.

Memories also flooded back to a terrible year for our family in 1979, when we lost both our mother and our "in between" brother. On the 16 April that year, our mother, Elizabeth (Betty), passed away due to bowel cancer at the age of only 49. She left behind our father, Artie, and seven children, the eldest, Michael (aged 22), and the youngest, twins Sean and Cathal (aged just 10). I was 18 at the time. It was a terrible blow to the whole family, but it wasn't until I myself lost Jacqui, 36 years later, that I could begin to truly understand what it must have really been like for my father to have lost his wife to cancer at such a young age. Unfortunately, there was still worse to come. The cruel hand of fate was not finished with the Breen family yet.

On 22 July, just three months after our mother had passed away, our brother, Brendan, who was only 20 at the time, was killed in a road accident along with his best friend, Peter, when their car collided head-on with another as they were returning from a night out. To say that our family was left reeling from this second tragedy within the space of three months is an understatement. It was certainly very hard on me and on my remaining brothers and my sisters, Ann and Teresa, who were 17 and 13 respectively at the time. But I still find it very difficult to fully comprehend how it must have felt for my father to have lost his wife and then a son within such a short space of time. But he managed to come through it all. He never talks about it, but somehow he found the strength to carry on and to take care of the rest of the family, despite the desolation he must have faced. He is nothing short of amazing in my eyes and is living proof that people can and do get through the most devastating of circumstances.

As for me, I was enrolled to begin a four year civil engineering course at Queen's University Belfast in October of that year and I decided that it was best to attend as planned. Looking back on that time, and after what I have been through more recently in losing Jacqui, I can now recognise the value in having my university course to focus on to help get me through that very difficult period. Brendan and I had been very close as brothers. We had even been practicing our skills at hurling (an Irish team sport played with wooden sticks and a small leather ball) together on the afternoon before he died. He was already at Queen's studying physics and I had been looking forward to joining him on campus later that year. Losing Brendan and my dear mother had been earth-shattering and when I came to Belfast to begin university life, I was in a very dazed and confused state. My fortunes were about to change though. I first met Jacqui through mutual friends at a Boomtown Rats concert at the Ulster Hall in Belfast and, although we only exchanged a few words with each other on that first occasion, something had definitely sparked! When I saw Jacqui again at a party at one of the Queen's Halls of Residence, I made an arrangement to phone her at the weekend, which I subsequently did, much to her surprise! And the rest, as they say, is history. I can't emphasise enough how important meeting Jacqui was in helping me to turn my life around from one of despair to one of hope. She was much more outgoing than I was and was quite bohemian in her style, while I was quite reserved and conventional. I had never met anyone like her before. She brought me out of my shell and we soon discovered that we were actually very much of a like mind. We were kindred spirits, so in tune with each other right from the start. It was Jacqui who saved me and who brought me "back to life". Who was going to save me now, I wondered.

The next couple of hours were spent winding our way around a series of country roads, and at times I lagged behind my big brother, who is a seasoned walker and often leads walking groups on treks around the mountains and hills of County Sligo and beyond. The competitiveness between brothers never completely disappears! I was glad that he had draped a fluorescent jacket over the rucksack he was carrying, as it meant it was easy for me to spot him in the distance, when he got too far ahead. I am of course exaggerating a little, but his walking ahead did bring to mind a time back in March when Hannah and I had gone down to Enniscrone to stay with Michael for a few days, just a number of weeks after Jacqui had passed away. The three of us had gone out for a walk one day in the dunes above Enniscrone Beach, a place where Jacqui and I had occasionally walked before.

On returning home to Belfast, I had composed a poem simply called *Following*.

Following

We walk through the rolling dunes
Single file on a narrow path of sand
Big brother leading, daughter behind
You alongside me, holding no hand

Tall grass waving in the wind
Constant noise of the grey sea
Your gentle voice fading in and out
Your whispers heard only by me

Following along in a sort of trance
One foot placed in front of the other
Heart so heavy with your absence
Taking steps we once took together

When I look behind me I realise
You've been following all this time
For you live on through our children
They will always be yours and mine

The weather remained damp around Omagh, but we made good progress and it wasn't long before we arrived at our end point for the day, where the country road we had been following met with the main road between Omagh to Gortin. For the last 15 minutes or so, I had been on my mobile, on and off, to give directions to a photographer from the Ulster Herald, who was on an assignment to meet us at the finishing point for some photographs. He eventually found us, after Michael and I waited around for a time and I guided him in by phone. However, the delay actually worked in our favour as it also gave Ann and my father time to arrive so we could get a group photograph of the four of us together. With the photos in the bag, it was then time to pick up Michael's car again, have something to eat at Ann's and then head back to Belfast.

It had been a long week and I certainly felt that I was entitled to a well-earned rest over the remainder of the weekend. It was then back to work for a few days before I would be able to get out on the road again the following Friday.

Mind the Gap

Friday 14 August – Gortin Rd to Barnes Gap

I drove from Belfast to the road junction on the main Omagh to Gortin road, where Michael and I had finished the previous Saturday. I parked in a lay-by outside a nearby house and called to let the occupant know that I was leaving my car there for the day. After I had pulled my boots on and made ready for the day ahead, I met with two lovely ladies from the Omagh CRUK Committee, Laraine and Yvonne. They had very kindly come out to give me some sponsorship money they had collected and to wave me off at the start of the day's walk. Once again, it was fantastic to have this support and to know that there were lots of people out there following my journey and rooting for me. After a few photographs with Laraine and Yvonne, I set off along the main road for a short distance before turning onto a minor road that led towards Gortin Glen Forest Park. For the next few miles, it was quite a climb up this road, followed by a forest track, which took me up and over Tirmurty Hill, and into the morning's low lying cloud. On my descent from Tirmurty Hill, I met the Pollan Burn and enjoyed a pleasant walk down the track alongside the water as it bubbled and flowed.

For me, there are few things more relaxing than the sound of flowing water and, alongside the walk through the Cladagh Glen at Marble Arch, this was one of the nicest forest walks I had enjoyed on the Ulster Way to date. I used to come to this forest quite often as a child and teenager with family and friends, but I had forgotten, or perhaps never fully appreciated, just how wonderful a place the Gortin Glen Forest Park is. I also made a very brief detour off route to take in the deer enclosure and was fortunate to see some of the herd and get a few good photos.

I then headed out of the forest park and after a short walk along a couple of roads, turned into another forest track that took me uphill and round the lower slopes of Curraghchosaly Mountain in the damp drizzle before descending to meet and cross the main Omagh to Gortin Road again. The origin of the name Curraghchosaly is unclear, but it may be derived from the Irish Corrach Cois Saili, meaning "bog beside the willow". The route then took me up past the Boorin National Nature Reserve and two of the Gortin loughs, New Lough and Oak Lough. The weather had started to clear up and I soon had good views across the Sperrins and was able to spot Gortin village nestling down in the Owenkillew valley to the north-west. I looped round Lenamore and Boorin Wood before joining the road from Greencastle for the last three quarters of a mile into Gortin. I was quite amused by the sign erected by a Greencastle running club along the roadside, which read "It's just a hill....get over it!!"

I decided to treat myself to lunch in Gortin and was outside one restaurant when three local teenagers came past and I asked them if there were any other places to eat in the village. One of them said that there was "Fuitells" up the street but it was "wild deer". Luckily I was originally from Omagh, which was only eleven miles away, and so I was able to understand that he meant that the place up the street was rather expensive and not that it was running amok with escapees from the Gortin Glen Forest Park. I decided to check it out anyway and found the place he was talking about called "The Foothills", which looked very nice and in fact appeared to be very reasonably priced. It turned out to be a good choice and I had a lovely lunch. When I went to pay the barman-waiter, Rory, who I'd been chatting to over lunch, he returned the money and told me to put it towards my charity. He then also presented me with a £20 voucher for a meal at The Foothills to sell or raffle to raise further funds. Yet another unexpected act of generosity.

From here, I nipped into the small supermarket next door to have a quick look at the Newsletter, which had run a nice article on my walk – I had become a bit of a publicity hound, but for all the right reasons I hoped. The sun had now really broken through and it was turning out to be a glorious afternoon. After checking out St Patrick's Church and the very attractive little Beltrim National School building at the top of the village, I took a road out of Gortin and climbed steadily up through woods to reach the lower slopes of Slievemore. I then followed a series of narrow roads and tracks for the next three miles or so, following the contours of the mountainside high above the Owenkillew valley, enjoying the superb views as I went, until I arrived at Barnes Gap. The Barnes Gap cuts through the southern Sperrin Mountains, between the hills of Mullaghbane and Mullaghbolig, and was formed during the last Ice Age, some 20,000 years ago. I must say that a rather beautiful glacial landscape has been left behind and I found the smooth lines and curves, dips and bends of the Gap quite stunning in the early evening sunlight. Legend tells how St Patrick spent his nights in this area praying in the solitude and (of course!) a small local well carries his name and attracts pilgrims from near and far for cures and miracles. This pilgrim was happy to give this particular well a miss though, as it was a bit off route and I was in no need of a cure or a miracle - or so I thought!

I had earlier contacted my sister Ann by mobile to say that I could be picked at the Barnes Gap crossroads in about half an hour, but if I wasn't there, it meant that I had decided to walk on along the Ulster Way route and she would pass me somewhere on the road. Unfortunately, this turned out to be an error of judgement on my part. I hadn't allowed for a combination of factors at Barnes Gap, including a complete dead zone for phones signals, a confusing web of minor roads and some inaccuracies in the map and directions I was relying on. This put us both within a hundred yards of each other at times but unable to see or contact each other. Realising that there must be problems when nearly an hour had passed, I had turned back to retrace my steps to the crossroads. At one point I spotted Ann's car coming up the lower road as I was walking on the higher road and I frantically tried to attract her attention by waving like some demented creature. I saw her driving up to the crossroads and with some relief saw the car pulling in. I thought that she must have spotted me waving and was now waiting on me to get back down to the crossroads. However, my feeling of relief was short lived, as within seconds I watched the car pulling away again and heading back towards Omagh. I couldn't believe this was happening. I was getting very tired by this stage, but I resisted the temptation to just sit down on the spot and give up. Instead I trudged on in the direction in which Ann's car had disappeared. Just as I was considering seeking out St Patrick's Well after all and praying for a miracle, a large blue pickup truck came sailing up the road towards me and, as I stepped up onto the verge to get out of the way, I recognised a familiar face in the passenger seat. It was Ann! She had enlisted the help of the local mountain rescue team to come find me – well, if the truth be told, it was in reality a local farmer by the name of Richard. I was so relieved and grateful to see them both. I slung my backpack into the back seat of Richard's pickup, pulled myself in after it and was ferried back down to his farmyard where Ann had left her car.

I thanked Richard profusely for his help. Ann, who had been frantically searching for me around Barnes Gap, had seen Richard out on his quad bike and she had simply stopped to ask him for directions. However, he told her that giving directions in this part of the world was pretty pointless unless you already knew your way around and instead he told her to follow his quad down to his farm. Ann was, understandably, a bit wary at first but when she got to the farm and saw that there were other family members about she relaxed and put her trust in this good Samaritan. Richard then swapped his quad for the pickup truck and set off to find me with Ann on the lookout in the passenger seat beside him. Ann was as relieved to see me as I was to see her. This was yet another fantastic act of kindness by a complete stranger to add to my growing list. This journey was really restoring my faith in humanity. Time and time again, people were reaching out the hand of friendship and support to me, people I didn't even know. Not for the first time on this journey, it occurred to me that perhaps "someone up there" might actually be looking out for me and that it didn't only extend to the weather conditions. I had written a letter to Jacqui a number of weeks ago, but I now began to think of how magical it would be if I could have a conversation with my guardian angel.

A Touch of Magic

Saturday 15 August – Barnes Gap to Moneyneany
Hi love.

Hi my dear. Well, where did you walk today?

Ha! Do you not already know?

I do, but I would still like to hear you tell me.

Well, I started out from Barnes Gap Road, about six miles from Gortin, and walked to Moneyneany.

Moneyneany? Where's that?

I know, I had never heard of it either until I decided to do this walk. In fact, it's a little village that sits at the base of the Sperrin Mountains, just a few miles from Draperstown. The Irish name for it translates as "bog of wonders" and legend has it that it was a favourite place for the old Irish warriors to learn their exercises and perform great feats of magic. It still has a touch of magic about it. The sun was shining when I arrived and the people there were really nice and laid on a wonderful welcome for me.

Yes, I hope you appreciate mine and Rosaleen's efforts to try and make sure the weather is nice for the days you are out walking.

I certainly do and mostly it's been great. But what happened that Wednesday when I was walking from Lough Navar Forest to Belleek – it practically poured the whole day? Noah would have started building again if he had been there!

Ah, well we're still pretty new to this game – we still haven't earned our wings yet, you know. Anyway, we thought it would be better to get rid of all the rain in one fell swoop rather than letting it through in dribs and drabs over a number of days. Sure weren't the next couple of days great?

Yeah, I have to admit they were. Anyway, I suppose you'd like to hear more about today's walk.

Well, we don't have Facebook here, thank God! Oops!

Ha! Ha! Careful now, you never know who might be listening. Well, I stayed at Ann's again last night and then we both took our cars to Moneyneany, where I left my car in the chapel car park. Ann then gave me a lift back to Barnes Gap. Gee, we had some "fun" there the previous day!

Yes, I saw that. Rosaleen and I were in stitches at the sight of you frantically trying to wave Ann down when she drove past on the lower road. Rosaleen said it looked like you were being attacked by wasps! Anyway, when we stopped laughing we took pity on you and set a rescue plan in motion.

You done that?

Not so much 'did' that, as just provided a helping hand. It's a matter of helping things to align. Often you just need to provide the right opportunity for the natural goodness in people to come out.

Too true! I am certainly finding that to be the case with this walk! I'm glad you two thought it was funny though. Anyway, after exploring the Barnes Gap area a little more to try and figure the place out, Ann dropped me close to where I had got to the day before. It had been a beautiful morning since leaving Omagh and was still a very nice day when I started walking – thanks to you and Rosaleen for that I suppose.

You're welcome

It didn't last though.

Oops!

Ah, it wasn't too bad. I just had to get the wet gear on a few times. I followed a country road that hugged the southern slopes of the Glenelly Valley for the next two and a half hours, covering about seven miles. There were some lovely views, both in front of me and behind, as I headed up this long valley alongside the Glenelly River flowing way down below. The landscape was forever changing as rain-front chased after rain-front up the valley. I eventually crossed over the river close to the little hamlet of Sperrin and then walked along the main Glenelly Road for the next four and a half miles, stopping off in the sunshine at Leagh's Bridge, to have the tasty sandwiches that Ann had made for me.

Glad to hear that you are still eating well.

Well, you know me love – I've never liked to go hungry. And sure, I have to keep my strength up for this walk. Nearly everyone I've stayed with has ensured that I don't leave without a good breakfast or a good lunch, or both! Anyway, about another half a mile after Leagh's Bridge, I left the Glenelly Road to follow a stony track up the slopes of Crockbrack Mountain.

Really! Any good looking cowboys up there?

Ha! Ha! No, it's Crockbrack Mountain; not Brokeback Mountain! Crockbrack actually means "speckled hill" and, I can tell you, it was fairly speckled with raindrops today! The stony track soon became what I now know to be a turbary track, which is a deep cut path through the peat. I then had to follow the way markers as best I could across the peat bog towards the summit of the mountain. Unfortunately, it rained nearly the whole way up Crockbrack, but thankfully it was starting to clear when I reached the top and I had some pretty good views over the Sperrins, both North and South, and was even able to see Lough Neagh away in the distance. This might sound daft, but I have been wondering if I'm any closer to you when I'm at the top of a mountain?

Ha! Ha! No love, not physically closer anyway, if that's what you're asking. But darling, you know, we will always be close in other ways. I'm never far away from you. You just have to learn how to see and listen in a different way.

I'm not sure I understand.

Well, you know the way we had such an understanding between each other that we sometimes didn't even have to speak to know what the other was feeling or thinking?

Yeah.

Well, you can still do that. You just have to free your mind and allow yourself to. That's what you're actually doing now without even realising it.

Oh yeah, I see what you mean. And you're right. I hadn't even realised. It just seemed like such a natural thing to do. You are still here; inside my head.

And you thought you were rid of me!

Ha! Ha! Never! Ok, that's good to know. It's not going to keep me warm at night or take my hand when I'm out walking, but I suppose it is something to hold on to.

Just remember, I'm always here dear. You don't even have to call. Anyway, what happened next on your walk?

Well, I had a pretty hard trek across some very boggy ground at the top of Crockbrack, heading towards Crockmore, which just means "big hill", before I joined the top of a stony track that zigzagged down the slopes of Crockmore for about a mile and a half. Towards the bottom I passed an abandoned clachan called Crocktaggart.

Sorry, a what?

Ha! Ha! I thought that would get your attention. A clachan – it's a Scottish Gaelic word referring to a small settlement, usually just a small cluster of farm houses. From here a farm laneway led onto a country road, where Danielle, a Cancer Research UK employee from Moneyneany, met me and walked with me for the last three quarters of a mile into her village. When we arrived, I was very warmly welcomed by a small delegation of her family members and friends from the Moneyneany community, led by Danielle's parents, Patsy and Annis. The people of Moneyneany were just brilliant and I was handed over £100 in donations before the evening was out. Danielle's family welcomed me into their home like I was one of their own and provided everything that I needed and more. These acts of kindness from strangers just keep coming!

Strangers are just friends that you haven't met yet.

Oh God (Oops!), I can't believe you just said that! But I suppose there is a lot of truth in it. By the way, speaking of God, can you tell me anything about him?

Hmmm, not really allowed to. There's one funny thing I can tell you though. He would really like everyone to ease up on the same old prayers and hymns. After centuries of listening to them he has gotten pretty weary. He knows people mean well, but you know what it's like when someone keeps saying the same thing over and over, again and again – you just want to switch off. Believe it or not, he puts his fingers in his ears and hums to himself a lot! And when it comes to the hymns, well let's just say, he finds some people more tuneful than others! He does love people talking to him though, in a natural way, and he doesn't care who they are or where they are when they do it.

Why did he take you from me? And please, please don't tell me that he works in mysterious ways!

Oh love, I really don't know yet. I just know that I didn't want to leave you any more than you didn't want me to go. I didn't want to leave you, or Matt, or Hannah, or my sisters and brother or anyone else, but the choice was simply not mine to make. You know that I've always believed that we live on through others and I still believe that. I asked people at my service to always carry a little piece of me around in their hearts. I truly meant it and I can see that people are doing just that, which gives me more comfort than you can imagine. Keep doing what you are doing also. I am with you every step of the way.

I know.

I have to go now. Choir practice beckons! Give my love to everyone.

I will. Love you.

Love you more.

Ha! Ha! Some things never change.

As I was waking the following morning I experienced another touch of magic.

Sweet dreams are made of this

I held your hand this morning
Your touch was so real and so warm
I reached away for just one second
When I returned, your hand was gone

Though a fleeting moment of contact
In that space between sleep and awake
Your warmth has remained with me
What magic you continue to make

Flying

Sunday 16 August – Moneyneany to Dungiven

I was up early this Sunday morning as I had a very important family engagement to make later on in the day in Letterkenny. Danielle and her husband, Barry, came over early to start preparing a great fry-up for breakfast, which I enjoyed with them and Danielle's dad, Patsy. After breakfast, Danielle drove over to Dungiven and I followed her in my car, stopping occasionally to allow sheep to cross the road. I parked up opposite St Patrick's Catholic Church in Dungiven and then got a lift back to Moneyneany with Danielle. We arrived back to the day's starting point at the village's community centre to find Orla waiting to walk with us. Orla is one of the most successful fundraisers ever for Cancer Research UK in Northern Ireland and Danielle had filled me in on some of her impressive achievements, such as collecting £2,500 by herself in a single day through a street collection!

The three of us headed out of Moneyneany to Moydamlaght Forest and followed the Ulster Way way-markers uphill towards the imposing cliffs of Craig-na-shoke, known locally as Eagle Rock. Craig-na-shoke, or more correctly in Irish, Carraig na Seabhac, actually means the rock of the hawk. There were also way-markers for Hudy's Way along the route and Danielle had explained to me the previous day that this walking route was named after a local man, Hugh "Hudy" McGuigan, who had convinced himself, that he could fly. One day he set off to prove it by launching himself off the top of Eagle Rock with homemade wings "fashioned from half doors and goose feathers!" He didn't get very far – well, not in a horizontal direction anyway. So Hudy's Way was created in his honour. We do love to celebrate our spectacular failures.

I had thought that I was reasonably fit, but I must say that I was labouring for breath at times as we headed up the forest tracks towards Eagle Rock. It didn't seem to take much out of my companions though, and they chatted away as we went, while I struggled to complete a sentence and hoped that they would soon stop asking me so many questions. After about three miles, we came to a junction in the forest track and the girls decided to take the left turn that would take them in a loop back down to the forest entrance. So after saying our goodbyes, we parted company and I took the right turn which climbed on

The wooden stairway that brings you up Cuilcagh Mountain

The famous and picturesque Belleek Pottery on the banks of the River Erne

The author, second left with, from left, his father Artie, brother Michael and sister Ann

A beautiful 'wild deer' at Gortin Glens Forest Park

for about another half mile to the foot of Eagle Rock. The cliffs at Eagle Rock were quite impressive and provided some stunning views of the countryside below. This marked the end of the formal pathways for now and I was now advised by the directions to work my way up and round Eagle Rock, as the route scrambles uphill. This section was quite challenging and I have to say that I might have managed it better with a pair of hooves rather than a pair of feet.

The directions then advised that I should follow the way-markers closely over the boggy ground that links Moydamlaght and Glenshane forests. What way-markers, I asked myself. Unfortunately, I have to say that I only ever saw one way-marker between this point and my final destination at Dungiven, which was still some ten miles away. I'm not saying that there weren't others, just that I didn't see any. However, the maps I had were pretty good and with the occasional aid of my compass, I was able to follow the route fairly closely. It was still very difficult crossing over the very boggy ground between the forests though. Such terrain really saps your energy as you go. It's almost as if the wet ground, sucking on each boot in turn as I pulled it out to move another step forward, was at the same time sucking any reserves of energy I had out through the soles of my feet. It was a hard and tiring slog.

It took quite a bit of searching to find the style leading into Glenshane Forest that the directions referred to. I eventually located it and climbed wearily over the slight wooden structure and finally left the bogland behind to enter the trees. From here the path was very steep and muddier than expected and I went "flying" on my backside pretty early on when my feet suddenly left me. But there was no harm done. I just made my way to the bottom a little quicker than planned; perhaps not as quickly as Hudy achieved at Eagle Rock, but quick none-the-less! I picked myself up, wiped the mud off the backside of my trousers and moved on through the forest. I came to a small clearing where a "mass rock", used as a place of worship during Penal times, was located and then followed the forest track down through the trees. I eventually emerged from the forest again and picked up a grassy track that followed the contours around the lower slopes of Corick Mountain, which takes its name from the Irish Cnoc an Chomraic, meaning "hill of the combat".

Thankfully things were fairly quiet as I made my way round this hill, apart from a lone shepherd and his dog, who were about to head up the hill in search of some stray sheep. We chatted briefly before both going on our separate ways, but I watched him for a bit and was mightily impressed with how effortlessly he seemed to be able to cross the steep and rough ground. If only I had legs like his, I thought. The track was now essentially running parallel to the Glenshane Pass and following a route above the River Roe in the valley below. I could see the traffic in the distance across the valley on the Glenshane Road, which passes though Dungiven. Thankfully it was far enough away at this stage for the traffic to have any impact on the peacefulness of the route on my side of the valley. The grassy track later became a farm lane that took me gradually down off the slopes of Corick Mountain to join the Corick Road and I followed this quiet county road until I came to Cluntygeeragh Bridge, which crossed the River Roe. I stopped here and sat on the stone wall of the bridge for a "Rachel break" and for something to eat, while enjoying the beautiful pastoral scenes around me in Benady Glen. It was a very pleasant place to stop for a short while, particularly in the early afternoon sunshine. Cluntygeeragh, the townland from which the bridge takes its name, I believe means "meadow of sheep". There were no sheep visible from where I was sitting, but I watched a rather magnificent stallion in the field next to the bridge slowly amble across from the far side of the meadow once it had spotted me – or perhaps more accurately, once it had spotted me eating. I have always loved animals and find it hard to pass a horse, pony, donkey or dog by, without stopping to give it a bit of attention. This one was no exception and I was happy to share a piece of my apple with it for its trouble. Apart from the yappy little mutts I endured near Lough Scolban in Co Fermanagh, all of my four legged friends have been friendly and only happy to be petted and talked to.

From the bridge, I followed the country road for about another mile before I unfortunately left the rural solitude behind and joined the very busy Glenshane Road for the last mile and a half into Dungiven. Thankfully this road had a good footpath set well in from the road, which at least made for very safe walking. However, the traffic on this road was pretty continuous and so it was time to stick the ear buds of my iPod in again and turn up the music in order to help drown out the constant road noise. Before I knew it I was entering Dungiven and admiring the lovely floral displays in the flower beds on the edge of the town. Dungiven comes from the Irish Dún Geimhin, meaning "fort of the hide". Between the twelfth and seventeenth centuries the area was ruled by the Ó Catháin clan, one of the most influential clans in Ulster at the time. On the way into the town, I passed Dungiven Castle, which was originally built by the Ó Catháins in the early seventeenth century, but has more recently operated as a restaurant and guesthouse. Amongst many other things, Dungiven is also notable for two very different musical connections. Firstly, the world famous song "Danny Boy" is taken from a melody composed by the Ó Catháin bard, Ruairí Dall Ó Catháin, and secondly, Dungiven is also the town that gave us Eoghan Quigg, who finished third in the X Factor final in 2008. I have great admiration for one of the two, but I'm not saying which!

I arrived back at my car parked opposite the very attractive St Patrick's Parish Church. I had made good time and it gave me sufficient time to change out of my boots and drive to Letterkenny in County Donegal to join the family celebrations for my sister, Teresa's, very significant birthday. It was lovely to rest the feet for a couple of hours and unwind with family for the remainder of the afternoon. After the celebrations, I drove to Portrush. I am very fortunate to have a holiday home on the North Coast, which Jacqui and I had bought about ten years before, prior to the property prices going crazy. We had spent many days and weeks here together, and with the children as they were growing up, and we really loved the place. Both the house and the town are filled with the happiest of memories and we had both made many good friends here over the years. I still loved the place and the people, but it certainly wasn't the same any more without Jacqui being around to enjoy it with. However, this was going to be my base for the next number of walking days and many of our friends had already been lining up to lend a hand – or foot!

Unfortunately, returning to an empty house filled with happy memories proved difficult. Everywhere I looked there were memories of Jacqui – photographs of us together, smiling and happy, pictures and ornaments that she and I had bought together while wandering round the local shops and fairs, the settee in the living room where we curled up together to watch TV or read our books, her dressing gown still hanging on the back of the bedroom door, her clothes still hanging in the wardrobe, her toothbrush still in the holder in the bathroom. I still hadn't mustered up the courage to clear Jacqui's things from either our home in Belfast or this house in Portrush. Even the thought of doing so was too painful. It would feel like a huge betrayal – as if I was keen to get rid of all remaining traces of her. I knew that it was something that I would have to face some day, but at this stage I didn't even want to think about it. The house was therefore still filled with emotional booby traps. Any one of these objects could potentially trigger a small explosion that would see my emotions being torn to shreds once again. It was often impossible to tell what might set things off, or indeed when. This wasn't the first time that I had been back to the house since Jacqui's death and I knew that it was an emotional minefield. On this occasion, I seemed to be doing fine to begin with. But when I was in the kitchen fixing myself a late tea, I opened a cupboard door to lift out a plate. Then it was nothing more than the sight of a coffee mug, Jacqui's coffee mug, that was enough to tilt the switch and suddenly I was on the floor, sobbing uncontrollably and fighting for breath. The pain I felt at her loss was just too much to bear at times and there was nothing I could do in these circumstances except let it out and wait for the worst of it to subside. I had loved Jacqui so much that I just didn't know what to do now that she was gone. I wanted to forget everything and at the very same time I didn't want to forget anything.

I Want To Forget

I want to forget
Not your smile
nor your laugh
Not your talk
nor your call
I want to forget
that they are lost

I want to forget
Not your warmth
nor your touch
Not your embrace
nor your love
I want to forget
that they are past

I want to forget
Not your face
nor your hands
Not your lips
nor your kiss
I want to forget
that you are gone

A Tale of Two Hills

Tuesday 18 August – Dungiven to Cam Forest

It was a beautiful morning when I left Portrush to drive to the Ringsend Road at Cam Forest to meet with my mate and driver for the day, Conn. Conn had brought Hudson, his one year old dachshund, along for the ride and I had the "pleasure" of nursing him on my lap as Conn drove me in his car on to Dungiven. Hudson is a lovely little dog, but I have to say that he is definitely on the hyper end of the activity scale. It was like trying to hold onto a large brown four legged eel that twisted and turned even more frequently than the narrow country roads we were travelling on.

Conn dropped me off opposite St Patrick's Church again at the top of Dungiven and, after the obligatory photographs, I set off walking. The first major challenge of the day came into view almost immediately - the mountain of Benbradagh, which dominates the landscape for miles around. I headed out of Dungiven via the Curragh Road that wound its way up the sloping southwest side of the mountain, the summit of which stands at an impressive 465m. It took about an hour and a half of steady climbing to reach the top of the steep roadway in the warm morning sunshine. I honestly don't believe that I have ever sweated as much so early in the morning before! It was a relief to reach the end of the roadway and to enjoy the cooling breeze coming over the top of the mountain.

At this point I had to decide whether to immediately continue along the Ulster Way route to the right, or to turn left and take the two mile detour out to the summit that overlooks the very steep north face of the mountain. It was a beautiful morning and the summit promised spectacular views, so I headed left. It was well worth the additional effort. Benbradagh is from the Irish Binn Bhradach, meaning "thief's peak", although no-one is sure why. I would volunteer that it may be simply because both the climb up and the views from the summit can steal your breath away. The views back over the Sperrins to the south and the countryside below were fabulous. Much of the view to the north was obscured by a sea mist that hadn't burned off yet. It rolled across the low-lying countryside below like dragon's breath, which was how Jacqui and I always referred to such mist after seeing John Boorman's movie, Excalibur, years ago. The effect was quite magical.

I stood on the summit for quite a while, lost in my thoughts - some of them good, some of them not so good. It was undoubtedly a spectacular location, but I have to admit that it was sometimes difficult for me to fully enjoy such glorious views without them being overshadowed by the pain of loss. The beauty around me at times felt superficial. I could certainly appreciate the splendour of what my eyes were seeing, but the effect it had on my soul seemed somehow filtered or deflected. It was as if grief had created a barrier that prevented beauty from permeating below the surface. Just as sunshine cannot penetrate the depths of the oceans, so it seemed it could no longer reach the depths of my heart, as it once had. As I stood on that mountain in the glorious sunshine, I should have been experiencing a real "top of the world" moment, but instead my mind sank to the lowest of places as the darkest of thoughts began to take form. It was several minutes before I could pull myself together and drag myself away from the summit. I slowly retraced my steps back to re-join the official route once again.

I then had a long walk down the American Road, passing the rather unnerving and desolate remnants of an old US Navy Cold War signal base on the way. Lenamore Forest came into view on the left as expected, but I failed to find the promised way-marker posts that were supposed to guide me across the open bogland and into the forest. This turned out to be a blessing in disguise, as I would experience quite enough bogland later on. I could see from the map that the road I was on would meet up with the official route again after a couple of miles, so I continued on down the roadway rather than risk getting "bogged down" and possibly lost in this bleak wilderness. From here I followed a number of roads and tracks for about five miles before arriving at my second major challenge of the day, Donald's Hill. Again a simple short sentence in the directions, ".....and then turn right again, following the fence line steeply to the summit of Donald's Hill, an effort of around 45 minutes", belied what was really ahead. This hill, and the subsequent trek across the blanket bog and heather to the turbines at Rigged Hill, was, without a shadow of a doubt, the most exhausting section of the Ulster Way I encountered.

After lunch, I started up the steep slope of Donald's Hill and quickly began to realise that it wasn't going to be easy. Once again, I would have gladly swapped my own flat feet for a pair of hoofs. Numerous sheep ran around the hillside and looked on bemused at this strange two-legged creature struggling up the slope and having to take frequent rests to catch his breath and wipe the sweat from his eyes. Admittedly, at 399m above sea level, there were super views from the summit over the Roe Valley and Lough Foyle, but I'm not sure I fully appreciated them at the time. However, what followed made the climb up Donald's Hill seem like a walk in the park! Bog hell awaited!

The absence of way-markers ahead meant that I had to simply head off in the direction of the radio masts and wind turbines in the distance and pick my way through the very rough bogland as best I could. There were plenty of stumbles and falls along the way, accompanied by even more sweat and curses, and for a long time the masts and turbines just didn't seem to be getting any closer. The sun was really beating down on me at this stage and, for the first time on my pilgrimage, I was really glad to have my floppy sun hat. I dreamt of the cold beers waiting in the fridge in the Portrush house for me when I got back.

The ground was incredibly rough in places and I probably walked twice the distance the crow would have taken, as I constantly had to weave and turn, and even back-track at times, in an attempt to find the best route through the bog. There was even some jumping and climbing involved in getting across some quite deep gashes that ran through the bog in places, as if the earth's skin had become too small to contain the hill underneath and it had split open as a result. I felt truly alone and abandoned while crossing this wild and desolate landscape. The dark thoughts from the summit of Benbradagh returned. At times I just felt like giving up and lying down in one of those cool crevasses to wait for the earth to close in around me and envelop me in its cold embrace, sparing me any further physical or emotional torture. If I was to disappear here, I would probably never be found again. But I would be at peace and all the hurt would be at an end; the terrible crushing sense of loss would be over. It wasn't the first time, and it wouldn't be the last, that the temptation to remove myself from this world of torture and heartache presented itself to me. After all, what did the future hold for me now with Jacqui gone? I felt that my whole reason for living had disappeared when Jacqui had died. What reason was there for me to go on now? I really didn't want to live the rest of my days without her. It just seemed utterly pointless. Better to just lie down, give up and die. It was hard to stop such thoughts infiltrating my mind when I was walking on my own through such difficult terrain and in such isolation. I had to dig very deep and remind myself of the purpose behind my walk in order to keep going. I could imagine Jacqui's voice urging me on and encouraging me not to give up. I had to keep going.

I finally reached Rigged Hill Wind Farm. I have never been so happy to reach a proper track and I fell to my knees and literally kissed the ground in thanks. It was almost in a state of euphoria that I wandered through the ten wind turbines that made up the wind farm. It was pretty amazing being so close to these huge machines. In fact, I was able to touch the masts of some and I found the shadows of the rotating blades on the ground to be almost hypnotic. From here I picked up a forest track that led down through Cam Forest. Once out of the forest, I joined a number of lanes and tracks through fields and eventually reached the Ringsend Road after about another three miles, although it wasn't particularly easy to navigate this final section. I finally reached my car almost ten hours after leaving Dungiven! I wearily changed out of my walking boots into a comfortable pair of shoes and then set off by car back to the Portrush house. As soon as I got into the house, I made straight for the fridge, opened the door and pulled out one of the cold bottles of beer that I had been fantasising about for much of my trek across the bogland between Donald's Hill and Rigged Hill. I think that I had well and truly earned it. It and the two or three other bottles that followed! It had indeed been a tale of two hills. It was the best of times, it was the worst of times..............the weather and scenery had been fantastic, but it had certainly been an incredibly hard day's walk!

However, no matter how tough my walk became, it was absolutely nothing compared to the challenge that Jacqui had faced in dealing with cancer. Just imagine for one moment how you might feel if you were told today that you were going to be taken away from everyone and everything that you loved and that you would never be able to see them again, ever! That your very existence on this earth was going to end with absolutely no hope of reprieve or pardon. That you were never again going to witness another crisp and clear winter's day, another spring bursting forth with hope, another summer enjoying the cool water of the sea as you take a stroll along your favourite beach, or another warm sun on your back as you kick your way through the Autumn leaves. How would you deal with it? Would you rail against it? Would you get angry or would you simply lose it and go to pieces? You won't be able to answer that of course. None of us can possibly know how we would deal with such a situation unless faced with it in reality.

Jacqui unfortunately had to face it for real. However, she did so with her characteristic calmness, strength and grace. Her bravery throughout her final months, when we realised that there was no further hope, was quite simply remarkable and her acceptance of her situation was nothing short of heroic in my eyes. And if I had to use just one word to sum up her state of being during that time, that word would be "equanimity". Equanimity is defined as calmness and composure, especially in a difficult situation, and it perfectly sums up how Jacqui dealt with her impossible position. That is not to suggest that she cruised through her illness and then gently slipped away without any difficulties. Cancer does not allow you to do that. Cancer is a bastard - a completely indiscriminate, uncaring, heartless, cruel bastard. And almost worse than the cancer itself at times was the treatment; the needles, the chemotherapy drugs, the hair loss, the sickness, the weakness, the wasting away, the bed sores, the swelling, the drains, the restlessness, the loss of appetite, the constipation, the shear indignity of it all.

Jacqui had always been a physically fit and very active person. Before her diagnosis, we would have gone out running together and she regularly attended kick-boxing and other exercise classes. In the final weeks, she could only go out in a wheelchair and I had to carry her up and down the stairs at home and even help her to shower. Neither of us ever imagined that life would change so much for us in such a short period of time. I remember asking Jacqui in the final weeks if she was frightened or felt any anger at the fact that she was dying. She very calmly replied that she wasn't frightened nor was she angry. She just felt very disappointed that her body had let her down. She had always looked after herself; she ate healthily, exercised regularly, never smoked, only drank in moderation and had regular health checkups and tests. She had followed all the recommended guidelines, but it still hadn't protected her. In effect, she felt that her own body had betrayed her. I suspect that most people faced with this betrayal would have been livid, but Jacqui wasn't. That just wasn't her. She certainly didn't like her situation, but she accepted it with equanimity.

I have no doubt that we will, eventually, beat cancer. We will find a cure and finally rid humanity of this awful scourge. It will of course come too late for Jacqui, and too late for many others also, but I believe that in the end cancer research will triumph over this evil.

I Am Cancer

I am a stowaway, remaining hidden for as long as I can
I am a sleeper, awaiting the signal to follow my plan
I am an illegal, doing all it takes to avoid being found
I am an assassin, awaiting the command to cut you down

Your wish and desire is that you might live forever
My modus operandi is for us to die together
I am cancer, I am fear, I am hate, I am within
You are human, you are hope, you are love
You will win

The Highwayman

Wednesday 19 August – Cam Forest to Castlerock

The Lough Navar to Belleek washout was on a Wednesday and this Wednesday was not much better weather wise. My weather angels must have had Wednesdays off. However, overall it turned out to be a much more varied and interesting journey than the one a fortnight before, despite the rain.

I met Conn again, this time at the promenade at Castlerock, and got a lift with him to the Ringsend Road at the entrance to the northern section of Cam Forest. No Hudson this time. Conn claimed that his little dog was a bit tired that morning and so he had left him at home. I wasn't buying that at all – I don't think Hudson and tired can be used in the same sentence. I really think Conn was just trying to spare me another morning of having to wrestle with the energetic little dachshund.

The morning had been fine weather wise up to now, but it started to rain just as I was getting ready to set off. I waved to Conn as he drove off home to shape a few more surfboards and I set off up the hill into the forest, only to stop after 100 metres to pull on my wet gear, as the rain had started to get much heavier. Unfortunately, the rain stayed with me for pretty much the rest of the day. The directions recommended stopping at a clearing that I soon came to, to look back and take in the views of the Sperrins, including Benbradagh and Donald's Hill that I had encountered the day before. Unfortunately, there was nothing to be viewed through the rain. However, I can't say that I was too disappointed at not seeing Donald's Hill again – I didn't care if I never set eyes on that particular hill ever again!

After Cam Forest, I passed through Springwell Forest and emerged onto the Windyhill Road, which is known locally as Murder Hole Road. Apparently, in the 1700's an infamous highwayman, called Cushy Glen, spent his time robbing travellers on the mail coach road between Limavady and Coleraine. He is reputed to have murdered several travellers and dumped their bodies in the 'Murder Hole' at the foot of Windy Hill. I love this reference that I came across when looking into the history of the highwayman – "Many tales refer to Cushy Glen's wife (Kitty) aiding and abetting him in his dastardly deeds – helping him to bury the bodies, encouraging him with wifely inquiries such as 'Did you get him Cushy?', and generally being a real bad lot." For 170 years the old coach road was called the Murder Hole Road, but was renamed Windyhill Road in the 1970's. Apparently there is a sculpture of Cushy Glen, at a nearby picnic site, that depicts an eerie representation of Cushy lying in wait in his den for passing travellers, but unfortunately I didn't get to see it as it was off route. Nevertheless, I have to say that the Murder Hole Road was a bit unnerving, particularly given the dreary weather conditions, and I had to resist the temptation to keep glancing over my shoulder to check that I wasn't being stalked by Cushy's ghost!

After just over a mile on this road, I turned off at a junction that had a sign pointing towards Moorbrook Lodge Angling Park, with the promise of rest and eating facilities. At last there was a chance for some respite from the relentless rain that had, particularly on the open road sections, been accompanied by a strong wind, which had actually been quite chilly at times despite the fact that it was mid-August. The road had indeed been well renamed as Windyhill Road. Unfortunately, my hopes of a hot coffee and a dry resting place were soon dashed, as the route took another turn, which headed away from the prospect of shelter. Moorbrook Lodge wasn't marked on the map and so I had to assume that it might be too far away to justify a detour. So it was a case of keeping the head down and ploughing on along the official route of the Ulster Way.

The route took me through Grange Park Wood, where I encountered a couple of men out walking an assortment of exuberant, friendly and very wet dogs. These were the first people I had come across since I had waved Conn off that morning, apart from those whizzing past in a car or van on the main roads. They were certainly very surprised to see someone "as crazy as themselves" out walking in the relentless rain and I didn't even have a dog! We chatted only briefly, as the weather wasn't particularly conducive to stopping for a long exchange. They wished me all the best on my walk and I pushed on again, with the dogs eagerly following their newfound friend until their owners called them back. About three miles after entering Grange Park Wood, I emerged out the other side and joined Bishop's Road for around two and a half miles until I reached Gortmore viewing point. Here the rain eased off for a short time and I found a spot sufficiently sheltered from the wind to allow for a quick lunch, while taking in the mostly grey views of Binevenagh Mountain to the left and Magilligan Point and Inishowen peninsula straight ahead. Gortmore viewing point had once been the site of a six foot high sculpture of Manannán Mac

Lir, a sea god in Irish mythology, until it was cut down and removed by persons unknown earlier in the year. He could be viewed as a Celtic version of Neptune and local people believed that his spirit was released during fierce storms. Apparently some elderly folk in this area are still heard to remark "Manannán is angry today," when Lough Foyle below is rough and they also refer to the angry waves as "Manannán's seahorses". Those who made off with the sea god sculpture left a wooden cross with the words "You shall have no other gods before me" in its place, so their motives would appear to have been "Christian" in nature. I would have liked to have seen what must have been an impressive statue at this elevated site with its commanding view over Lough Foyle.

Unfortunately, the rain started again before I had finished my lunch, so I quickly wolfed down the last of my sandwich, pulled on my backpack again and re-joined Bishop's Road to walk on eastwards towards Downhill, which, not surprisingly, was all downhill for the next two miles or so. However, before reaching the village of Downhill itself, the route turned off into Downhill Forest. Even though it was still raining, I really enjoyed the half-hour walk through the deciduous trees of this forest, which, in parts, followed the path of a fast running river, the name of which still remains a mystery to me. When I emerged from the forest, I turned right and passed Bishop's Gate and the rather quaint gothic style gate lodge beside it, which is now used as a private residence. Bishop's Gate is the entrance to the National Trust owned Downhill Demesne, which was home to the Bishop of Derry, Earl Frederick Hervey, in the late 1700's. He chose this spot to build his country residence, Downhill House, which is now unfortunately in ruins. He also built Mussenden Temple, a small circular building located on the cliffs at the edge of the demesne overlooking the North Sea. This temple was built as a library and was modelled on the Temple of Vesta in Italy and, unlike Downhill House, it was still in pretty good condition. Apparently the Bishop tried to buy the original Temple of Vesta, which he planned to dismantled and rebuilt at Downhill. His offer was thankfully turned down by the Vatican and that's why he had to have his own temple built from scratch. I shuddered to think what might have become of the Temple of Vesta if it had been relocated from its home in Italy to this part of the world. The fundamental Christians of Gortmore might have toppled it over the edge of the cliff into the wild seas below and stuck a wooden cross up in its place saying, "Vestal virgins not welcome here!"

I followed the main road for three quarters of a mile before passing Hezlett House, a very attractive 1690's thatched cottage also owned by the National Trust, and then heading down Sea Road to reach my car in Castlerock in the late afternoon. I then headed for home in Belfast, as I had to return to work for a couple of days before resuming my pilgrimage at the weekend. I was planning to take on the Magilligan Point to Binevenagh leg on Saturday. I was hoping for an improvement in the weather, so that I could fully appreciate the beautiful views from the top of Binevenagh. What I didn't realise then, was the impact that those same views were going to have on me emotionally, as I stood at the edge of Binevenagh's cliffs, staring into the abyss and battling against my dark demons once again.

Temptation

Saturday 22 August – Magilligan to Binevenagh

> *For what is it to die but to stand naked*
> *in the wind and to melt into the sun?*
> *And what is it to cease breathing,*
> *but to free the breath from its restless tides?*
> *Only when you drink from the river of silence*
> *shall you indeed sing.*
> *And when you have reached the mountain top,*
> *then you shall begin to climb.*
> *And when the earth shall claim your limbs,*
> *then shall you truly dance.*

The Prophet
Kahlil Gibran (1883 - 1931)

Saturday turned out to be a superb day for walking. Dry all day, hazy sunshine, not too hot and a nice gentle breeze to keep things comfortable. After my second wet Wednesday earlier in the week, my weather angels had returned! I had taken the next fortnight as annual leave from work to concentrate on finishing my pilgrimage, which I planned to complete on 2 September, in twelve days' time. Today was certainly a great start to this stage – weather wise anyway! Unfortunately, the same could not be said for my state of mind! It was seven months since Jacqui had died and I was missing her more that words could say. I was feeling really low and vulnerable and it was at times such as this that my inner demons came to the fore. It really felt like they were gaining control as they constantly tried to fill my head with dark thoughts of hopelessness and despair. Once again, I was thankful to have the challenge of my walk to give me some focus and to help keep me going.

Conn had returned for his third tour of duty as my driver for the day. He met me at the car park beside Binevenagh Lake and drove me over to Magilligan Point, stopping briefly at St Aidan's Church on the way to "enjoy" a drink from the holy well. The water is believed by some to have healing powers and we both had a good cupful – I don't believe in such things but, at the same time, I thought it couldn't do any harm. However, it wasn't until after drinking that I noticed that there were some pairs of socks draped on the stones just above the well. Conn explained that people with verrucas and other nasty foot conditions left them there in the belief that the waters would cure them. I really wished he had told me that before I had swallowed a cupful of the stuff!

With one of us feeling healed and the other feeling mildly infected, we drove on to Magilligan Point and parked up near the Martello Tower. Conn walked the short distance out to the beach with me, and we stopped to admire the tower on the way. The Martello Tower is a well-known landmark at Magilligan. It was built in the early 1800's, during the Napoleonic Wars, to guard against possible French invasion. It was one of 74 constructed in Ireland and is one of the best preserved of the 40 or so that still remain. The top floor housed a twenty-four pound gun able to swivel and shoot in any direction and, together with a similar tower standing across the water in Co Donegal at Greencastle, it controlled entry through the narrow mouth of Lough Foyle.

After a few photos, both at the tower and on the beach right out at the "point", I thanked Conn for his help and for the "refreshing" drink, and then I set off once again. It was only a very short stroll along the small beach before I joined the roadway at the Point Bar and the Magilligan to Greencastle Ferry Terminal. My destination for the day, Binevenagh Mountain, was clearly visible in the distance. Dominating the skyline as it does, it rarely disappeared from my field of view, or from my subconscious mind, throughout the day's journey. I headed on inland, following the roadway for about three and a half miles and passing the MOD firing ranges and Magilligan Prison on the way, thinking that all the gunfire must act as a great deterrent to anyone thinking of going over the walls! Beyond the prison, I stopped for a while to pet a very friendly "tribald" pony – its body was brown and white, but it had a wonderful two-tone, black and white mane and a black tail. I then joined the A2 Seacoast Road and once again I wondered just how many A2s there were in Northern Ireland? Having finally looked it up, I now know that there is in fact only one A2, but it stretches for 239 miles and runs practically the whole way around the entire coast of Northern Ireland from Derry-Londonderry (so good they named it twice!) to Newry. So it was actually different sections of the same road that I kept encountering as I meandered around the coastal sections of the Ulster Way.

This particular section of the A2 road was very busy indeed and the route map indicated that I should follow it for the next three miles. I didn't fancy that at all, so I turned off the A2 at the first opportunity and followed a number of country roads instead. This only added about half a mile onto the journey and turned out to be well worth it as it was much quieter and passed close to the lovely eighteenth century Tamlaghtard Parish Church and the aforementioned St Aidan's Church and Holy Well. I enjoyed my lunch at the former and managed to resist the temptation to stop for another drink at the latter. Tamlaghtard means "the cemetery on the height," and the name is derived from its ancient burial-ground, which is still in use. It was a very peaceful place to have a break and a bite to eat, sitting on the steps at the front entrance of the church, with my back resting against the heavy wooden doors, and enjoying the views of Binevenagh towering above. Binevenagh marks the western extent of the Antrim Plateau formed around 60 million years ago by molten lava. The plateau and steep cliffs extend for over six miles across the peninsula of Magilligan and dominate the skyline over the villages of Bellarena, Downhill and Castlerock. The name Binevenagh comes from the Irish Binn Fhoibhne, meaning "Foibhne's peak". Foibhne (pronounced "Evena") was the son of a Celtic chieftain and legend has it he was killed on the mountain in pre-Christian times by Fergna, known as "the man of the broad spear". It was easy to visualise a "Highlander" style fight taking place at the edge of the cliffs above where I was sitting and poor Foibhne being fatally wounded and falling to his death on the rocks far below. I shivered at the idea of such a horrific fall, but somewhere in the deep recesses of my mind a very dark, subconscious thought had taken root. Perhaps a cemetery hadn't been the best place to stop for lunch!

When I took to the roads again, I had the pleasure of following a pheasant and its single chick for a short distance before they veered off into a field. Although these country roads were generally very quiet, the skies above were anything but, and I enjoyed several sightings of buzzards, helicopters and gliders, at least some of which had probably come from the nearby airfield at Bellarena. Unlike most other place names in Northern Ireland that have their origins in the Irish language, this one was named by the Earl Bishop of Derry from the Italian Bella rena meaning "Beautiful sand or strand". It seems that the Earl Bishop had certainly left a lasting stamp on the area and he very obviously had a great passion for all things Italian.

After about three miles of quiet country roads, I re-joined the A2 for a short time before turning into Ballycarton Forest. Here I followed a twisting and turning route through the forest along the lower slopes of Binevenagh, before climbing up and round the shoulder of the mountain. A hard track roadway then brought me back to Binevenagh Lake and my car by late afternoon. But I wasn't quite finished for the day yet. I retrieved my camera tripod from the boot of my car and headed over the grassy pathways that led out to the top of the spectacular cliff face of Binevenagh. It was just stunning as I approached the cliffs and looked over the edge to see the landscape of Magilligan and beyond appearing below - laid out before me like the most incredibly detailed map. As l took in the magnificence and grandeur of the view before me, I was reminded of a verse from the bible about the temptation of Christ, "Again, the devil took Him to a very high mountain and showed Him all the kingdoms of the world and their glory".

It must have been somewhere like this. But temptation comes in many forms. The cliff face at Binevenagh is approximately 170 metres at its highest point. From this height it takes an object, inanimate or otherwise, approximately six seconds to complete the perpendicular journey from top to bottom. As I stood on the edge of the abyss, the dark thought given birth to earlier by the story of Foibhne's fall, suddenly came to the surface and hijacked my mind.

"It could all be over in a matter of seconds!" my demons taunted.

I took a few steps back from the edge to prepare myself. This was it. The moment had arrived. Eyes wide open. I may as well enjoy the adrenaline rush. One chance only. Deep breath. No more stalling. Just do it. Start running towards the edge. Resolve. No hesitation. No slowing. My right foot hits the sweet spot. Perfection! Launch forward into space. Jesus, what a view! Enough to take your last breath away. Spread-eagled. Confident. I seem to hang in the air for a long second - no doubt a trick of the mind - just as time appears to go into slow motion during an accident. But this is no accident. This is purposeful. Deliberate. Planned. The landscape below me looks so clear. The ultimate satellite view.

The spell of hanging in the air suddenly evaporates. The inevitable force of gravity kicks in and I drop more quickly than I ever imagined possible.

A dilapidated shack with Barnes Gap in background

Spectacular views back over the Sperrins from the summit of Benbradagh

Tamlaghtard parish churh (left) with Binevenagh towering above

Dawn over East Strand, Portrush beach

One, acceleration

Two, cliff face blurs

Three, air whistles past

Four, jagged rocks below

Five, ground rushes up

Six, ...

"Please, my love, come away from the edge", my angel whispered.

I snapped out of my dark fantasy with a jolt. I moved back from the edge of the cliff slowly and sank to the ground to catch my breath and to wait for my head to stop spinning. Sometimes I wished I wasn't such a coward.

My thoughts could be extremely dark sometimes. You definitely wouldn't want to have been left alone with them! Here I was at the top of these wonderful cliffs with fantastic views and on a fabulously warm and sunny day. Outside my body it was perfection. Inside my head it was turmoil. The one person I wanted to be by my side enjoying the views with me, making the scene complete, giving my world meaning, had been taken from me. Could I continue to live without Jacqui? Yes, of course I could. I could still breathe, still eat, and still sleep. I could still function quite well in some sort of quasi human-being mode, going through the motions mechanically. So yes, I could live without Jacqui. But was life worth living without Jacqui? That was a much more difficult question and one that I wrestled with every day. I really just couldn't imagine myself ever being truly happy again and that was an incredibly hard thing to have to accept and resign myself to living with. Grief is an incredibly powerful and overwhelming emotion. It reaches into yoru chest and grabs your heart, and yes, it feels physical, it feels very real. I'd been on the floor, literally on my hands and knees, overcome with grief. At its worst, grief was like a huge unbearable weight, not from above but from within, as if my heart had suddenly turned to lead. It would drag me down and it would hold me down as it tried to wrench the very soul out of me. It would kick me in the gut until I felt absolutely drained and hopeless, totally empty and numb, an emotionless husk. Going on living in this kind of undead state, interspersed with episodes of painful anguish, seemed totally pointless at times. Each time the tsunami of grief passed, it was so tempting to just stay down and accept defeat. To give in and to give up.

So yes, desperate thoughts had entered my head. And God only knows, I had had enough opportunities to end it all during my walk round the Ulster Way. As well as the dizzy heights of Binevenagh, there had been other high spots, such as Cuilcagh, Magho and Benbradagh. Either of them would have served the purpose well. I could even have followed the "flight-path" of the poor, deluded Hugh "Hudy" McGuigan off the face of Eagle Rock near Moneyneany. Or I could have thrown myself into the tumbling torrents of the Sillees River near Lough Navar, with its ancient curse, "bad for fishing and good for drowning".

However, there were a number of factors that had together conspired to keep me shuffling along this mortal coil. Firstly, I would always be far too concerned about the poor people that would have to deal with things in the aftermath, the dreadful mess of my smashed or bloated body. Then there was the fear of the physical pain that I might experience in making the transition from this world to the next. And, thinking of the next world; is there actually life after death? What if there is absolutely nothing beyond this world that we all currently live in. Apart from escaping my pain, the other attraction in ending it all was the hope of being reunited with Jacqui on "the other side"; but what if there is no other side? We all like to believe in something, but, let's be honest, none of us really knows for sure.

And then there was the fear of botching my attempt to end it all. Nothing on this earth would terrify me more than the thought of lying paralysed in a hospital bed, body destroyed but mind still alert – trapped with a head full of loss and no means of escape. And of course, there was the not insignificant matter of the effect that such an act, whether successfully executed or not, would have on friends and family. All these factors and all this reasoning of course provided a very strong logic against taking one's own life. I fully realise that those who truly are suicidal have probably reached a place of such overwhelming desperation and depression that they are totally incapable of calmly applying such logic and reasoning. Of course, my logic and reasoning may all just be lame excuses to cover up the fact that, when all is said and done, I am just too much of a coward to face the music and voluntarily dance off this mortal coil. Perhaps there are some benefits to being a coward after all. I did worry though that my demons might be able to push me "over the edge" if they really got to me at a vulnerable time and place. The cliff edge at Binevenagh was the closest they had come to achieving that so far!

After quite a time on the ground, safely away from the cliff edge, I gradually regained my composure. I wiped my eyes and then slowly picked myself up and retrieved my camera and tripod from where I had placed them earlier. Once again I reminded myself of why I was on my pilgrimage, and who I was undertaking it for, and I set about doing what I had really come out to the cliffs of Binevenagh to do. I set the camera up on its tripod and switched it to video capture mode. I then very cautiously positioned myself on a rock near the cliff edge with the dramatic backdrop of Magilligan, Lough Foyle and the Inishowen Peninsula directly behind me. I had a script already prepared and so I switched the camera on and shot a little video to post on Facebook later as a further appeal to people to support my fund raising efforts.

"Hi everybody. Thank you for watching this video. If you have been following my updates on Facebook, you will know that I have now completed over 500 miles of my walk round the Ulster Way in memory of my very dear wife, Jacqui. You will also know that I have been using the walk to help raise funds for cancer research so that one day we might be free of this horrible and indiscriminate killer. To date we have raised over £7,000, but we still have a bit to go to reach my £10,000 target. Although the reason for me doing this walk is routed in the personal tragedy of losing my wonderful wife, it has also proved to be a very positive and life affirming experience for me. It has taken me to many new places around Northern Ireland and has also reacquainted me with many familiar ones. It has certainly made me realise just how beautiful a part of the world we have here, right on our own doorsteps. But what has impressed me most, above everything else, is the kindness and generosity of the people I have encountered on my travels, many of whom I had never even met before but who were somehow touched by my story and instinctively wanted to help in any way they could. However, walking round the Ulster Way has proved to be a tougher challenge than I expected. It has resulted in many blisters, sore muscles, shin splints and aching joints. It has brought with it moments of exhaustion, saturation, depression, even frustration and of course, lots and lots of perspiration. It's been incredibly hard at times.

But what you have to do is so easy. All you have to do is visit my Just Giving page or pick up your phone and click a few buttons to make a donation. It's as simple as that. If you are one of the many people who has already donated, then thank you so much. However, if you haven't quite got round to it yet, then what are you waiting for – just do it. Details of how to donate are on my Facebook page. Thank you."

I had kept my sunglasses on during the recording. This was mainly in an effort to disguise the fact that I was reading the script from a few pages propped up against the tripod, but it also served to hide my reddened eyes from the camera. Temptation can indeed present itself in many forms I thought. On this occasion, it had been the chance of a quick way out, a chance to escape my pain and mental anguish once and for all. Perhaps even a chance to be reunited with Jacqui. But the dark demons had failed in their attempts once more. My angel was still looking out for me.

I eventually dragged myself away from the dramatic views and the taunting precipice and headed back across the grassy paths to my car, still parked beside the lake. I was initially minded to just head straight back to Portrush and hide away for the night. However, I fought the temptation to withdraw from the world and instead headed to Castlerock and joined a group of my surfing buddies for a very pleasant evening in the water. It was the perfect therapy after a traumatic day. Afterwards, when heading back across the long beach, the sky became the deepest, most intense dusky pink I had ever witnessed. It was my weather angels signing off and wishing me goodnight. "Goodnight", I softly replied, "and thank you".

The Ports

This Sunday turned out to be a very special day indeed. After my traumatic episode on the cliffs of Binevenagh the previous day, I needed to stay closer to sea level and I needed to have good people around me. Today's walk thankfully offered both in abundance.

The day started with my Portrush neighbours, Noreen and David, giving me a lift out to Hezlett's Cottage at Castlerock, where I had arranged to meet Diane and her husband, Peter. They had come up from Belfast for the day and were going to walk with me as far as Portstewart. Diane had been one of Jacqui's best friends and belonged to a small group known affectionately as the "Stran girls", who were five friends who had remained close throughout all the years since they had graduated from Stranmillis Teacher Training College in Belfast in 1985.

Just as we were setting off, I got a wonderful surprise when Karen, a colleague from work, her husband and gorgeous little daughter, appeared to wish me well - it was a lovely gesture and the first of many to come today! Diane, Peter and I then headed along the A2 for a short distance before turning off to follow a number of country roads for about four miles, enjoying some glimpses of the River Bann, or at least the masts of a few yachts sailing up river, along the way. We eventually reached the outskirts of Coleraine and began weaving our way through the south side of the town until we reached the footbridge over the River Bann, near the town centre, and we stopped here for a few photos. At this point, the River Bann had almost completed its 80 mile journey from the Mourne Mountains to the ocean. I'm sure that the water, that had passed under my feet as I crossed the fledgling river below Spelga Dam some seven weeks earlier, had reached this point in Coleraine well before I had. But then, I had taken a more circuitous route and, of course, a river never has to go uphill!

We headed on over the footbridge and stopped for a comfort break at the town's Methodist Church, where a service appeared to have just finished. On leaving the church building again, I was approached by two young teenage parishioners who had been talking to Peter, and they handed me a small cash donation. Peter explained that Oscar and Rowan had seen my 1000K4J T-shirt and had asked what I was doing. When he told them, they immediately wanted to help. I was really touched by this spontaneous act of kindness by these two young people.

It was lunchtime as we began our journey out of Coleraine towards Portstewart and we therefore stopped at the marina on the banks of the River Bann to enjoy the very tasty lunch that Diane had prepared for us. We then got back onto the main road again and followed it for another two miles, all along good wide pavements thankfully, until we reached the outskirts of Portstewart. Here, I was delighted to also be joined by Gerard, another one of my surfing buddies, who was going to walk with me on to Portrush. Our party had now grown to four and we soon joined the coastal path near the end of Portstewart Strand. This took us past yet another St Patrick's Well! This well was originally used by prehistoric communities as a source of water, as well as being venerated by pagan pilgrims looking for medical cures – no sign of any socks at this one though. Later, when St Patrick passed through the area (on his Ulster Way hike!) around 450 AD, he blessed the spring and it became equally important for Christians, who used it as a source of holy water. Apparently the canny locals sold the water to tourists until the 1940s. I knew that there was somehow money to be made out of all those St Patrick's wells!

The coastal path headed on towards the crenellated outline of Dominican College, which sits rather dramatically on the cliffs overlooking the Atlantic Ocean and the town of Portstewart itself. The college was originally a castle called Rock or O'Hara's Castle, which explained the crenellations. The delightful coastal path squeezed past the seaward side of the college, climbed up onto a balcony built into the cliff and then descended via a flight of stone steps to meet the main promenade into town. With it being a warm and dry Sunday afternoon, it was very busy along the main street. So we were surprised to find a coffee shop that wasn't too crowded and we all stopped for a "Rachel break" and a very welcome cup of coffee. We were joined here by two friends of Peter and Diane's, who were also very happy to give me a cash donation on the spot.

It would have been so easy to have sat on and enjoyed the chat, but Gerard and I still had another few miles to do. So we said our farewells and left the good company and the comfortable surroundings of the coffee shop to pick up the Ulster Way again close to the town's small but picturesque harbour. It was a very pleasant walk along the coastal track, with the sea never far from us on the left hand side and the fairways and greens of Ballyreagh Golf Course on the right. It was an up and down and rather winding journey, but that's the nature of a coastal track when it's hugging a jagged and rocky coastline such as this. As we approached Rinagree Point, the path climbed steeply to a headland, which provided us with great views along the coastline in both directions. We continued along the edge of the cliff, occasionally dipping down to cross a cove, and passed a promontory that once held Ballyreagh Castle, though very little remains of the building today.

After about four miles of coastal path we dropped down into West Bay at Portrush. Here I bumped into the always enthusiastic Ricky from Alive Surf School and parted him from some of his hard earned before heading up to the car park to meet Gerard's partner, Kirsty. It was at this point that Gerard had to bow out and so I said my farewells to him and Kirsty and headed on round the long promenade that sweeps around West Bay Strand, passing the screams coming from Barry's funfair on the way. I made a quick call into Babushka Cafe at the harbour to say hello to the young and energetic proprietors, George and Shonee, and then headed through the harbour and up and round Ramore Head, enjoying the panoramic views along the North Coast to the west and east as I went. These were views I had seen many times before, as Jacqui and I had often walked the path round Ramore, but they were views of which I will never tire. Portrush had been mine and Jacqui's second home for many years. It would definitely have been our first home if it hadn't been for little inconveniences, such as schools and careers, that kept us shackled to Belfast. If that sounds as if living in Belfast was like a prison sentence, it certainly wasn't. We loved life in Belfast also, but it was always a wonderful feeling to be able to escape the big city for the more relaxed and chilled world that the North Coast offered. We had always hoped to move to the North Coast together when we retired; but that dream, like so many others, had now turned to dust.

Rather than heading directly to East Strand, my intended finishing point for the day, I made a quick detour into the town to meet up with my good mate, Andy Hill of Troggs Surf shop and his wife, Frankie. Andy kindly invited me across the street to Kiwi's Bar for a very welcome pint, where I met barman, "Long John" McCurry. I was now in the company of two of the town's top surfers, as Andy and John were both Irish Champions many times over! New Zealander Kris, who runs Kiwi's, very kindly slipped me another cash donation before I left. It was "Brews and Blues" night at Kiwi's and it would have been nice to sit on and enjoy the music and craic, but I still had a few yards to walk. So I said my farewells and thank yous and headed on round to East Strand car park, where I was met again by my Portrush neighbours, Noreen and David. They drove me back to their house where I enjoyed a lovely meal and a few drinks. It was very relaxing and just what I needed after a long and warm, but very enjoyable day's walking.

There was little doubt that the miles passed much more easily when I was in the company of good people and, on all of the occasions I had company, I really enjoyed it. But it was also very important for me to have time on my own; time to think and to reflect. Time to deal with my grief and the demons that followed closely in its wake. Company distracted me from my grief, which was good in itself, but I also felt that I would never be able to deal with my grief effectively by either trying to ignore it or by allowing myself to be constantly distracted from it. So, yes, I really enjoyed the company when I had it, but at other times I wanted to be on my own, really needed to be on my own – hard as that might have been on occasions. Most of the following day was going to be walked on my own and the day's walk was also going to begin at a place of great personal significance to me (and Jacqui!). East Strand in Portrush was one of three special places that Jacqui had requested that her ashes be left, the others being in Jacqui's favourite spot in our garden at home in Belfast and at Ramoan Church in Ballycastle, where her parents lay in the embrace of Knocklayde and Fair Head. East Strand was a place that held many happy memories, but it was also a place of sad parting, a fact reflected in a poem I had composed back in April after I had carried out Jacqui's final wish.

Farewell

A cherry tree planted together all those years ago
Now standing mature and strong, keeping watch

Knocklayde mountain bathed in glorious golden sunlight
Fair Head majestically sweeping down to touch the sea

Wet sand reflecting the warm colours of the rising sun
The gentle wash of the tide creeping up the beach

A hand written note on a fish shaped piece of paper
A wise old bookmark, a small elephant carved from wood

Special places, special things, special meanings
Honoured to carry out these final tender acts

Fortunate to have known such undying love
Farewell until we find each other once again

Shipwrecks

I woke up to another glorious day in Portrush and after a quick bite of breakfast, I got a lift down to Portrush Harbour with Noreen. Here I was met by three lovely ladies from the local committee of Cancer Research UK from Coleraine. They had gathered at Babushka Kitchen Café to show their support for my walk and also to give me a generous donation. I also met George again and he very kindly invited me for lunch the following day, which was one of my scheduled rest days.

After saying farewell to all the well-wishers at Babushka, Noreen then left me round to East Strand car park and I headed down onto the beach to begin my walk. However, before setting off, I paused here for a few minutes reflection, as I recalled a beautiful morning back in April when I had performed a little private ceremony here at sunrise to carry out part of Jacqui's final wishes to have some of her ashes scattered on this, her favourite beach. She had told me that she felt that she would still be able to be close to me when I came here to surf. East Strand will therefore always be one of those special places where I will feel particularly close to Jacqui. It had been the starting point for countless numbers of our walks out towards Whiterocks and back, Jacqui and I unashamedly holding hands as we went, never out of love and forever comfortable in each other's presence. I smiled at the memories and particularly at the fact that it was invariably me that would say "right, that's far enough, my short legs have had it". Today, I would be walking all the way to Whiterocks and then some! Unfortunately, I would have no hand to hold on this occasion. I felt that Jacqui was not far away though, as she and her fellow weather angel, Rosaleen, worked their magic yet again to produce another fabulous day. So I lifted my head and set off on my unlikely pilgrimage once again.

The walk along East (or Curran) Strand, which merges with Whiterocks to form nearly two miles of beach, was lovely, with the sand dunes to my right and the sea and the Skerries to my left. The Skerries, or Skerry Islands, are a small group of rocky islands just off the north coast. The term skerry is derived from an Old Norse word *sker*, which means "a rock in the sea". The dunes along this strand are covered with a thick coat of Marram Grass and Jacqui and I often imagined the dunes as a huge sleeping green monster, especially when the wind blew over the grass and made it look like fur being ruffled in the breeze. Behind the dunes, and hidden from view when on the beach, lies the world famous Royal Portrush Golf Course. There were plenty of walkers on the beach and a horse and rider came thundering across the sands at one point. As I approached the limestone cliffs that make up Whiterocks at the end of the sandy beach, the rider had taken her horse into the sea for a bit of a paddle. It was an idyllic scene with the blue sky and sea and the Skerries in the background. Upon reaching Whiterocks, I decided to take a new pathway that had only recently been created, rather than follow the way markers and maps, which hadn't yet caught up with this recent development. I was certainly glad I had, as the new footpath followed a trail across the tops of the white limestone cliffs for quite a distance and provided much better views than I would have had if I had followed the official route.

When the path eventually met up with the roadway, it was only a fairly short walk along a good sidewalk before reaching the Magheracross viewing point, which offered superb views to the west towards Whiterocks, the Skerries, Portrush and Donegal beyond, and to the east towards Dunluce Castle, the Giants Causeway, and even the island of Islay off the coast of Scotland. I arrived here at the same time as a German family of four, who were cycling around the coast, and I took the opportunity to ask them to take a few photographs of me and I did the same for them. We got chatting and I found out that they were the Theil family, who were originally from Stuttgart, but who had been living in England for the last 15 years or so. This was their first visit to Northern Ireland and they were enjoying it very much, particularly now that the weather had improved! Mr Theil wouldn't let me go without giving me a donation. The kindness of strangers demonstrated once again!

After wishing each other well on our respective journeys, I headed on along the A2, passing the magnificent ruins of the medieval Dunluce Castle on its dramatic setting, perched on a crumbling basalt outcrop above the sea. There has been a castle here since the thirteenth century, and it was the seat of power for the MacDonnell clan who dominated this part of Ulster during the sixteenth and seventeenth centuries. Dunluce Castle has also made its way into more modern culture, having been cited as the inspiration for CS Lewis' description of Cair Paravel in the Narnia books and also famously appearing on the artwork of the Led Zeppelin album, "House of the Holy". Just beyond the castle, I paused for a while to watch a man and two boys "tombstoning", jumping into the sea from the cliffs. They were well kitted out in wetsuits, buoyancy aids and helmets and they certainly seemed to know what they were doing. It definitely looked like great fun. Certainly more fun than what I had been contemplating only two days previously at Binevenagh!

From here it was on along the pavement towards the holiday resort of Portballintrae, but just before turning off the A2, a car pulled in a short distance ahead of me. I assumed it was someone pulling in to use their mobile or something and so I was very surprised and delighted when another one of my many surfing mates stepped out of the car to greet me and wish me all the best. Rory was on his was to meet his wife in Portballintrae, when he spotted me walking and decided to stop to say hello. Walking the Ulster Way can certainly be a lonely business at times and it's little unexpected moments like this that would sometimes brighten up my day.

I then followed the road down into Portballintrae, past the pretty bay and harbour and on round to the public car park overlooking Runkerry Strand. Remembering once again Rachel Joyce's advice, I stopped here for a little rest and a snack at one of the picnic tables, enjoying the views over the bay to Runkerry House. After my short break, I followed the path from the car park down to the footbridge over the River Bush. On the other side of the bridge, I joined the wooden boardwalk running behind the beach and the dunes and this took me along the riverbank and subsequently to a path running alongside the tracks of the Giant's Causeway and Bushmills Railway. This is a narrow gauge heritage railway that runs for just two miles along the track bed of the former Giants Causeway Tram and it provides a passenger link between the historic town of Bushmills and the famous stone columns of the Giants Causeway World Heritage site.

At the far end of Runkerry Strand I followed a path that brought me round the front of the splendid sandstone building of Runkerry House and up onto the cliff tops of Runkerry Point. I stopped to take a photograph here and a lovely elderly gentleman, who was out walking with a woman that may have been his daughter, offered to take one of me. I took him up on his offer and we got talking and before leaving he reached into his pocket and handed me some cash, saying that he could relate to my story as he had been through something similar himself a number of years ago. Another unprompted act of kindness by a total stranger; as well as a reminder that my loss was in no way unique. From here I proceeded on round Runkerry Point and soon found myself standing on a flat grassy area that was extremely busy with tourists. I then noticed that this flat grassy area had rows of reinforced glass panels in it and it suddenly dawned on me that I was actually standing on the roof of the Giant's Causeway Visitor Centre. This centre is without doubt a genius of architectural design. From above, it blends in with the hillside perfectly and yet it presents a striking facade to the visitor arriving at ground floor level. It was my first visit and I was hugely impressed; almost as much as I had been when I had first visited the Causeway itself with Jacqui years before.

I enjoyed a lovely lunch in the company of a nice Spanish couple from Madrid who were visiting the Causeway as part of a coach party that was travelling around Ireland, North and South. They were very interested when I told them about the historical connection between the Causeway and their home country – the wreck of the Girona, a Spanish galleon, lay just a short distance further along the coast. The visitors' centre was thronging with people and it was great to see so many foreign visitors now coming to these shores – changed times indeed!

After lunch, the directions for the Ulster Way gave a choice of two options at this point; either to take the low route to visit the Causeway itself at sea level or to follow the Red Trail along the cliff path. I had been to see the fabulous hexagonal stones and columns of the Causeway several times before, most recently just the year before with Jacqui and my son Matthew from the ocean side, courtesy of Portrush Sea Tours, which had been wonderful. So on this occasion, I chose the cliff path and enjoyed the almost aerial views of the Causeway as I proceeded along the high road. It was simply stunning to view the rock formations from this elevated position, approximately 100m above the ocean, and I saw the Causeway in a totally new light. The fabulous weather helped immensely! I wondered if my weather angels were also enjoying the views.

I continued along the cliff path for many miles and many headlands and coves. The cliffs along this stretch are no ordinary cliffs. They are cliffs that are made up of tall vertical columns of basalt rock that formed from cooling lava flows millions of years ago and the almost corrugated effect in the rock faces that has resulted is truly a wonder to behold. In a number of places, the columns appeared between layers of more regular rock and it almost seemed as if the columns had been inserted in order to support the layers above – nature's architecture at its most splendid. On one headland called Chimney Tops, with its impressive rock pinnacles or "chimney stack" formations, I met a young Chinese man who wanted me to take a photograph of him on the very edge of the cliff. After taking a couple of shots of him, he kindly returned the favour as I posed rather precariously on the end of the headland directly above the stacks. Memories of my experience on the cliffs at Binevenagh returned, but thankfully on this occasion my demons did not make an appearance, probably because I was in company – my demons were devious and would only ever appear when they knew I was alone and vulnerable.

Directly below this headland there is a finger of dark rock that extends treacherously into the sea from the edge of Port na Spaniagh cove, as if waiting to snag anything that might pass too close. And it is indeed this finger of basalt, called Lacada Point, that ripped open the hull of the Girona, one of the ships from the ill-fated Spanish Armada, back in 1588, with the loss of an estimated 1,300 lives. It had been carrying so many as it had picked up 800 survivors from two other Spanish shipwrecks that had floundered off the Irish coast at Mayo and Donegal. The bodies from the Girona were washed into Port na Spaniagh and written accounts tell of a pile of white bones that once existed in the bay just above the shoreline, which were known locally as "The Spaniard's Bones". In the 1960s, a team of divers investigated the wreck of the Girona, which still lies below the waters in Port na Spaniagh, and they salvaged the greatest haul of Armada treasure ever recovered, which is now on display in Belfast's Ulster Museum.

Thoughts of the Girona brought to mind some words I had read recently, in which the anonymous author had compared losing a loved one to being shipwrecked. The words had really struck a chord with me.

"....As for grief, you'll find it comes in waves. When the ship is first wrecked, you're drowning, with wreckage all around you. Everything floating around you reminds you of the beauty and the magnificence of the ship that was, and is no more. And all you can do is float. You find some piece of the wreckage and you hang on for a while. Maybe it's some physical thing. Maybe it's a happy memory or a photograph. Maybe it's a person who is also floating. For a while, all you can do is float. Stay alive..."

And I suppose that's what I had to do now – stay afloat; stay alive. So, not wishing to add my bones to Port na Spaniagh, I left the Chinese man to take more of his precarious photos and I returned to the safety of the cliff path to continue eastwards along this stunning stretch of coastline. The path undulated past the dramatic rock scenery around Benbane Head and climbed very gradually to the highest point at Hamilton's Seat, at the tip of the headland. From this point, I began a steady descent around more headlands before stopping at Port Moon to take in the magical views across the sea to Rathlin Island and Scotland. I noticed that there was a little cottage down by the shore in Port Moon, which looked to be very well kept. I later learned that this was a shelter or "bothy" that is managed and maintained by the Causeway Coast Kayak Association and it can be booked to stay in for a small fee. A real get away from it all spot, but a trip here requires a fair bit of preparation beforehand as it has no mains water or electricity and can only be accessed by suitable landing craft – not unlike to the lunar rock that Port Moon takes its name from.

Not far beyond Port Moon, I came upon the sparse ruins of Dunseverick Castle. Little remains of this ancient promontory fort. – in fact, only the ruins of the gate-lodge actually remain standing. However, despite its rather dilapidated condition, it still makes for quite a striking sight, given its commanding position on the rock promontory high above the ocean. The terrain became a little more challenging beyond the ruins of Dunseverick Castle. I started to tire and, despite the spectacular scenery still on offer, I found the final mile and a half of this stretch quite a struggle. There were quite a few styles along this bit of the walk and at one, rather than stepping nimbly off the high step to the ground below, I sort of hesitated and teetered on the edge before half falling forward and only just managing to stay on my feet as I landed on the other side. If you have ever seen the Father Ted episode where Mrs Doyle falls of the window sill, you will have a fair idea of how my dismount from the style must have looked!

I struggled on though and the route gradually dropped in level and brought me to Dunseverick Harbour and on towards Gid Point. Here, I passed through a natural, but quite magical, basalt archway in the rocks that suddenly revealed stunning views of the wide sweep of Whitepark Bay and the coast beyond. Beyond the arch, I had to clamber over a very stony area that led round to the very quaint little hamlet of Portbraddan, with what is reputed to be the smallest church in Ireland, the tiny St Gobban's Church. Noreen arrived in her car from Portrush to pick me up just as I approached the church – perfect timing! She got out of her car to join me and enjoy the beautifully calm and balmy evening and the sight of the magnificent Whitepark Bay laid out before us. From here, there were also wonderful views of Rathlin Island and Fairhead in the distance, with clear views of Scotland's Mull of Kintyre beyond that. We then headed back to her house where I joined her and David for a lovely evening meal. Both Noreen and David had been wonderful over the last couple of days. Thankfully, I had the following day off in Portrush to rest my weary legs, and to take George up on his offer of lunch at Babushka, before setting off again on Wednesday for Jacqui's hometown. No doubt another very emotional day lay ahead. I was pleased that my daughter Hannah and her boyfriend, Jonny, were going to join me for the next section. My walk was now covering the land of Jacqui's childhood – around Ballycastle and the North Antrim coast. Her voice was steadily becoming stronger in my head as I travelled around this coastline and passed through the many places where we had once walked together.

Teardrops

Wednesday 26 August – Portbraddan to Breen Bridge
Hi love.

Hi sweetheart. I see you had Hannah with you today.

Yes, and Jonny too. Matt would have loved to have joined us also, but, as you know, he's in Berlin at the moment. And Christine left us over to Portbraddan from Ballycastle this morning and made us our lunches also!

It was lovely to see them supporting you. I'm so pleased that Matt went to Berlin with Finn as planned and it doesn't surprise me at all that my big sis looked after you all. I bet there were some wee treats in with the lunches as well?

There were indeed! And listen, your hometown done you proud!

Hmm, I think you mean "did you proud."

Ha! Did, done, do'd, whatever. I told you I would never learn. Anyway, before we left for Portbraddan, we met a group of people from the local Cancer Research UK Committee in the Marine Hotel. It was the largest turnout from the local committees so far! I think we have Christine to thank for rallying the troops. She has also been doing a fantastic job raising funds and the local community has been extremely generous to date.

Aw, that's lovely to hear, but again it doesn't really surprise me – about Christine or the community – they have always been wonderfully giving. You're not doing too bad yourself either in the fundraising stakes from what I see.

I thought you didn't have the internet and such things?

Ah, we have others means of finding these things out, you know. I could be looking over your shoulder right now!

That's nice to know. It would be even nicer to feel your hand on my shoulder though and to...

I know love, but better not go there. Tell me about the rest of your day.

Ah, I suppose you're right. Well, when we arrived in Portbraddan, it was a lovely day and I shot a little short video outside the very pretty little St Gobban's Church. Hannah, Jonny and I then waved goodbye to Christine and set off around the rocks at the base of the cliff face towards White Park Bay. It was quite a tricky start, clambering over the slippery rocks, but we soon reached the long stretch of sandy beach.

Such a gorgeous beach. I've always loved it.

It is, although today it was not without its challenges. Heavy rainfall overnight meant that we had to cross several small "rivers" that were flowing down the beach and some of them were quite wide. Anyway, when we got to the other end of the beach, you know where Elephant rock and the other arches and stacks are, we clambered over more boulders to reach a grassy area, which was alive with rabbits!

I don't think we ever walked that far round before?

No, we always stopped at the rocks and turned back – probably at my insistence too! Sorry.

Never be sorry, my dear. I always enjoyed our walks, no matter how short they were. In fact, I always thought that I did quite well to get you as far as the rocks.

Ha! That's a fair point. Anyway, today we followed a path through the grass until we reached Ballintoy Harbour, which, as you know, is now famous for being one of the locations for Game of Thrones.

Hmm, I really miss that series – you'll have to let me know what happens next.

I will, if I ever get round to watching it again. Anyway, despite it now being on the Game of Thrones tour route, Ballintoy was really peaceful when we were there and so we stopped for a wee break and also to take a few photos. We then headed up the road for a bit, before turning off at Ballintoy Church onto a wide grassy path that led around fields, past Sheep Island, and on to the car park at Carrick-a-Rede Rope Bridge. The weather had been lovely so far, but we could see the dark rain clouds coming in from the west. We went into the little cafe at the car park, where the girl behind the counter was happy for us to eat our packed lunches after we had ordered our drinks; coffee for me and Jonny and hot chocolate for Hannah, of course!

Of course! Always the sweet-toothed girl.

Yep, no change there. We had timed our lunch stop perfectly, because while we were in the cafe, it started raining quite heavily. However, by the time we had finished lunch and were ready to head on, the weather had cleared up again – thanks to you weather angels I suppose!

You're welcome.

We had decided not to make the one and a half mile detour to the rope bridge and back as it was very busy and we had all been to it before. We also reckoned that we had far enough to walk today as it was. So we climbed up the access road, past that quirky house on the corner, to join the main road and then turned left towards your home town. It was then a long four mile walk along this busy road, but there was plenty to see on the way, including views out to sea towards Rathlin, Islay and the Mull of Kintyre, and some four-legged friends, including an apple loving donkey! Unfortunately, we also saw quite a bit of rain along this stretch, although it was strange how Ballycastle, Fairhead and Knocklayde Mountain always seemed to be bathed in sunshine ahead of us! On the approach to Ballycastle, we took a planned diversion to stop at Ramoan Church to........well you know why.

I know dear. And all that rain was to help wash away the tears that I knew were coming.

Jesus Jacqui, between the tears and the rain you nearly drowned us in that graveyard!

Sorry, I hadn't allowed for my own tears also!

That's alright. Raindrops and teardrops. It's what connects us now. Hannah said that the weather matched our moods and she was perfectly right. Anyway, when the rain and the tears eased off, we headed on into The Diamond, where the Lammas Fair had only just been held a couple of days before.

"Did you treat your Mary Ann to some Dulse and Yellow Man at the Ould Lammas Fair in Ballycastle-O!"

Ha! Ha! I was just waiting for that! Christine met us again here and she took us round to briefly meet with Sean McKay, the butcher, who has been very supportive of the fundraising in Ballycastle. I think she might be hoping to get a wee bit more discount off her sausages as well, ha! ha! We then headed for the entrance to Ballycastle Forest, but we had to take shelter under the little covered gateway here as another heavy downpour came through, accompanied by some very dramatic thunder this time!

We were trying to encourage Hannah and Jonny to turn back. I thought that they had walked far enough at this stage.

Ha! Ha! Well it didn't work. They were pretty determined to stick with me right to the end. So, when the rain eased off a bit, we started off along the Moyle Way and headed down the track under an old stone bridge and along what used to be the line of the old Ballycastle Railway. We then had a long steady climb up through the forest and over the shoulder of Knocklayde. You know, I would really love to come back to this area sometime and climb to the summit of Knocklayde. I only found out recently that there's a cairn at the top called Carn na Truagh in Irish, which means "Cairn of Sorrows".

Hmm, sounds like a cheerful place. You might want to wait a while before doing that.

Aye, you're probably right. Anyway, once we got to the top of the rise, the going became considerably easier, although we still had a fairly long walk along some narrow roads around the south-eastern slopes of the mountain. After about three miles, we approached the junction with the Glenshesk Road and were met by Christine, who had parked her car at the entrance to Breen Wood and had come to walk the last few hundred metres with us.

Ah, Breen Wood! An appropriate place to finish. And I'm sure Christine had a nice meal waiting for you when you all got back to hers.

She sure did and it was lovely. So, we had a fairly hard day's walk. But it was very special too, as we passed through many very familiar places – although there was that one particular place at Ramoan Church that I wish we weren't familiar with at all.

Ah, me too love, but I'm afraid that's just the way things are and there isn't a thing we can do about it.

I know, but it really is just bloody awful being stuck down here without you. Sometimes….sometimes I really just don't feel like I want to go on.

But you must sweetheart. There are too many people there who care about you and Matt and Hannah need you more than ever now. We will be together again someday, but you can't do anything to make it happen sooner so please don't try. No more cliff top dramas please!

Okay, I'll try.

There's no guarantees that you'll be accepted into the place I'm in anyway, you know. The standards are pretty high.

Ha! Cheeky sod!

Look, you are doing great and I am really proud of what you have achieved so far. Please keep it up. I know it's hard, but believe me, what you are doing is helping more people that you would ever believe. And you are enjoying your walk, aren't you?

Well yes, I suppose I am. You know, you really see things in a new light and from many different angles when you're on foot and have the time to fully appreciate it.

Hey, talk about different angles, love. You want to see it from where I am!!

Ha! Ha! I certainly hope to sometime, but only if they let me in, of course!

Ha! Ha! Just be a good little boy. And talking of being good, it's time you were in bed. You have a tough walk ahead of you tomorrow.

How do you know that?

Well, you'll be going through Breen Wood, won't you?

Yeah, it's right at the start.

Well, in my experience, the Breen's have always been a right awkward lot!

Ha! Ha! Very funny.

Good night, sweetheart.

Night night, my angel.

Crashing

Thursday 27 August – Breen Bridge to Glenariff Forest

Today was a day of obstacle courses, very steep hills, sunshine and rain, forest firebreaks, and lots of wet and very boggy ground! It started with me driving to the entrance to Breen Wood, where my sister-in-law, Christine, had collected me, Hannah and Jonny from at the end of the previous day's walk. It was a damp and grey morning as I left the car here and set off into the wood.

Surrounded by a more recently planted coniferous forest, Breen Wood is one of the few remaining areas of natural oak wood in Northern Ireland. Centuries ago, Ireland was covered in oak woods, but over the years they were cleared for farming or timber. The reason that Breen Wood survived is not really known, but an earth fort or rath that was once located here was believed by some to have been a sidh (pronounced shee), which was a mound under which it was believed the fairies lived in their "Fairy Palace". Since it was considered by many to be very unlucky to interfere with land associated with the fairies, this may have been why Breen Wood was spared, while the rest of the original oak woodland around it was destroyed. Incidentally, sidh is also the origin of Irish Bean sídhe, or banshee, a female spirit in Irish mythology that could strike fear into the bravest of souls. I therefore hurried on quickly, following the track around the wood for a little under two miles before turning off along a fire break between the pine trees.

The ground along this firebreak was very wet and boggy in places, but fairly manageable as I was able to use my walking poles to test the ground ahead. At the end of the firebreak, the route turned down a track running between the edge of the forest and a boundary fence and then weaved in and out through the trees themselves. At several places, I came up against a tangle of fallen trees across the pathway. It wasn't possible to find a way around them, so there was nothing for it but to crawl under and clamber over the fallen tree trunks. At times it more resembled a "tough mudder" obstacle course than a walk through the woods! Breen Wood had certainly proved to be pretty awkward alright, just as Jacqui had predicted. If only I'd thought to bring a chainsaw with me! It was therefore with much relief that I finally exited the forest to cross a wooden footbridge over the Glenshesk River and join an earthen track that led upstream. It was great to be out in the open again and I was walking along quite happily, when I rounded a bend in the track and was suddenly confronted with the very unexpected sight of hundreds of mallard ducks sitting in my path! They parted as I moved towards them but didn't appear to be overly concerned by my presence.

I reckoned that the ducks must have been farmed and my suspicions turned out to be correct when, a short while later, a man came down the hillside on a quad bike with a hunting rifle slung over his shoulder. Before I managed to "duck" and run for cover, he pulled up alongside me on the track and stopped his quad. He turned out to be a really friendly guy and we had a great chat. His name was Seamus and he farmed the ducks alongside the Glenshesk River for hunting purposes. He told me that they organised an annual shoot to raise funds for a cancer charity and said that his daughter was currently battling the disease, but thankfully doing well. He had, let's just say, some rather "unorthodox" views about cancer and why a cure wasn't available to the common man, but I didn't feel like getting into that area. So I sidestepped the conversation by asking him for a photo. I took a selfie with him and he had to get the rifle into the picture. *"Don't fuck with the mountain men!"* was his comment as I took the photo and we both burst out laughing. He then headed on up the track, splashing through a stream cutting across the track as he went. *"Damn,"* I thought, as he sped away, I should have hitched a lift over that stream! As it turned out, I just about managed to leap across it without getting my feet too wet.

I met Seamus again further on up the track and he helped direct me across to another firebreak in a forest plantation, which required a climb over some fairly rough, boggy ground to get to. This firebreak linked up with a forest track, which I followed for just over a mile to reach a road that took me down to the entrance to Orra Beg, where I stopped to have the lovely sandwiches that Christine had prepared for me that morning. From here, I made the steady climb up the track through the trees and then on up to the 508m high summit of Slieveanorra. The ground either side of the track was pretty rough and the directions suggested that one should spare a thought for the doomed members of the McQuillan and O'Neill clans who perished here with no such firm surface to save them. Slieveanorra is from the Irish Slieve-an-Aura, meaning "hill of battle", and it was here that the Battle of Aura was fought in the middle of the sixteenth century between the MacDonnells, led by Sorley Boy MacDonnell, against the McQuillans and O'Neills. Before the battle, the

MacDonnell clan covered the boggy ground with rushes to make it appear solid. Members of the rival McQuillan and O'Neill clans were tricked and floundered into chest-deep bog, only to be slaughtered as they tried to struggle free. It seems that we have always been fighting among ourselves in this wee land of ours. Thankfully, it was peaceful today, as I enjoyed the superb views from the summit, looking back at Knocklayde to the north and ahead to Trostan Mountain to the southeast.

I also came across a memorial erected on Slieveanorra to commemorate the lives of the American Service men who perished here when their B17 Flying Fortress bomber crashed in mist during WWII, on 3 October 1942. It had lost its way in cloud cover and had become separated from six other bombers en route from Newfoundland to Scotland. The crash killed eight of the ten personnel on board, all but one of them in their 20's. The Slieveanorra crash reminded me of another air crash in the area that had happened one year later, the facts of which I had only become aware of recently. On 18 October 1943, a British twin-engine Anson based in Blackpool, was flying near Ballycastle when it was caught in a downdraft, which caused it to strike high ground. The pilot attempted a forced landing, but the aircraft struck a tree before crashing into a house in Glenshesk owned by a Charles Blaney. Mr Blaney's wife and their five children were at the house at the time, along with a young girl from County Donegal, 22-year-old Josephine McGroarty, who was staying with the Blaney family. Josephine was standing outside the house with her boyfriend, as the aircraft came sliding into its final impact with the house. Josephine was tragically killed as were two of the crew on board the plane. Miraculously, Josephine's boyfriend was thrown clear and survived. The pilot was thrown from the aircraft and he landed in the children's room and they also all miraculously survived. It turns out that Josephine's boyfriend was none other than John Greer. He was known to everyone as Jack and he would later marry Annie Christie and have four children - three girls and a boy. The youngest girl was born in 1961 and was named Jacqui and in 1987 she became my wife!

Jack carried the tragic story of Josephine around with him for the rest of his days and never spoke of it. Neither Jacqui, nor any of her siblings ever knew of it and no one knows if Annie, Jack's wife and Jacqui's mother, ever knew of this remarkable story either. Both Jack and Annie passed away a number of years ago and Jacqui's sister Christine only found out about the events by chance a few months after Jacqui's death, when she was sent a copy of an official account of the tragedy. As I stood at the top of Slieveanora, I wondered at the vagaries of life and of death. What would have happened if Jack had also died in the air crash back in 1943? Or what if Josephine had also survived and she and Jack had subsequently married? Jacqui would never have existed. I would never have met and married her. We would never have had Matt and Hannah. I wouldn't be grieving now. Everything would have been totally different. For a split second back on 18 October 1943 all the possible outcomes must have hung in the balance as fate casually flipped its coin. I'm glad it happened the way it did though. Obviously not that Josephine and two of the crew were killed. I'm glad that Jack survived and married Annie and that they had Jacqui. Although it ultimately ends with me in this awful place of mourning, the thought of never having met Jacqui, never having married her, never having loved her, was incomprehensible. As so eloquently expressed by Alfred Lord Tennyson, "Tis better to have loved and lost, than never to have loved at all." I could not bear the thought of Jacqui never having been in my life. I never wished for "the eternal sunshine of the spotless mind".

Between sixteenth century battles and WWII aircraft crashes, all these stories of life and death and fate were weighing too heavily on my mind. I needed to get off this mountain fast and I set about just that, as I attempted to suppress the dark thoughts that were in danger of overwhelming me. Unfortunately, progress was slow as there followed yet another interminably long tramp over very wet and boggy ground. However, there were occasional little round mounds of earth, fringed with spiky grass, that provided a lighter moment as well as some firmer steps through the bog. They looked like a series of little bald heads, fringed with green hair, poking up just above the surface of the bog. I couldn't help imagining that I was walking on the heads of those poor McQuillans and O'Neills as I went. I almost apologised as I put my foot down on each of their bald pates! Anyway, heads or not, I eventually reached another firebreak through another forest plantation. The going here was again extremely boggy in places and, not for the first time, I was very glad to have my walking poles, both to test the ground ahead and to help lever myself over the worst bits. Although, for the first time on the entire walk, I felt the water get inside my boots.

With much relief, I finally reached a gravel path and then a roadway. However, this in turn led me to a point where a sign directed me off the road again and up the slopes of Trostan, Antrim's highest peak at 550 metres. The ground was rough and wet in places and it was quite a steep and demanding climb, but at least the route was well way-marked. The rain came in as I made my way up Trostan, which only added to the challenge. Thankfully the route didn't take me all the way to the summit, but instead skirted round it and down the south-western shoulder of the mountain. However, it was around this point that my emotional defences finally crumbled and the pain of my loss came screaming in at me again out of the blue and I was brought to my hands and knees. Grief was like that. One minute, I was cruising along steadily, enjoying the world around me, and the next thing I knew I was under attack, being forced into a tail spin and heading for a crash. After a time I slowly regained control and I struggled to pull myself up. I climbed to my feet and, as I descended towards Glenariff Forest, I was greeted with the sight of a glorious rainbow, the first of many that would dramatically and reassuringly steak the dark skies with colour in the coming days. Wherever there was darkness, there could also be light.

There were more forest firebreaks, boggy tracks, fallen trees and streams to cross, as I trudged onwards through Glenariff Forest, eventually emerging from the trees to pass the beautiful Essathohan Waterfall and follow the river downstream into Glen Ballyeamon. I then followed a number of gravel tracks for about a mile through another section of Glenariff Forest to meet the main entrance into Glenariff Forest Park. Cue the next downpour! Fortunately, I was able to take partial shelter under one of the large trees at the entrance to the Park and watch the fairies dancing with abandon on the roadway. I waited until the deluge eased enough to allow me to press on for the final three quarters of a mile, which took me up to the main visitors' car park. Here, in spite the poor weather, I was still able to enjoy impressive views of the cliffs and waterfalls of Glenariff valley, although the promised views of Scotland's Mull of Kintyre across the Sea of Moyle were out of the question today!

Christine arrived at the Forest car park to rescue me before closing time and drove me back to Ballycastle. We enjoyed some stunning skies and intense rainbows out over the sea along the way and I was treated to another wonderful meal once again at Christine and Nigel's before heading back to base at Portrush, absolutely exhausted and so glad that the following day was a planned rest day. I certainly felt that I needed a bit of time to recover from what had been a couple of physically and emotionally challenging days.

The Prisoner

Saturday 29 August – Ballycastle to Waterfoot

Following my Friday rest day, I drove over to Ballycastle from Portrush on Saturday morning and parked opposite the Marine Hotel at the seafront, where I met Noelle, a good friend from university days. Noelle was also one of Jacqui's best friends from way before that, when they were brought together as part of a cross community initiative during their school days in Ballycastle.

I probably need to explain why I was back in Ballycastle again, having already passed though it only a few days previously. It so happens that the Ulster Way offers two alternative routes between Ballycastle and Waterfoot. The first route is the Moyle Way, which I had largely already walked on Wednesday and Thursday – that was the inland route via Breen Wood, Glenshesk, Slieveanorra, Trostan and Glenariff, leaving only the stretch from Glenariff to Waterfoot yet to complete. The second route follows a more coastal route by road around the north-east Antrim coast and is really intended as a "wet weather" alternative to walking the inland route should the weather be too poor to allow for safe passage through the glens and over the mountains. I had decided right from the planning stage that, if weather permitted, I was going to walk both routes. Ballycastle was Jacqui's hometown and if anywhere on the Ulster Way deserved special attention from me, it was this very town.

Noelle and I set off from the front, close to the very striking Children of Lir sculpture, crossed the footbridge over the Margy River and then stepped onto the marvellous Ballycastle Beach. It was a beautiful morning and Ballycastle was looking at its best as we headed across the golden sands, taking in the views that Jacqui grew up with and loved – the town and harbour behind, Rathlin over the sea to the left, the golf course and dunes to the right, and Pans Rocks and Fair Head ahead of us. Before reaching the end of the beach we cut up onto the road towards Corrymeela. We weren't too far along it before I had the lovely surprise of bumping into a work colleague, John, and his wife, Yvonne, coming the other way. They were up for a break in their motor-home and had just set off on a mornings walk themselves. It was great to meet them and of course a few photos had to be taken! After a brief chat, Noelle and I headed on and it wasn't too long before we reached Corrymeela, a residential centre on the north coast that has promoted the principles of peace and

Dunluce Castle, with Runkerry Head and the Giant's Causeway in the distance

A serene Ballintoy Harbour

A rainbow takes a seat on the throne that is Red Bay Castle

The Children of Lir take flight with Fair Head and the Mull of Kintyre in the background

reconciliation in Northern Ireland for over 50 years. It was here that Noelle had to bow out as she had other pressing engagements for the day.

From Corrymeela, I soldiered on alone and joined the main Cushendun Road for half a mile before reaching the Barnish Coffee Shop & Tea Room in Ballyvoy village. It is run by my sister-in-law, Christine, and her daughter, Emma, and I couldn't have passed by without dropping in for a quick hello and a coffee. I was delighted that a lady called Kate, one of my growing army of supporters, came into the café to wish me all the very best. As usual though, I had to pull myself away from the good company sooner than I would have liked, to get back on the road once more. I continued along the main road for a short distance before joining the narrower and quieter Torr Road. This road climbed gradually for the next four miles and I kept turning to look back at the ever present and ever changing mountain much loved by Jacqui, Knocklayde, and the island of Rathlin that Jacqui saw from her family home on North Street practically every day of her childhood.

As I approached the headland of Torr around the shoulder of Greenamore Mountain, the views across the sea towards Scotland began to open up before me. Today was a particularly good day for spotting Scotland and, as I travelled round this north-east coast of Northern Ireland, I was able to clearly pick out the Mulls of Oa and Kintyre, the islands of Isla and Jura, Cnoc Moy and Sanda Island and even the distinctive conical shape of Ailsa Craig in the distance. Coolranny, on round the coast from Torr Head, is only 12 miles away from Scotland, which is reputed to be the shortest distance between Scotland and Northern Ireland. The descent to the hamlet of Torr itself was quite steep, but it was a delight to walk down through the fuchsia lined roadways in the early afternoon sunshine, with Torr Head and the sea views beyond always providing an interesting backdrop. Jacqui always thought that fuchsia blooms looked like little angels and I will forever think of them as just that! Both sides of the roadway were just a mass of blooms – a multitude of angels.

To say that the next few miles were rather hilly would be a bit of an understatement and I was envious of Mickael, a guy from Brittany, who I met. Mickael had been on "The Wind Trip", riding around the coast of the UK and Ireland since mid-July on his specially designed trike with a sail to promote travel without fossil fuels. He was heading towards the Giant's Causeway and was covering more ground than I was in a day. I waved Mickael on his way as he glided off effortlessly. I meanwhile climbed back up on "Shanks's pony" (my own legs) and headed on slowly to the very picturesque village of Cushendun, which means "foot of the dark brown river".

It was still a beautiful day and Cushendun is a beautiful place, so I stopped here at a picnic area by the sea to enjoy my lunch, which Christine had kindly prepared for me that morning. It was an absolutely delightful spot to relax and refuel and it was lovely to see lots of other people doing the same – lots of happy families enjoying the day out. But once again, I experienced the now familiar feeling of bitter-sweet emotions as I recalled the last time I had been here. It had been on another beautiful, sunny, summer's day in 2012, two years BC – Before Cancer! Jacqui was of course with me and life then was just wonderful. I struggled to fight off the demons I could feel gathering around me. I needed to move again and so I quickly finished my lunch and I crossed over the River Dun, where I came upon the strange sight of a bronze statue of a goat that had a real live goat tethered to it. "JOHANN" was the name of the bronze goat and, according to the inscription on the statues plinth, it was erected to mark the fact that a goat was the last animal to be culled in the foot and mouth outbreak of Spring 2001. As to why there was a live goat tethered to the statue, I have no idea, but then perhaps it should just be viewed as another quirky little thing about this unique village.

Much of Cushendun looks like it's been relocated from Cornwall, as most of its old-fashioned cottages were designed specifically to look like they came from that part of England. The idea was developed in 1912 by Lord Cushendun, who wanted to pay tribute to his Cornish wife and he enlisted the help of a renowned architect, Clough Williams-Ellis, to carry out the work. Williams-Ellis would subsequently achieve lasting fame by putting the Italian-style village of Portmeirion in the unfamiliar surroundings of the Welsh west coast. Many people of my vintage will probably remember Portmeirion best from the 1960's TV series 'The Prisoner', where anyone who tried to escape the village was hunted down and trapped by "rovers", which were large, mysterious, balloon-like objects. It starred Patrick McGoohan, who was known only as Number Six and was always heard declaring *"I am not a number, I am a free man"*, at the start of each episode.

It was still a gloriously sunny day as I started to make my way out of the village of Cushendun, but suddenly, the emotions I had been attempting to suppress since sitting down to lunch, caught up with me. My own form of "rovers", my demons, swooped in and pulled the dark, smothering cloak of grief around me. What good was it being in this lovely place on this gorgeous day without Jacqui by my side? I felt totally abandoned and so alone. I was of course free to leave this village, but I certainly didn't feel like I was a free man. I felt trapped in this world, condemned to spend the rest of my days on this lonely planet without the one I loved. I hoped that the "gift" of longevity on my father's side of the family had missed me out; for me, longevity would be a curse, imprisoning me on Earth for many years to come with little hope of early release. I was heading into a tail spin again. I had to really fight to pull myself up before crashing. I tried my best to shrug off my demons, and the heavy cloak they would have me smother in, and just kept right on walking until I escaped the claustrophobia of the village.

Although I had left Cushendun in a dark mood, it had still been a gloriously sunny day. But only 15 minutes later I was caught in the first cloudburst of the day. The remainder of my journey was punctuated by sunshine and showers and yet more hills, but I recalled the Greencastle motto, "It's just a hill, get over it!" It had brightened up again as I approached the village of Cushendall, meaning "foot of the River Dall". The route into this village was along a very pleasant cliff pathway that led past the ruins of Layde Church, one of the oldest and most important historical sites in the Glens, and then hugged the coastline in a fairly elevated position that provided superb views of Cushendall Bay as I went. Cushendall is also known as the "Capital of the Glens" and I was initially intrigued by the Curfew Tower in the centre of the village. It was built in the early nineteenth century and its design had been influenced by towers seen in China at the time. I then learned that its original purpose was to imprison "idlers and rioters". I swiftly moved on – I had had enough thoughts of prisoners today already!

The sight that impressed me most when approaching and passing through Cushendall was without doubt the magnificent flat-topped Lurigethan Mountain that towered over the village. Its shape reminded me of the famous Table Mountain that overlooks Cape Town in South Africa – admittedly on a smaller scale though. The top of Lurigethan apparently hosts one of the most spectacularly situated Stone Age promontory forts in Ireland. I surely must have seen this mountain before on journeys by car up and down the coast, but I have to admit to never really having noticed it properly before. There is little doubt that you become much more aware of the landscape when you are on foot and have the time to fully appreciate it.

More showers and more rainbows were experienced as I headed out of Cushendall along the back roads to Waterfoot. As I approached the ruins of Red Bay Castle, I spotted a potential photo opportunity in the making and I rushed along the road and managed to get one of a rainbow "landing" on the castle, which appeared throne-like from the angle I shot it – it almost appeared as if the rainbow was having a seat! As I passed the small caves along the roadside into Waterfoot that looked like Hobbit dwellings, it reminded me that my son, Matthew, had recently messaged me from Berlin to say that I must have "feet of steel by now; either that or feet like Frodo Baggins!" I think the latter was closer to the truth. When I reached Waterfoot, I was picked up there by Christine, who took me back to Ballycastle for tea once again. Then it was back to Portrush to prepare for the next day's walk.

Despite another difficult episode as I was leaving Cushendun, it had been a gorgeous walk around the North-East Antrim coast, with beautiful new vistas constantly opening up before me as I proceeded along the local coastline. This was one of the things that I loved most about walking along the coast; how new and sometimes dramatic land and seascapes often suddenly revealed themselves as I came over a rise or round a bend. In many ways it had similarities to what I now recognised as the emotional, even spiritual, journey I was also on, as I walked around the Ulster Way. New insights into my grief, and my responses to it, and new perspectives on the innate goodness of people were being revealed to me almost on a daily basis.

When I had originally conceived the idea for my pilgrimage, it was mostly about walking miles and about raising money. Now I was beginning to realise that my pilgrimage was offering me so much more. It was also teaching me how to deal with my grief and my dark demons when they suddenly and unexpectedly appeared, and how to pick myself up and move on after each bruising assault. I was also being taught to be more open to appreciating the kindness of friends and strangers and recognising that people will always help if they can. And it was now also becoming clearer to me that, even though Jacqui had gone, there was still light and there was still hope and that her presence would always be there to guide me towards it, whether that be over the bridge, down off the hillside or back from the edge of the precipice.

Blackbirds Return

Sunday 30 August – Glenariff Forest to Glenarm

I drove to Glenariff and met Noelle at Laragh Lodge as we had pre-planned the previous day. She left her car here and took a lift with me up to the visitor's car park in Glenariff Forest Park. The kind gentleman at the pay-booth let us park for free when I explained that we were walking for charity. Noelle accompanied me down through the forest trail for about a mile, as far as Laragh Lodge again. Unfortunately, she hadn't time to walk further, but I was really touched that she had driven all the way over from Ballycastle to lend her support so early on a Sunday morning. We said our goodbyes and she headed back home again, as I headed on down the Glenariff valley, along a narrow country road.

Laragh Lodge sits just on the edge of the forest, so the views during the rest of my journey down the valley were not constrained by foliage and I was able to enjoy the magnificent landscape as I went. And there was much to see on this stretch, ranging from the cliffs and waterfalls at either side of the valley to various farming activities and life along the Glenariff River in the valley itself. The Ulster Way directions informed me that the name Glenariff translates from the Gaelic as "ploughman's glen", probably in reference to the fertility of its soil, and that it is the biggest of County Antrim's nine glens, often being referred to as the "Queen of the Glens". My weather angels were obviously on duty today and doing a fine job, which made the journey down this glacially formed glen all the more pleasant. As I was passing a farm yard, I spotted a nice vantage point for a photograph and signalled to the farmer, who was on a quad bike in the yard, to ask if it was okay to step in to his property to take a picture. He called out to me that it would be no problem, but said that I had better wait a minute as one of the two dogs that were with him was "none too sociable". So I waited patiently until he had gathered the two dogs up onto the quad with him, one up front and one behind, and he headed out of the yard and on down the road with a wave. A few moments later I stepped into the yard to get my landscape shot, but not before I captured one of the farmer and the two dogs on the quad heading down the road!

Further on down the valley, the route took a left turn over a style and along the edge of a field heading towards the banks of the Glenariff River. It looked like someone had tried to block off this route at several points but, to the determined walker (and I now counted myself as such) it offered little in the way of resistance. Although it did involve some climbing over barbed wire fencing, which I am never too keen on! I was puzzled as to why this attempt to block the route had been made, until I met a fisherman on the river further downstream. He informed me that the farmer who owned the land had deliberately blocked it off after a walker had slipped on his land and tried to sue him for compensation. Now I have no idea if the attempt to sue was successful or not, and I don't know all the facts, but based on what I heard I certainly hope that it wasn't. Quite a bit of the Ulster Way relies on farmers allowing people to pass through their property – they are not rights of way as far as I understand it. For a farmer to be sued for a slipping incident (in a field for goodness sake!) seemed, on the face of it anyway, to be utterly ridiculous.

I followed the rest of the very pleasant grassy path along the banks of the river (thankfully unobstructed) for about one and a half miles and eventually reached the main road at the appropriately named village of Waterfoot, which sits at the mouth of the Glenariff River. This marked the end of the mountain and glens route between Ballycastle and Waterfoot, the Moyle Way, and meant that I had now completed both of the alternative routes, having also walked the coastal route to Waterfoot the previous day. I was pretty determined not to leave any part of the Ulster Way un-trodden! At Waterfoot, I left the road for a while to walk along the beach instead – always a much more pleasurable proposition in my opinion! At the end of the beach, however, I had to join the road again and I followed it round the coast for a couple of miles, passing the limestone White Arch, the remains of Ardclinis Bridge and Ardclinis Church, the White Lady rock formation and the impressive stone facade of St Killian's College, better known perhaps as Garron Tower.

After another couple of miles, I stopped for a bite of lunch at a pleasant spot just above the stony shoreline, enjoying the views out across the Irish Sea. Although quite enjoyable, it certainly wasn't the quietest of spots as every motorcycle in the land seemed to be on the coast road today, roaring past on the road just above where I was sitting. After lunch, I continued along the coast road for about three miles to arrive at a very, very busy Carnlough. It turned out that I had arrived in the middle of Carnlough's "Blackbird O'Bash", a family fun day organised by the Honda Blackbird Club. The highlight of the day for the bikers was a ride-out from Carnlough to Portrush and back. So that explained the numerous motorbikes roaring along the coast road. Prior to stumbling upon this event, I had never even known that the blackbird had a motorbike named after it! It was hard not to view their presence here today, on the very day that my pilgrimage took me through Carnlough, as yet another positive sign that there were greater forces at work that I, or anyone else, fully understood. Sheer coincidence or not, it was another magical confluence of circumstances that filled my heart with hope. In stark contrast to the hustle and bustle of the event's various entertainments, the waters of Carnlough Harbour, and the boats moored there, presented a picture of pure tranquillity. However, I couldn't hang around to either enjoy the entertainment or admire the views and so I weaved through the crowds to continue with my solitary pilgrimage.

Once again, as I had done at Waterfoot, rather than heading out of Carnlough along the main road, I took a set of steps down onto the beach and headed over the sands. Here I enjoyed the sight of a horse being ridden leisurely through the shallows as well as a curlew, strolling casually through the water with its long and slender bill, characteristically curved down at the end and perfect for sifting through the sand. At the end of the beach I worked my way back up onto the main road again, but it thankfully wasn't too long before I reached the pretty little fishing village of Glenarm, well known for both its castle and its salmon fishery. Glenarm is from the Irish Gleann Arma, meaning "valley of the army" and takes its name from the glen in which it lies, the southernmost of the nine Glens of Antrim. The village was the family seat of the MacDonnells, who once occupied Dunluce Castle on the north coast and of course trounced the McQuillans and O'Neills at Slieveanorra. Glenarm Castle dates back to 1750 and its imposing entrance, the Barbican Gate, is at the heart of the village. Glenarm also claims to be the oldest town in Ulster, having been granted a royal decree by King John in the twelfth century. From here I had only another two miles to go to my prearranged pick up point. But they were two miles that surely tested my stamina, as they involved a steady and steep climb up a series of country roads to reach a point where the route left the road and crossed over a style to take off over the open wilderness of the Antrim Hills. But those hills were for another day. Today I was very happy to stop at the style after that long, tough, road climb and wait to be rescued by my brother-in-law Jonathan, and his wife Heather and their two young daughters. I thankfully didn't have long to wait for them to arrive and ferry me all the way back to my car in Glenariff Forest Park.

Before driving home, I made a quick visit by car back to Laragh Lodge and walked the short distance behind it to visit the lovely Ess-na-Crub Waterfall, which translates from the Gaelic as "the fall of the hooves", and the water was thundering down it today. Irish mythology relates how Glenariff's waterfalls were created by the warrior Oisín. Oisín was being pursued up the glen by Vikings and tried to climb a cliff to safety. A rope suddenly appeared to help him, which he realised was the tail of a huge horse. Once Oisín had safely reached the top of the cliff, the horse's tail then transformed into a stream and ran over the cliff edge, plunging the pursuing Vikings to their deaths. I found these tales from Irish mythology quite fascinating and they certainly added an extra dimension to my travels around the Ulster Way, often bringing the landscape vividly to life. Jacqui had always loved Irish folk-tales and I had bought her several books of such stories over the years. One of her favourite tales, partly because of its association with the North Antrim coast, was the Children of Lir. This told the tragic story of a wicked stepmother who, jealous of the love her four step-children had for each other and for their father, an ancient Irish king, used her magic to transform them into swans and banished them for 900 years, 300 of which were spent in the Sea of Moyle.

Out with you upon the wild waves, Children of the King!
Henceforth your cries shall be with the flocks of birds.

After 900 years of suffering, the spell was broken and all four children changed back into human form, but as they were now over 900 years old, they rapidly withered and died. Some versions of the tale go on to add a happier ending that says that the children then lived happily ever after as angels in heaven with their father and their birth mother. Although a terribly sad tale, even taking the "happy" ending into account, it is nonetheless a highly evocative story of love surviving throughout the centuries, regardless of the suffering and loss endured over all that time. I hope and pray that I meet my angel once again someday, no matter how long it takes.

Strangely though, I didn't ever dream of meeting Jacqui again. Not because I didn't want to, but simply because I never did. The peculiar thing is, that when I was asleep and I dreamt of Jacqui, we were at once back in a world where nothing had changed. She was with me as she always had been and everything was normal. It was always in a world prior to her illness and her death, which had not happened yet. It should have felt fantastic, but my own mind was also back in that time and place. Her illness and death were unknown to me in my dreams. So I wasn't, as you might expect, rejoicing to see her again because in that dream world she had never been away. When I woke out of the dream, however, I once again had to confront the reality that she was gone; that she was not lying beside me in bed waking up as normal also. These dreams were sweet and cruel at the same time. I looked forward to them and loathed them in equal measure. If only I would never wake up so that I could remain in the dream forever – always back in that happy, carefree time before cancer had destroyed our lives.

The Teacher

Tuesday 1 September – Glenarm to Ballynure

After enjoying another day's rest on Monday, I was up early to drive from Belfast to Ballynure to meet up with Jonathan again. I left my car in the Presbyterian Church car park in the centre of Ballynure. I was happy to use a church car park of any denomination – so long as it was free! Jonathan then gave me a lift back to the point on the road two miles out of Glenarm, where I had finished on Sunday evening. It was good to know that I had already completed that long, steep road climb out of Glenarm! I waved Jonathan off and climbed over the style into a field and began the penultimate day of my 1000 kilometre pilgrimage. I followed the way-markers up through fields and across several rocky hillocks for about a mile and a half to reach the summit of Black Hill at 381m. From here there were pretty good views back over the coast towards Garron Point and ahead to Larne Lough and Islandmagee. The unmistakable shape of Slemish Mountain was also clearly visible inland. Slemish is the core of a long extinct volcano and this was where, according to legend, St Patrick was brought as a slave in his youth to work as a shepherd – long before he set off on his Ulster Way pilgrimage of course!

The next four miles saw me traversing over fairly rough and grassy high ground close to the eastern edges of a series of hills. Many of these hills, such as Ballygilbert Hill, Scawt Hill, Robin Youngs Hill and Sallagh Braes, were edged with sheer cliffs that faced out over the east coast and the Irish Sea beyond. I would have to be careful up here! Given the elevation of this section of the route, there were certainly great views as I went. But the over whelming sense I had on these heather covered hills, segmented by occasional dry stone walls, was one of total isolation and of being in a complete wilderness. Apart from a few sheep, I never spotted another living thing the entire time I was in the hills. I had experienced a similar sense of isolation on many parts of the Ulster Way before, but perhaps never for such an extended period of time and in such an open and windswept landscape. You could easily lose yourself up here; and in more ways than one! Previously, such isolation had left me vulnerable to dark and dangerous thoughts. I remembered my feelings of despair between Donald's Hill and Rigged Hill, and at the cliffs of Binevenagh in particular. But thankfully, for some reason, my demons didn't descend today.

The lovely Ess-na-Crub Waterfall behind Laragh Lodge on the edge of Glenariff Forest

The wilderness of the Antrim hills with Agnew's Hill in the background

Hannah and I are welcomed back by the pupils of Greenisland Primary School

Some of my work colleagues who joined Hannah, Jonny and I at the Knockagh Monument

Perhaps I was beginning to cope with my grief better. A good friend had told me after Jacqui's death that I would probably never get over it, but that I would learn how to live with it. I'm not sure that I fully understood what he had meant at the time, but I could now totally relate to it. I hoped that perhaps the waves of grief might be starting to get further apart. Being a surfer I know what it is like to be caught in a series of breaking waves that never let up. No matter how hard you paddle, you just can't make it out through the succession of white water waves to reach the relative calm "out back", behind where the waves are breaking. It can be utterly exhausting trying, and sometimes simply impossible, to reach those calmer waters. Often I have been paddling against white water for ages only to realise that I have made no headway whatsoever. I have even had to admit defeat and give into the ocean and let the waves carry me back to shore, beaten and drained. However, at other times, even when the waves are breaking powerfully, there is sufficient time between them to allow me to make progress and slowly but surely make my way out to reach the calmer waters "out back". I felt that my waves of grief, which still swept over me powerfully at times, were beginning to hit me a little less frequently and allowing me some time for recovery, perhaps even progress, in between. I also felt that my pilgrimage, and the focus and purpose it gave me, played a significant role in holding back the waves of grief at times, allowing me to make this progress. Of course, I knew that getting through the grief each time was only a temporary measure. In the ocean, even when you get "out back", there is always the possibility of a larger wave coming through that catches you out and forces you back into the white water zone to face a struggle once again. Similarly, I had to accept that I would never truly get to the other side of grief and be able to remain there safely in the belief that grief has been finally defeated and left behind for good. Grief never goes away for good, just as surely as the ocean's waves will never cease for good. There may be periods of calm, but the waves will always return. Similarly with grief, there will be periods of calm, but grief will always return. I will never beat it. I must accept it as part of my life and learn how to live with it.

The cliffs at Sallagh Braes were quite dramatic with superb views over Ballygalley and beyond. Sallagh Braes is a semi-circular basalt escarpment that was created when glaciers cut into unstable slopes and caused a massive land slip. The cliffs of this natural amphitheatre are some 100 metres high and two kilometres long. I climbed over the fence here to get a better feel for the drop and capture some photos. At 100 metres, it would only take four and a half seconds to make this drop. I knew this because, believe it or not, there is a free-fall calculator on a website used by climbers that estimates such things – quaintly called "The Splat Calculator"! On this occasion, however, I was content to simply take in the views and take some photos. It was only when I climbed back that I saw a sign warning of dangerous cliffs and advising people not to climb over the fence. Oops!

From Sallagh Braes the route turned more inland and after about a mile and a half I stopped for lunch. Sitting on a style at the roadside, I enjoyed the impressive views of the next challenge ahead of me, which was Agnew's Hill. With a summit at 474 metres and an eastern face of dramatic cliffs, I thought that labelling Agnew's Hill a "hill" was rather unfair, particularly as I knew that, geographically, hills greater than 300 metres (1,000 feet) above sea level are normally regarded as mountains. After my lunch, I headed up the road for about half a mile and then climbed over another style to begin the steep ascent up the northern slopes of Agnew's Mountain – I had decided that for today at least it was going to be a mountain. If some people can make mountains out of molehills, then surely I can make one out of a bloody big hill!

It was about a mile to the summit of Agnew's Mountain and it was quite a strenuous climb for the most of it – a real "hands on the knees" job! There were super 360° views though when I reached the top; Slemish and Garron Point to the North, Larne and Larne Lough to the East, Ballyboley Forest and the distant Belfast Hills to the South, and Lough Neagh and the very distant Sperrins to the West. From here the mountain dipped a little and then rose again to a smaller peak and just beyond this point the route suddenly veered off, in a south-westwards direction, towards Ballyboley Forest. There then followed a mile of often very wet trudging through increasingly boggy land to reach the trees, but the route was very well way-marked so that at least I always knew that I was squelching in the right direction! It was with some relief though that I finally reached the forest boundary and picked up the forest track which led me through the trees for the next two miles. It was fairly easy going through the forest, but, as has often been the case in forests, it made for a fairly long and boring walk – at least my iPod was fully charged on this occasion. I eventually emerged out of the southern edge of the Ballyboley Forest to enjoy fine views ahead of South Antrim and the Belfast Hills – the end of my 1000K4J walk drawing ever closer. From here, I joined a series of minor roads that took me on a zigzag journey down off the southern Antrim

Hills for four miles to reach the village of Ballynure. It was a long but very pleasant walk in the early evening sunshine and I reached my car at the church car park, after a good eight hours out on the hills.

As I drove back home to Belfast, I found it hard to believe that tomorrow was going to be the final day of my unlikely pilgrimage. I only had another 13 miles to go to complete the challenge I had started out on two and a half months ago. In fact, I had already covered well over the 627 miles walked by the fictional Harold Fry, so I could have hung my boots up at this point if I had wanted to! But that was never a thought I was ever going to give any serious consideration to. There had only ever been one place to finish this walk and that was back at the place that I started out from on the 12 June. That was, of course, at Greenisland Primary School, where Jacqui had taught literally hundreds of young children over the 25 years plus that she had devoted to her profession, a profession that she was born to and loved. It takes a very special kind of person to teach, particularly infant children, and Jacqui was definitely one of the best. In the words of her Principal, Brian Stirling, who had worked with Jacqui for most of her career at Greenisland:

"Jacqui was an outstanding teacher, in that most demanding of settings, the teaching of young children – a demanding role both physically and mentally. Those children loved her. Jacqui was professional, caring, dedicated and any complementary adjective you care to think of. She was a natural leader. Jacqui's example influenced and inspired her colleagues. Head of the Infant Department was the original title; "Chief Breen" was the affectionate nickname of her friends. When she spoke in either formal or informal settings, everyone listened. Her judgment was mature and at a higher level. She never had to force her leadership role. People were happy to follow."

That night I wondered what sort of welcome would await me at the finish tomorrow. Would it be a total anti-climax or would it be a grand homecoming to remember? I already knew that the total raised by 1000K4J to date for Cancer Research UK had exceeded the £10,000 target and was still being added to, which was absolutely fantastic. However, over the last week or so, as the final day of my journey had been drawing ever closer, I had been becoming more and more apprehensive about finishing my pilgrimage. I had become so accustomed to being on this journey that I wasn't sure if I was ready to stop. My body would certainly appreciate a good rest, but I wasn't sure that my mind was in the same place. I had invested so much time and energy in my Ulster Way walk that I really didn't know how I was going to react when it all came to a sudden end. My walk had given me a purpose; a reason to get up and get out in the morning. How was I going to fair when I didn't have my journey to continue with; when it was all over? Was I going to forfeit any progress that I felt I had begun to make in dealing with my waves of grief? Was I going to end up back on the shore, beaten and drained? It was certainly going to be an emotional day and I just hoped that I would be able to get through it and not let everyone down at the final furlong.

Hannah and Jonny were going to walk the last day with me and I was entirely okay with this; in fact I really welcomed and appreciated their support. But there were a number of friends and work colleagues who were also very keen to join me and I wasn't quite so sure how I felt about this. I certainly had no desire to shun anyone and didn't want to disappoint folk. These were friends who had shown tremendous support for me and for my 1000K4J challenge right from the outset and, in a very real sense, I felt that I owed it to them to allow them to share in a part of the walking experience with me. However, at the same time I felt that this journey, and particularly the return to Greenisland Primary School, was so personal that it deserved to be, cried out to be, completed alone – in true pilgrim fashion. But then again, it was me, the most unlikely of pilgrims, who had created all the publicity around 1000K4J. I couldn't very well just turn it all off again at the eleventh hour, could I? And, if I am being totally honest, a small part of me actually enjoyed the attention and focus I was getting and was even looking forward to the grand homecoming. So it was quite a maelstrom of thoughts and emotions that coursed through my mind as the final day approached and, in true prevarication fashion, my mind would settle on one option and then drift to another before heading back to the first, in an endless cycle of indecision.

So, how did I deal with all this confusion in the end? I decided to take my lead from my angel, my guiding light, my teacher. I felt that I had already learned a number of valuable lessons by remaining open to Jacqui's voice and one of the most important was to always have faith in the goodness of others. I relaxed and simply decided to accept and embrace whatever came my way. Not to push or resist, but to go with the flow and let Jacqui bring me home. And as it transpired, I hadn't a single thing to be worried about. Even now, my teacher was still teaching me.

The Beginning

Wednesday 2 September – Ballynure to Greenisland
Hi love. I know it's late, but today was just so special that I can't even think about going to sleep without telling you all about it first.

Hi dear. Sounds like you had a good day?

I certainly did. It was just wonderful. I completed my walk for you and the fundraising target has been smashed.

That's fantastic. Well done you. Of course, I always knew that you would do it!

So many people turned out to show their support and just wait 'til you hear about what your school did!

Can't wait. I'm all ears. Well I'm now mostly wings if the truth be told.

Wow, so you've earned your wings now. That's great news. Well done. Will you have to wear an "L" plate for a bit?

Ha! Ha! Very funny. Nope, I'm fully fledged now! Anyway, come on; tell me all about your day.

Well for starters, Hannah and Jonny wanted to walk with me today, so we were all up at six-thirty this morning so we could be out to Ballynure for eight.

Sorry, did you just say that Hannah was up at six-thirty?

Ha! Ha! Yeah, she and Jonny were determined not to miss the final day's walk no matter what and I was so pleased that they wanted join me. We had Skyped Matt in Berlin yesterday evening and he was so sorry that he wasn't able to join us also, but said he would be with us in spirit all the way.

That's nice, but it's probably just as well that he couldn't join you. None of you would have been able to keep up with him!

Yeah, you're probably right. Anyway, we headed out of Ballynure, following the roads for about three miles, first to Straid and then on to Woodburn Forest.

Good Heavens, you were hitting some quare tourist spots today, ha! ha!

Yeah, not the most spectacular part of the Ulster Way route I have to admit, but we found it quite a pleasant walk none-the-less. It took us through some lovely countryside and it was quite a nice morning for walking also. But there wasn't much that stood out or warranted a photo, apart from the views back to Agnew's Hill, or Agnew's Mountain as I prefer to call it! Anyway, we walked through Woodburn Forest, following the twists and turns of the pathways for about two miles. There were no way-markers or signs, but thankfully the map was pretty easy to follow. When we reached the other side of the forest, we were only a few minutes from Monument Road, which leads out to the Knockagh Monument. It's not on the Ulster Way route, but it was only about a mile and a half diversion there and back. And besides, we had arranged to meet some folk there.

So glad you did that. Gee, the number of times we passed that monument, way high up on the hill, and wondered what it was like up close. And it overlooks Greenisland Primary of course!

Oh yes, and we were able to spot the school way down below when we got out to it. There were some fantastic views from up there over Belfast Lough. We could see Kilroot Power Station and Carrickfergus Castle to the East, Scrabo Tower to the South and Belfast to the West – not all at the same time mind you, as rain showers had started to drift across the landscape below. The monument itself was much, much bigger than I had expected and it was quite impressive both in stature and location. It's certainly a very fitting tribute to those who lost their lives in the two World Wars. We had our lunch beside the monument, on a park bench, and, while we were there, we started to notice some cars arriving in the small car park behind the boundary wall. It was the first wave of my work colleagues arriving to walk the final stretch with us. We finished our lunch and went up to the car park to meet and greet them. I couldn't believe it when I saw that they were all wearing 1000K4J T-shirts!

Really? That's fabulous! Who all was there?

Well, there were ten of them all together! Nikki, Ronan, Alison and seven others.

That's fantastic.

Yeah. Nikki and Alison had organised everyone to come and Ronan had sorted the tees. We all set off together between the beech hedges of Monument Road and then followed the Knockagh Road for about a mile and a half downhill towards the main road to Carrick. I had to split away from the rest of them at this point, so that they could head straight on down to the part of the main road that had a sidewalk. I meanwhile tried to follow the Ulster Way route, but the road I was looking for wasn't the easiest to find as it wasn't signposted or way-marked. I was up and down the Knockagh Road several times searching for it. Thankfully, I met a very friendly man in a van called Jim and he was able to point me in the right direction.

He was pretty easy to organise really.

You're kidding?

Ha! Ha! No, not at all. Rosaleen and I could see you looking lost again, a bit like that time back at Barnes Gap. So we intervened a little to make sure you got back on the right path again. Jim was supposed to have been away a few minutes before you arrived, but low and behold his favourite song just happened to come on the radio and he decided to stay parked up for a bit longer while he listened to it. We couldn't very well have you getting lost on your final day, now could we?

Good Lord! I had no idea. Thanks for that. I had been starting to get a bit flustered alright, as there were so many folk waiting on me. Anyway, I managed to make it down to join the main road to Carrick, right opposite the entrance to the Three Mile Water Park. And at this point, believe it or not, I had actually completed the entire circular route of the Ulster Way!

Hooray! But you weren't quite finished walking yet, right?

That right. I had started my walk at Greenisland Primary School and that was where I was going to finish it.

You know Dermot, that was such a lovely thing to do. That school meant so much to me. Not just the building, but the people – the staff, the pupils, the parents and grandparents – it is a real community and it was wonderful being part of it for so many years.

Well, I can tell you that they are so proud that you were part of it also. You know that they dedicated the new outdoor play area to you and there's a plaque erected in your honour?

Yes. Who would have ever thought that I would have a plaque, hey? It was a super gesture by the school. It's a lovely play area and from time to time I love to watch the pupils play there. Life is more fun if you play games!

It certainly is, love. Well, back to the walk. As you said, I wasn't finished yet. I headed along the main road towards Carrick. As you know, it's a very fast and busy road with no footpath. That's why I had sent the rest of the group the other way. It would definitely have been too dangerous for a large group to walk along this stretch.

Safety first!

Ha! Ha! Too right. Thankfully, it was only about 15 minutes of stepping on and off the grass verge to avoid the traffic, before I reached the footpath and joined up with the rest of the group that were patiently waiting there for me. And the group, including Hannah and Jonny, had now swollen to 17.

You were becoming the right Forrest Gump, ha! ha!

Yeah, it felt a bit like that as I headed on towards Greenisland with my dedicated followers falling in behind. It was really lovely to have so many come out and support me though. I had been concerned that it maybe wasn't the best way to finish my walk, but that couldn't have been more wrong. In reality, it was great to have so many friends with me and the company meant I didn't have time to dwell on any dark thoughts.

I'm so glad you had such good people around you dear. I know that you feel like being on your own sometimes and that's absolutely fine, but be careful not to become too isolated. You need to keep in contact with other people. You need to keep your friends close. Remember, it's harder to cry when you're smiling or laughing. And they will know and understand when you need your own space also.

Yes, I'm starting to realise that.

You must have been quite close to the school now.

Yeah, it only took us about another 25 minutes to reach the top of the Station Road. Mandy phoned me along the way to say that reporters and photographers from the Belfast Telegraph and the Carrick Times were awaiting our arrival and to let me know what they had planned.

If you need something organised, Mandy's the girl.

That's for sure. She was just brilliant organising everything at the school. As we came down Station Road, we were met with the wonderful sight of more friends, work colleagues and parents and there were hundreds of pupils lined up to welcome us and cheer us in. It was a fantastic reception and by far exceeded any expectations that I might have had. The school really did you proud!

Ha! Ha! You got it right again. That's the second time you've used "did" correctly tonight!

Maybe an old dog can learn new tricks after all.

It's never too late. You certainly deserved that reception, dear.

Oh, it wasn't just for me love. This was another opportunity for everyone to express their love for you and to show how much they still think of you. It was for you and me, for us! And I was delighted to see my Dad, your "wonderful Artie", standing out amongst the crowd. Ann and Rosaleen were also there and Christine and Nigel.

Ah, that's fantastic. I'm so glad they were all there to welcome you back. Ann and Christine certainly did a great deal to help you along the way.

They certainly did. There was then a whirlwind of interviews, photos and videos with lots of cheering and clapping and Hannah and I got to walk through a sea of children giving "high fives" and hugs as we went. In fact, we had to do it a few times, so that the photographers and the guy filming the video got the shots they were after. Artie even had a go also. It was brilliant.

Ha! Ha! Trust him to get in on the act. Always playing to the audience!

Yeah, that's him alright. Afterwards, as the children headed back to class and the adults headed in for refreshments, I managed to grab a moment to myself and I headed round to your plaque in the playground to capture an image that had been in my head for weeks now. It was simply a picture of my hand resting on your plaque. In my own mind, only now was the walk truly complete. I had come all the way round the Ulster Way, the circular route was now complete and unbroken. Like our two wedding rings that I now wear side by side, I see it as another symbol of our unending love for each other.

Oh Dermot, that's beautiful – but you really are a big sop!

Yes, I suppose I am. I do really miss you terribly, you know – we all do.

I know, love, but remember what I said before – I'm never that far away. Others will have to learn how to listen and see things in a different way also, just as you have been doing.

Well, it's not easy, but I think I'm slowly starting to get the hang of it. It's obviously a very different sort of relationship and it certainly takes some getting used to. And, needless to say, it's often just not nearly enough. In many ways I don't even want to get used to it, as it just seems like I'm giving in.

Oh, but it's not giving in, love. It's just moving towards acceptance. Listen, do you remember my last few months?

I'm afraid I do, all too clearly!

Well, you know how difficult those months were. I didn't want to die. I didn't want to leave you all. I would have done anything to have stayed. But there did come a point, when I realised that it was simply a waste of energy trying to fight against the inevitable. Once I realised that, in a strange way I felt liberated. Once I had decided to accept the path I was on, it allowed me to see things much more clearly and to focus on the important things during the little time, the precious time, I had left. I was so pleased that I was able to concentrate on saying goodbye properly to the people I loved the most, without being distracted by anger or regret or wasting energy on fighting against something that I was never ever going to beat. But I wasn't giving in, I was just accepting the way things were and making the best of it.

You were so brave during that time, my love. I really don't know how you did it, how you managed to hold it all together.

But don't you see, love? I wasn't being brave at all, not really. I was just doing what I had to do. My choice was to either go out kicking and screaming and making it so much harder for everyone, including myself; or to accept my destiny and leave with dignity whilst surrounded by calmness and love. There was absolutely no doubt in my mind what the best option was to take. In a similar way, you now have to accept what has happened and accept that the clock can never be turned back. You have to accept it and move on through it.

That's easier said than done.

I know it is, love, and it certainly won't happen overnight, but your being able to talk to me in this way is a sign that you are starting to move in the right direction. Remember the line from Gibran's The Prophet "And when you have reached the mountain top, then you shall begin to climb". Well you have reached the end of the Ulster Way, and now you must begin to walk.

That's pretty deep!

It is, but I think you know what I mean.

Hmm, I'm not sure I do.

In a sense, completing the Ulster Way is only the start of your journey. It has certainly brought you quite a distance and, although you have physically returned to the same place, I can clearly see that you are in a very different place mentally and spiritually from where you were when you started out two and a half months ago.

Well, the love and support from people, from friends and strangers alike, that I experienced on my walk was just incredible and it has certainly renewed my faith in humanity. I suppose I have begun to realise that life is not altogether hopeless and that there are good reasons to go on.

That's right and you now need to build on that and, as I said earlier, now you must begin to walk – metaphorically of course!

I'm glad you clarified that – I've walked enough miles for now, thank you very much.

You will be alright, my love. Just put your faith in the humanity that is all around you. Remain open to it. Don't shun it or push it away. As well as drawing strength from it you will also begin to contribute strength to it. I know it's not easy for you, or for Matt or Hannah, or for anyone else, but it is the only way forward. You are all in this together, so just be there for one and other.

I suppose you're right – as always. Some things never change, hey? Actually, when I left your playground and went back into the school to join everyone else, we had a wonderful gathering in the staff room. The school had laid on teas and scones and everyone had a lovely time. I have to say that the warmth in that room for the both of us was quite palpable. There was much talk of 'Chief Breen' and how much she was missed! It was just fantastic to see everyone there. I couldn't quite believe that so many folk had come along to welcome me back at the end of my unlikely pilgrimage.

Well it didn't surprise your weather angels, that's for sure. And it certainly was an unlikely pilgrimage. You were the last person I would have expected to embark on such a long walk. But I am so pleased that you did. You have achieved so much and involved so many people along the way. It was so much more than just a walk. It brought out the best in you and it also brought out the best in others. However, after walking more than 1,000 kilometres, I don't think that you'll be able to describe yourself as an "unlikely pilgrim" for much longer?

I guess not. What do you suggest instead?

What about the 'Proclaimer'.

Ha! Ha! Very funny. Just so long as you don't expect another 500 miles any time soon.

Oh no, dear. Next year will be fine.

Ha! Ha! We'll see. Anyway, listen, thanks for the chat, but it's getting very late now and it's been a long day. I should really be getting some shut-eye. Tomorrow, I am going to have the biggest sleep-in ever!!

I think you've earned it. Have a good sleep.

Oh, before you go, I really need to know that I will meet you again sometime – for real I mean.

Oh, you will. Be patient my love. You will.

That's all I need to know, love.

Night night, my dear. We'll chat again soon.

We certainly will. Good night, my angel.

My pilgrimage finally complete as I once again touch the plaque in Jacqui's playground

This is the picture that I had carried in my head for weeks before this photograph was even taken. This image, more than anything, represented in my mind the completion of my pilgrimage. It was an image that had driven me on through some of my toughest days, as for me it clearly visualised achieving my goal – my eventual return to the exact spot from where I had set off on my pilgrimage two and a half months earlier. I had indeed come full circle. I enjoyed the simple symmetry of this and the symbolism that it conveyed in conjunction with the two wedding rings, Jacqui's and mine, on my left hand (mine lost at sea and miraculously found again). Soppy or not, I believe that true love never dies – it is never ending, just like a circle or a ring has no end. Although, Jacqui may have gone, my love for her has not. I hope and pray that one day this love will be enough to somehow bring us back together again.

Epilogue

On 18th January 2016, the first anniversary of Jacqui's death, I returned to Knocklayde Mountain in Ballycastle and undertook a much shorter but very special pilgrimage. It was the fulfilment of a promise that I had made to Jacqui on previous visits to her final resting place, at Ramoan Church on the edge of the town. Knocklayde Mountain was clearly visible from Jacqui's graveside on a cold, damp winter's morning, as I whispered "au revoir" and headed out the gate and followed the road down to The Diamond in the town centre, where the Lammas Fair is held in August every year. From there I made my way up through Ballycastle Forest and up the steep slopes of the mountain to reach the summit. Once there, I had a very personal little ritual to perform at an ancient cairn, called Carn na Truagh, located on the summit. To me on that day, Knocklayde and that ancient cairn resonated with both history and mythology and, together with the land and sea around me, seemed to perfectly embody the very essence of this mystical land of ours. My act of leaving behind small symbols of Jacqui's love for life and for nature was another helpful step along the path I was still on and, I imagined, I would still be on for some time to come. But I was still walking, just as Jacqui had told me to – not just physically, but more importantly, spiritually. I was also making plans to walk the Camino de Santiago in Northern Spain, via the coastal Camino del Norte route, during the summer of 2016 – another 500 miles or so. I was about to become a Proclaimer after all. I felt that I was gradually moving towards acceptance. I hadn't yet found my place of sanctuary, but each day as I slowly put more distance between myself and the physical and emotional edge I had teetered on only months before, I certainly felt that I was heading in the right direction.

Carn na Truagh

Standing in a garden of marble stones
Looking up to the heather covered hill beyond
A place of current sorrows to one more ancient
A solemn promise is repeated

Leaving Ramoan with a heavy heart
First descending to the place of the annual fair
Then rising slowly, steadily through the trees
To emerge to a mountain exposed

Knocklayde, standing proud over Moyle
Where Lir's children were banished as swans
It has watched over many generations
Seen countless tides ebb and flow

A wall of stone and a fence guide him upwards
The ground is steep, sodden and exhausting
Still cold enough for patches of white snow
Each false summit taunts him further

Out of the mist an ancient mound appears
The pilgrim has reached his destination
Carn na Truagh, the Cairn of Sorrows
Secrets unknown, souls long forgotten

Here he places the things carried with him
Small symbols of a life full of beauty and love
From his very core, he cries out her name
Just then sunlight cuts through the gloom

His promise fulfilled, he turns to descend
Ballycastle, Fairhead, Rathlin Island now clear
East lighthouse signals that it is safe to return
His heart a little lighter, his sorrows shared

Author's note

A total of 38 days and over 300 hours were spent walking 654 miles, or 1052.5 kilometres. That's 27 miles further than the fictional Harold Fry! During that time I took over one and a half million steps over hugely varied terrain, including sandy beaches, rough grasslands, soggy bogland, rocky coastline, forest tracks and tarmac roads. And I took over 6,000 photos, of landscapes, seascapes, plants, people and creatures big and small – some of them decent enough to share on Facebook; most of them not! Very importantly, the walk and associated activities also helped raise over £20,000 for Cancer Research UK.

The sights I have seen, the places I have visited and the challenges I have faced over the course of my walk have undoubtedly made for an unforgettable experience. But looking back on my challenge, the one thing that really stands out for me is the support and generosity shown to me by practically everyone I met and relied upon along the way. So to all the folk who put me up for the night, provided me with meals, drinks and snacks, give me lifts to and from start and finish points, walked with me for some of the way (long and short), made donations and encouraged donations from others, offered words of support and encouragement, provided vouchers and gifts, followed my blogs with interest and shared them with others, I thank you all. I simply would not have been able to complete my challenge without your help, support and encouragement. And, of course, I have to thank my weather angels who generally looked after me very well – well, most of the time anyway!

I would also like to thank a number of people who were kind enough to read my draft manuscripts for this book and provide me with incredibly useful feedback. They include Nikki Monson, Barbara Lewers, Teresa Godfrey and Pip Crook. Special thanks to Brendan McManus SJ, a successful author, who has written extensively on the subjects of pilgrimage and surviving suicide bereavement. His insights and suggestions were invaluable and his gentle encouragement to be more "emotionally open" in my writing, I believe added a dimension to this book that would otherwise have remained suppressed. I also have to credit Brendan with the suggestion for the title of my book – it fitted perfectly!

I would also like to give a special thanks to the wonderful author, Rachel Joyce, who provided the inspiration for my unlikely pilgrimage and was also so supportive of my efforts in a number of special ways.

Thank you also to Outdoor Recreation Northern Ireland for permitting me to use some of the material from their excellent website in my book.

And lastly, I have to thank you for purchasing this book. By doing so, you have contributed to Cancer Research UK (CRUK), the cancer charity so dear to mine and Jacqui's hearts. Thank you very much.

Dermot Breen

P.S. If you didn't in fact buy this book, but borrowed it or acquired it by other means, fair or foul, you might be feeling a little guilty at this point. But don't worry, that can be easily resolved by making a donation to CRUK. Just go to:

www.cancerresearchuk.org/support-us/donate

or send a cheque to:

Cancer Research UK
PO Box 1561
Oxford
OX4 9GZ

The Ulster Way

The following information has been reproduced from the Ulster Way website with the kind permission of Outdoor Recreation Northern Ireland.

The Ulster Way can be broadly described as a 625 mile (1,000km) circular walking route around Northern Ireland.

The original Ulster Way was the brainchild of Wilfrid Capper MBE, who in 1946 had the inspiration to create a circular walking route taking in the six counties of Northern Ireland. It was originally planned to be a walking link between the ring of Youth Hostels which used to encircle Northern Ireland. There were about 15 hostels in total, sited in the most scenic areas, and the idea was that walkers could plan to tour the country sleeping in a different place each night. The Ulster Way became one of the longest way-markered trails in Britain and Ireland measuring 665 miles (1,070 kilometres) and was enjoyed by many.

The Ulster Way Today

The original Ulster Way route included a lot of road walking and some sections eventually began to suffer from increased traffic; there were also issues, in a few areas, about permission to cross private land. These factors resulted in a group being established in 2003 to examine how the Ulster Way might be best redefined. The Northern Ireland Environment Agency (NIEA) was identified as the most appropriate body to take over the co-ordination of the route and independent advice was supplied by an Ulster Way Advisory Committee which included members from walking groups and other agencies.

Many partners worked together from 2004-2009 to bring the new route and website to fruition and many thanks goes to each and every one. A new Ulster Way route was agreed in early 2009 and is designed to provide a high quality walking experience.

In order to deliver this quality experience, the route is divided into Quality and Link sections. The Quality sections are mainly on the already established Way-markered Ways which are predominantly off road and passing through Areas of Outstanding Natural Beauty. Walkers will be encouraged to use public transport along the Link sections as they are mainly on public roads. However really keen walkers will be able to include these sections as well and complete the circular route of Northern Ireland. A walk along all of the Ulster Way Quality sections, and using public transport to link them, will provide a truly memorable experience for any long distance walker.

Continued Evolution

Although the revised Ulster Way was launched in 2009 the vision is to constantly evolve the route in order to increase the mileage of Quality sections. For example it is hoped that a significant section of the Belfast Hills including Divis and Black Mountain – the famous backdrop to the city of Belfast will eventually be incorporated into the route. The majority of this area was secured and reopened by the National Trust in 2005.

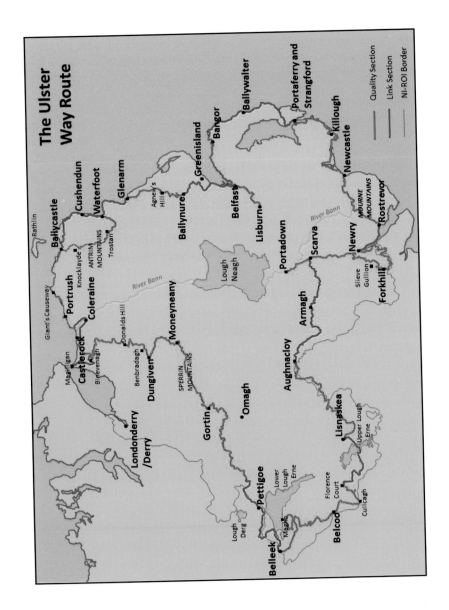

The Ulster Way Route

Quality Section
Link Section
NI-ROI Border

Rathlin
Ballycastle
Cushendun
Waterfoot
Glenarm
Agnel's Hill
Greenisland
Bangor
Ballywalter
Portaferry and Strangford
Killough
Newcastle
MOURNE MOUNTAINS
Rostrevor
Belfast
Lisburn
Portadown
Scarva
Newry
River Bann
Slieve Gullion
Forkhill
Armagh
Aughnacloy
ANTRIM MOUNTAINS
Trostan
Knocklayde
Portrush
Coleraine
Giant's Causeway
River Bann
Lough Neagh
Ballynure
Donalds Hill
Benbradagh
SPERRIN MOUNTAINS
Moneyneany
Magilligan
Castlerock
Binevenagh
Dungiven
Londonderry /Derry
Gortin
•Omagh
Lisnaskea
Upper Lough Erne
Pettigoe
Lower Lough Erne
Florence Court
Belcoo
Cuilcagh
Lough Derg
Maph
Belleek